# What others have said about Jungle Jewels & Jaguars

Thank you, Martha. What a spectacular idea! Link the exciting, blow by blow account of a real missionary career with specific chapters in the most widely used textbook on missions! Now the thousands of people who annually read the book or take the course *Perspectives on the World Christian Movement* can get a vivid, real-life picture of what those pages are talking about—as they read *Jungle Jewels & Jaguars* by Martha Tripp.

**Ralph D. Winter, General Director**
**Frontier Mission Fellowship**

As a lecturer on "Pioneer Church Planting" in the *Perspectives on the World Christian Movement* courses, I have used the 45 Amuesha churches in the jungles of Peru as an example of how God plants churches, indigenous from the very beginning. What the cross-cultural missionary should do and should not do and what the people themselves can and ought to do are shown not in theory but in an easy to read narration of what actually happened. Every Christian, not just missionaries, should read this book.

**George M. Cowan, President Emeritus,**
**Wycliffe Bible Translators**

Martha Duff Tripp's *Jungle Jewels and Jaguars* recounts how she and her colleague, Mary Ruth Wise, penetrated the domain of the Amuesha people in remotest Peru. Float plane landings on obstacled rivers, jungle trekking, bobbing down rapids, scaling precipitous ridges et al. were only a physical part of their incredible journey. Even more challenging was their quest to know the hearts and minds of Amuesha people, to share the feelings, fears and crises of a minority culture faced with the danger of drowning under the backwash of civilization.

Bigger than any geographical, medical or emotional tests Martha and Mary were to face was the task of learning the Amuesha language so thoroughly that they could translate the New Testament into it. Great the task, greater still the reward! Thrill to the climactic fruition of their labors—the beautifully indigenous birthing of 45 Amuesha churches, all of them nurtured by New Testament teaching in Amuesha and led entirely by Amuesha pastors!

It is impossible to read this book without envisioning other Amuesha-like cultures—perhaps 2,200 of them—hearing at last the footfalls of very special friends on one of their trails. Martha and Mary's unpretentious heroism, so humbly storied, beckons to a new generation.

**Don Richardson**
**Author of *Peace Child*, *Lords of the Earth*,**
***Eternity in their Hearts*, and *Secrets of the Koran***

Martha is a hero of mine and what she under the direction of our Father has accomplished is beyond description. The book is fantastic. I love it. I think God is going to use it in a significant way.

**Bernie May**
**Wycliffe-JAARS pilot in Peru,**
**former Director of JAARS, President of Wycliffe USA,**
**Founder and President of The Seed Company**

What does one look for in a really satisfying book? Often the answer is a worthwhile story. Or important information. Or entertainment. Finally—when possible—easy reading. No purely academic book can give us all four. I am glad to tell you that no one in his right mind could think that *Jungle Jewels & Jaguars* is a purely academic book!

Bible translation is certainly academic work, but the account in *Jungle Jewels & Jaguars* comes alive as Martha Tripp meets all the expectations I've mentioned. First this is the adventure story of two young women going deep into the jungles of the Andes and looking to the Lord to care for them, often in frightening circumstances. Second the book subtly supplies a great deal of information about Bible translation work. I use the word "subtly" because you do not realize the extent to which you're being taught. As for entertainment, it is first-class. Where else, for example, could you look over Martha Tripp's shoulder as she learns how the absence of head lice in a tribe interferes with bonding and communication! Best of all for tired readers: it is easy reading. The account of reaching the Amueshas zips along with a relatively simple vocabulary, and it is mainly told in the present tense making you feel that you are there.

It is a pleasure to commend this book to a wide range of Christian readers.

**Tom Wells**
**Author of** *A Vision for Missions*

The world is changing fast. But not so quickly for remote tribal peoples. And some things never change; steep mountain ranges; sweltering swamps and jungle; and lots of hiking and hacking through the bush. Just getting to the people is daunting enough. And staying there is not so easy either. Stifling heat, humidity and the constancy of mosquito inspired fevers and other exotic tropical inconveniences make life among the far-fetched tribes difficult. But these are the manageable externals. Attaining language and culture proficiency and the exhausting overt spiritual resistance from the enemy of souls is the rough and tough part. Through all of these obstacles and more, Martha Tripp's *Jungle Jewels & Jaguars* encourages us with the fascinating account of how the Gospel has gotten well-established among the Amueshas. I am happy to know their story in coming to faith in Christ.

There is one more thing that doesn't change, and that is the steady progress of the Kingdom of God throughout the nations. *Jungle Jewels & Jaguars* is further proof of God's faithfulness to give his Son an inheritance; a People from among all the peoples (Psalm 2:8). Cross the Amueshas off the unreached peoples list! A name has been made for Jesus there!

**David Sitton, President**
**To Every Tribe Ministries**

In these stories the reader is transported into another culture as two young women immerse themselves in Amuesha communities in order to bring them God's Word. You get a glimpse into the complexities of Bible translation as they discover and unravel the structure of the language and culture. This story is an excellent example of giving a people group God's Word and letting it penetrate hearts and lives with a minimum of outside influence. There are many great illustrations of principles which are taught in the *Perspectives on the World Christian Movement* course.

**John Bush, long time Wycliffe/JAARS member.**
**Presently in charge of Recruitment North East USA**

Martha as a speaker is a great story teller. You the reader, will be taken into the jungle to live those stories. I was one of the pilots who had the privilege of serving the Amuesha and the translation team. Today, there is an active church which is reaching out just like the New Testament Church of God's Word. Amazing! We all had a part.

**Eldon "Butch" Barkman**
**Peru Branch Pilot and Administrator, 1973-1987**

# Jungle Jewels & Jaguars

# Jungle Jewels & Jaguars

## Living with the Amueshas
## Translating God's Word

MARTHA DUFF TRIPP

Harvest
Day
Books

Traverse City • Michigan

## Jungle Jewels & Jaguars
Copyright © 2008 by Martha Duff Tripp

Page Layout Production by Lois Gable, Creative Touch Communications, Waxhaw, NC.
Layout and Cover Design by BookMarketingSolutions.com

Unless otherwise indicated, all Scripture references are from the New International Version of
the Bible, copyright 1973, 1978, 1984 by International Bible Society. Verses marked LB are
from The Living Bible, copyright 1971, by Tyndale House Publishers. Verses marked AMP are
from The Amplified Bible, copyright 1965, by Zondervan Publishing House.

*Published by*

**Harvest Day Books**
an imprint of **Book Marketing Solutions, LLC**
10300 E. Leelanau Court
Traverse City, MI 49684
info@BookMarketingSolutions.com
www.BookMarketingSolutions.com

Harvest
Day
Books

Printed in the United States of America


Duff-Tripp, Martha.
   Jungle jewels & jaguars : living with the Amueshas translating God's
   word / Martha Duff Tripp. -- Traverse City, Mich. : Harvest Day
   Books, c2008.
       p. ; cm.
       ISBN: 978-0-9790834-5-7
       Includes bibliographical references.
       1. Amuesha Indians--Missions. 2. Missions--Peru.
   3. Evangelistic work--Peru. 4. Bible. Amuesha language--
   Translating. I. Title.
BV2853.P7 D84 2008
266/.009839--dc22                                        0804

This book is available online
at www.ReadingUp.com and www.JungleJewelsJaguars.com

# Dedication

This book is dedicated to all the young people of this and future generations who will commit their lives to translating God's Word for those 2,200 language groups of people still in the world today who have nothing of God's Word in their own language.

# Acknowledgements

I would like to thank a number of friends who have been helpful and supportive in my writing this true story of God's faithfulness and enabling in *Jungle Jewels & Jaguars*.

In order of their occurrences, I remember Viola Galenzoski Escobar's suggestion that I write such a book and her encouragement along the way.

Various individuals have been helpful with editorial work, including my husband, Robert Tripp, who read my original copy and made many good suggestions. Loys Mundy of JAARS' Creative Services gave me helpful orientation in writing the initial chapters. Bob's niece-in-law, Margot Lewin, from her studies in writing at Dartmouth College, has also made many good suggestions and provided me with some late books on writing. Viola Escobar and Mary Ruth Wise (my former co-worker with the Amueshas) have also made extensive editorial changes.

Newton Frank, former Director of Research and Programs in Peru for Wycliffe Bible Translators, has reviewed the book and been my consultant in advancing it to the publishing stage.

I deeply appreciate the valuable editing of the book by Ilene Stankiewicz, Harvest Day Books editor. This has made the stories of *Jungle Jewels & Jaguars* more understandable to readers not familiar with the world of missions among indigenous, jungle people groups.

My grateful thanks go to Dr. Ralph D. Winter, co-editor of *Perspectives on the World Christian Movement*, for his desire to make *Jungle Jewels & Jaguars* available to students of the *Perspectives* courses.

# Early Amuesha Bilingual Schools

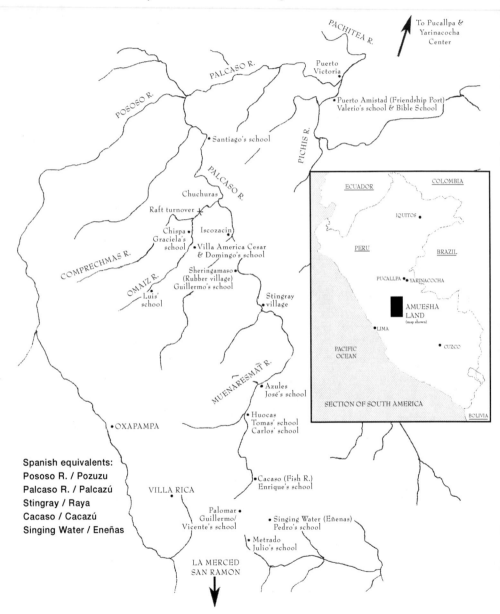

PACHITEA R.

To Pucallpa &
Yarinacocha
Center

PALCASO R.

POSOSO R.

Puerto
Victoria

Puerto Amistad (Friendship Port)
Valerio's school & Bible School

Santiago's school

PICHIS R.

PALCASO R.

Chuchuras

Raft turnover

Chispa
Graciela's
school

Iscozacin

Villa America Cesar
& Domingo's school

COMPRECHMAS R.

Sheringamaso
(Rubber village)
Guillermo's school

OMAIZ R.

Luis'
school

Stingray
village

MUENARESMATT R.

Azules
José's school

Huocas
Tomas' school
Carlos' school

OXAPAMPA

Cacaso (Fish R.)
Enrique's school

VILLA RICA

Palomar
Guillermo/
Vicente's school

Singing Water (Eñenas)
Pedro's school

Metrado
Julio's school

LA MERCED
SAN RAMON

**Spanish equivalents:**
Pososo R. / Pozuzu
Palcaso R. / Palcazú
Stingray / Raya
Cacaso / Cacazú
Singing Water / Eneñas

ECUADOR          COLOMBIA

IQUITOS

PERU          BRAZIL

PUCALLPA  YARINACOCHA

AMUESHA
LAND
(map shown)

LIMA

CUZCO

PACIFIC
OCEAN

SECTION OF SOUTH AMERICA

BOLIVIA

# Contents

# Foreword

The story in this book took place between 1953 and 1997, and is typical of the work of the Wycliffe Bible Translators during that period. The location is the eastern Amazon jungle and foothills of the Andes in Peru. The Amuesha people, one of thirty-seven minority languages in the area, number about 15,000. The work was carried on under the auspices of the Summer Institute of Linguistics in cooperation with agencies of the Peruvian government.

This is a story of isolated pioneer living and travel; of learning to speak a language by mimicry without textbooks; of devising a writing system for a previously unwritten language; of writing primers and teaching people to read; of watching indigenous authors produce their own literature; of translating the New Testament for the first time into this American Indian minority language; of documenting the culture and language in an Amuesha Dictionary and Amuesha Grammar; of observing but not guiding the formation of Amuesha indigenous churches (there are now more than forty-five fully indigenous Amuesha churches); and of the development of a government-sponsored bilingual school system incorporating the Amueshas into the life of their country.

This story is told not by some outside observer, but by someone who spoke the language, lived among the people, and personally witnessed the transformation. It is not a unique story — it has been duplicated in whole or in part in a number of other situations — but it is another powerful testimony to mother-tongue translation providing the Holy Spirit's tool to plant the seed that makes it possible for Christ to build His church.

Every Christian, not just missionaries, will learn much by reading this book. What the cross-cultural missionary should do and should not do, and what the people themselves can and ought to do are clearly shown, not in theory but in an easy-to-read narration of what actually happened.

There are still many such people groups without Scripture, without churches, without any way of hearing the Good News about Jesus Christ the Savior in the only or primary language they understand. The author wrote the book to challenge you, the reader, to get involved. I hope you will read it with an open heart and an attitude of "Here I am Lord, use me."

George M. Cowan,
President Emeritus,
Wycliffe Bible Translators

# Introduction

After finishing linguistic and Bible translation work with the indigenous Amuesha people in the jungles of Peru, South America, I was talking with a good friend, Viola Escobar, a former co-worker with Wycliffe Bible Translators, also in Peru. She showed me the book from which she was helping to teach a course in her church, *Perspectives on the World Christian Movement*, edited by Ralph D. Winter and Steven C. Hawthorne.

As she read from different parts of the book that dealt with the latest mission theory and practice, it would remind me of an occasion from my work with the Amuesha people, which I proceeded to relate to her. After about the third instance of doing this, she said to me, "Do you know what you should do? You should be writing down your stories that illustrate the validity of these recommended principles when they are used, including the story of the forty-five churches established by the people themselves as they received God's Word translated into their own language."

I had kept a ten-year journal during my work and had thought about writing a book, her suggestion clinched the idea. I trust that *Jungle Jewels & Jaguars* will not only complement the book *Perspectives on the World Christian Movement*, but that it will be a blessing to you and encourage many young people to become Bible translators and literacy promoters. There are some 2,200 language groups of people still in the world today without any of God's Word in their own language.

The following quote by Dr. Ralph D. Winter of *Perspectives on the World Christian Movement* is taken from his column in *Mission Frontiers*, September-October, 2006: "Wycliffe Bible Translators are right: once people get the

Bible in their own language, you can readily expect what in many cases will be explosive growth of "faith movements to Christ."

# 1

# Weak Knees

*Will these isolated people accept me? Will I be able to learn their unwritten language?*

Second thoughts begin to race through my head just as the small JAARS[1] floatplane splashes down on the tiny, clear river in the middle of Amuesha Indian country in the Amazon rainforest of Peru, South America. Not that I haven't already settled all these questions long ago. As we race along the river, spraying the water up on both sides of the plane in our effort to slow down, so race the uncertain anxieties through my head all over again. The moment of truth has arrived.

Happily, we begin to slow down before the short pool of deep water ends at the next rapids. But my second thoughts are still racing. My knees begin to feel as weak as the clear water below our floats.

The plane comes to a stop with a wake of water surging up from behind, rocking us forwards and backwards. Our pilot, Jim Price, starts to taxi the plane toward the bank of the river. As we turn, from my right seat position in the back of the plane, the entire riverbank comes into sight. People are lined up in a single row all along the bank, each one wanting to get a front-line view. After all, these isolated people have never seen anything like this.

They are dressed in long, dark robes. Some of them have their faces painted with red and some with black. Their long, black, flowing hair and dark, solemn faces do not help my weak knees at all; they look fearsome.

As we taxi closer to the bank, another anxious thought overwhelms me. From my back seat position, I realize that I will be the first one out of the plane since the door is on my side. My co-worker, Mary Ruth Wise, is in the front seat of the plane, but there is no door there. She will have to wait while the pilot turns off the engine, jumps out, and tosses a rope to some of the men, hoping they will catch it and hold on to keep us from floating down the river until he can get out and secure the plane.

As I think about how I will be the first one to step out onto the float of the plane to meet these people, my weak knees get weaker. I watch anxiously as the pilot and the men secure the rope to a nearby bush. Then I know my time has come.

With my "little faith," I open the door on my side of the plane. Despite all my uncertainties, I know this is the place to which God has brought me. This is why I committed my life to Him back when I was just fifteen years old. This is what I had studied for at Columbia Bible College. This is what I had trained for in linguistics at the University of Oklahoma. Yes, these people have an unwritten language that we not only want to learn to speak, but analyze its grammatical structures so that in time, with their help and God's, we will be able to translate God's Word into their language. We in Wycliffe Bible Translators[2] believe that all people have the right to read the Scriptures in their own language, the language of the heart, the language they understand best. Amuesha is only one of nearly 7,000 languages in the world today — more than 2,200 of them have nothing of the life-giving Word.[3] Yes, I am thinking, I'm sure this is the place God chose for me.

I deliberately slide down from the plane seat until my feet touch the plane float below me. I steady myself and begin to walk the length of the float to the riverbank. I almost wish that they had made the float a bit longer. *Are they going to receive me? Will I be able to learn their language?* I take another step and begin to see the end of the float sticking out over the land. I continue to keep my eye on it, knowing that this will be the greatest leap of faith I will make — I reach the end and take that "giant step" onto Amueshaland.

Just as my foot touches the ground, a wonderful thing happens. A young Amuesha girl of about thirteen years breaks from that crowd of people who are still standing there as if frozen and very quickly comes down the riverbank. By the time my foot touches the ground, she is there. She takes me by the hand and starts talking to me at full speed in her language. I understand nothing. I can tell she wants to be my friend. That's what I am looking for. My weak knees are scarcely holding me up.

She examines my dress, feels the material, and rubs her hand over it as she says, *"Cohuen, atarr cohuen."* I had purposely worn a bright, floral skirt. I had heard somewhere that Native Americans like bright colors. It works; I can tell she likes it. I suddenly realize that no one is going to interpret for me, so I make a mental note that *cohuen* must mean "pretty," or at least that's what I want to hear. I later find out that it means not only "pretty," but also "good, well" — everything positive. Little do I know at the time that this very first word I learn, even before leaving the plane, will be the most important word later as we translate "the good news of the Gospel of Jesus Christ" — *cohuen ñoñets* (the good words).

By this time, Mary Ruth and Jim are coming to where my new friend and I are standing. Other Amueshas are now crowding in too since they see there is no danger. We start to move up the steep riverbank to the thatched roof houses. My little friend is still holding onto my hand, for which I am very grateful. My knees are feeling a little stronger. As we slip and slide trying to get up the muddy bank, a passing buzzard swoops down over us and my little self-appointed teacher points to it and says, *"tse'm."* I pronounce it after her. There's no doubt about this word. A buzzard is now and forever a *tse'm.* I can see it written in phonetic script in my mind.

It is all so natural. I can hardly believe that God is already quelling my fears. Will the people welcome me? Yes, this young girl is already my friend. Will I be able to learn this language? Yes, I have already learned my first two words before scarcely leaving the plane. By the way, you may think there is no buzzard in the New Testament, but there is. These first two words will some day find their place in the Amuesha New Testament.

"Go . . . I am with you always, even unto the end of the world."
— Jesus Christ, (Matthew 28:19-20 KJV)

"Whenever I am afraid, I will trust in you."
— the Psalmist David, (Psalm 56:3 NKJ)

" . . . for when I am weak, then I am strong."
— the Apostle Paul, (II Corinthians 12:10 NIV)

(Thank you, Lord, for your faithfulness to me even when my faith is so small.)

# 2

# Stingray Village

We reach the top of the riverbank and the entire little thatched roof village of *Sheĩomas* (Stingray Water) comes into view. About twenty small houses are situated around a large open field in the center. The people take us toward a little basket-weave house (walls from strips of palm bark) to the left of the field and near the river.

By this time many have joined our group, with various volunteers carrying our baggage — duffel bags, boxes, and smaller bags. Each person seems to choose the item that best fits his or her size, from the strongest men with their heavy loads to the smallest children with their lightweight bags. Excitement is in the air as each child scrambles to get ahead and deliver his load first. What can be in these bags and boxes?

As we reach the house, the bigger boys immediately scamper up to the cross poles supporting the roof of the house. There they perch side-by-side like chickens on a roost, each wanting to get a bird's-eye view of what will come out of these bags. Hardtack candy comes out, enough for everyone to have at least one piece. They didn't know anything could be that sweet and good. They have only known natural sweets like honey.

While we can't express our thanks for their kindness in their language, the candy goes a long way in letting them know what we want to say. The senior missionary of our team, Peter Fast, who came here previously to make arrangements with the head man so we could live and work here in the village, taught us this secret of the candy.

Then something more comes from the baggage — the View Master, a small hand viewer showing various animals of the world. After teaching the first child how to use it to see pictures of things they have never seen before, the View Master becomes the most popular item in our new house. Thanks again to Pete for this idea. The first person then shows the next eager, waiting one how to use it. All the exclamations that come from the first sights — *"catoo! cohuen! añecmuen!"* — let us know they have many ways to describe wonders

never before seen. It is good language practice for us as we listen to them converse among themselves about the pictures.

My little buddy has hardly let go of my hand even yet. Since I need to help unpack our things, she lets me go, but stays near by. My knees are almost back to normal. From hearing the others call her, I learn that her name is *Shañe'*, the name of the giant anteater of South America. (This is the animal with the big, bushy tail that sticks out his long, thin tongue and allows innocent, unsuspecting ants to line up on his tongue. Then he makes one grand swallow, sending them all to their doom.) Any similarity between that animal and this sweet, young girl is nonexistent. Yet it is customary for Amuesha children to be given animal and bird names.

One of the first boxes we open is the shortwave radio that JAARS provides for us to keep in contact with our Yarinacocha Center.[1] We need to get it set up so we can inform our colleagues there that we have arrived and all is well. We will be given regular times for reporting in during the week. This is standard for all translation teams; lets our colleagues know that everything is okay as we continue our village stay over a period of months. It also allows us to get news from translation teams working in other areas throughout the jungle. In addition, we can order supplies and medicines for the people by radio and consult with our doctor on difficult cases.

Jim and Pete are working now on setting up the radio. One of the most agile of the boys is already climbing up the high pole to attach the antenna wire to the top. He is anxious to show off his great climbing abilities.

When everything is ready, we call in to Yarinacocha. Lo and behold, this black box starts to talk — almost as much a surprise to us as to the Amueshas.

"Yes, we have arrived at Stingray village, and all is well," we report. Then the radio operator gives us a call number and tells us the days and the hour we are to report. Although the people don't understand English, they realize we are talking with our friends far away in Yarinacocha. They can't believe it, but they like it. One of their main requests becomes, "Cause your radio to talk" *(Peñosat perratyo)*. We learn the whole phrase, but which part means "cause,"

which part "your," and which part "talk," we don't know yet. Can you tell?

After Jim is sure the radio is working properly, he bids us farewell and takes off from the river, going back to Yarinacocha, his mission completed.

We open up another box, take out a record player, and begin to turn the crank. All eyes are glued on this strange instrument. We put on a record and set the arm; this box starts talking in Amuesha! The people crowd closer and closer to see where the person is in this box that is speaking in their language. It does sound a little odd, but yes, it is our language. Is it someone else who has learned Amuesha? No, it can't be that. No one else has ever learned our language.

27

We try to explain that this is one of their people who lives way downriver and talks a little differently than they do. Then they listen more to what the voice is saying. It's our language, but he is saying strange things. What does it mean?

The box is playing a Gospel Recording record that Pete was able to have made while working with an Amuesha man who lives far downriver and knows some Spanish. Through Spanish, Pete was able to get a short Gospel message translated into Amuesha. Although the people don't quite understand all these new concepts, this box too becomes a favorite because "it talks our language."

As Mary Ruth and I continue to unpack, the people happily get to see what we have. As evening approaches, they leave quickly. They want to be home since they believe it is the time when the bad spirits come out. It's also the time they eat. Evening fires are started and blaze up in the darkness all around at the various homes. We begin to smell the smoke of the open wood fires mingled with that of boiling manioc root and boiling fish — the two main food staples. This smell becomes so ingrained in us that we can never escape from it, especially the smoke; it permeates even our clothes and hair.

We boil some water on our little one-burner kerosene pressure stove and have some instant coffee along with what food we can easily find in what we have brought. Now it is time to relax. Pete soon leaves to go to the neighbor's house where he is spending the nights. It has been a full day, yet even as we finally relax we see little eyes peeking at us through the cracks of the house. In a "face to face" society nothing is done in secret. Even little children know all the facts of life. As Mary Ruth and I look at each other, we realize that this lack of privacy is our first real culture shock.[2] But we will adjust.

We blow up our air mattresses and retire to what privacy our mosquito nets can give us as we spend our first night in Amuesha country.


" . . . If anyone would come after me he must deny himself . . . and follow me."

– Jesus, (Luke 9:23 NIV)

# 3

# Nothing to It!

We get up early the next day hoping to get dressed and finish our morning devotions before the curious once again arrive to peek through the cracks of our house. It's hard to beat them, so we soon learn it's easier just to forget we are being watched and go ahead with whatever we are doing.

There's no ready-to-eat cereal here for breakfast, but oatmeal never tasted as good at home as it does here. We hurry to be ready to talk on the radio about seven o'clock. We answer our call number and then hear our colleagues in their various locations throughout the Amazon basin taking part in the morning "roll call." Radio operator Luke Tanner is happy to hear we are getting set up and all is well. He will pass the word on to other Wycliffe workers at our Yarinacocha Center so they can keep up with us in their prayers.

These co-workers are mostly support personnel who work permanently at the Center. They consist of our director, medical doctor, nurses, pilots, mechanics, secretaries, print shop workers, finance workers, and teachers of missionary children. Each one is essential to our linguistic work among the various language groups. We count on their prayers as well as the prayers of our supporters at home. Without our prayer partners we couldn't be working in these very remote areas of the rainforest. With no roads here, the floatplanes are the only practical way to get in.

Our only furniture consists of two good-sized tables that Pete had made for us downriver where there is a sawmill. One table will be for our kitchen area and the other for our linguistic work. There is also a chair for each of us. The people here do not use chairs; they sit on the floor with their feet straight out in front of them. They find sitting on chairs very uncomfortable, especially the women. We get the tables and chairs set up. They look very elegant in our little one-room house.

We are now trying to get adjusted to walking on the springy bark floor made from the hard outer sheath of a certain palm tree. It is split lengthwise so that it spreads out, making a flat flooring. It's quite an art to walk in balance with the spring of the floor. You catch on to it after some practice.

Among the many people who visit us today is a woman with a small boy of about five years. We can tell from looking at them that they are the poorest of the poor. Their clothing is tattered and torn up from the bottom. The woman's hair seems never to have been combed. She scarcely talks, but she pushes the small boy up for us to see his bad arm. As we look at the swollen upper arm and compare it to his other broomstick-size arm, we realize this is a terrible infection, looking like a boil but having no head. I try washing it up first to get a better look. Pete suggests putting hot packs on it, however it is very painful. We decide to consult with Dr. Altig, our medical doctor at the Center, in the morning by radio. Although we have had some medical training, it is not enough to prepare us for the unusual things we find here.[1]

The next morning, as we explain the problem to the doctor, he casually answers, "You just need to lance it, that's all," as if there is nothing to it. I'm thinking, *that's all right for you to say, but what about us? We have not made a practice of lancing boils.* The three of us look at each other in desperation. Thankfully, the doctor goes on to tell us just how to do it.

"Take a new razor blade, single edge, sterilize it, and then make a quick, tiny quarter-inch piercing of the skin. Make the cut lengthwise of the flesh, not crosswise."

Again the three of us look at each other, and I think that surely Pete will volunteer to do this task since he has already been in the field five years and has no doubt done this before. Yet Pete says, "I'll furnish the razor blade."

"I just can't do it," Mary Ruth says.

I think I can't do it either, but one of us must. Since it's my case, I decide to try. As I'm preparing my things, I'm praying in my heart, "Lord, help me to do this."

Our operating table is the bare ground. The mother and child sit down confidently before me. Lord, do they know that I am a novice at this? They are not as nervous as I am, and they should be. I hunker down before them and start to clean the area with alcohol. Then, with the razor blade in hand positioned point downward in just the way I plan to use it, I quickly make the plunge lest I lose my nerve. Scarcely have I touched the skin when the pus starts spurting out with force. I move back quickly so I won't be drenched. Mary Ruth comes and we both start wiping it up with toilet paper. It looks like a cupful to me. As it stops draining, I can see the tiny quarter inch cut I made. Thank you, Lord. I clean it up and put on the dressing as doc had directed. Just like he said, nothing to it, but I know you, Lord, enabled me. As I hand the little guy a hard candy for his bravery, I think I can see a tiny smile.

"Vicky" comes back each day for me to check on how the cut is healing. Where did he get the name "Vicky"? That's what we nickname him since he becomes the first "victim" of our medical work. Even in years to come when we see "Vicky," he proudly shows us the little scar on his arm.

"... I can do all things through Christ who strengthens me."

    – the Apostle Paul, (Philippians 4:13 KJV)

"... whatever you did for one of the least of these brothers of mine, you did for me."

    – Jesus, (Matthew 25:40 NIV)

# 4

# Rain in Our Faces

We wake up in the middle of the night with rain coming in our faces. Our thatch roof works well in the middle of the house, but not at the end of the house where our cots are. We quickly remember the extra tarp we have and put it up in the opening, so a good night's sleep continues after all.

We will soon find out that the other end of our house, where the kitchen area is, is best left open. That way, when the rain comes in, we get our kitchen floor cleaned with little effort on our part. Can't beat those automatic floor mops in the jungle!

Pete, with the help of some of the Amuesha men, builds us a kitchen counter and shelves from lengths of split palm bark. It is so good to get many of our food items up off the floor and onto shelves. They also make us a lean-to on the house with its own thatch roof where we can store the generator (for the radio and tape recorder we will be using soon). It also proves to be a good place to store a whole stalk of bananas the people so generously give us.

The people have already started giving us other food as well. We offer to pay them with money, but they say no. They greatly appreciate the medicines we are now giving them and want to give us something in return. The oldest man, called To', chuckles as he throws a big fish he has just caught into our front doorway. We also find a bunch of nice, straight manioc roots (a starchy tuber) left for us. Grandma Santos likes to bring us the best of her *sachapapas* (potato-like roots) that we find make delicious French fries just like real potatoes do, only better.

I try my hand at cooking the first manioc roots given us. I've seen how the people boil them in pots. I do that, but then I think maybe they would be good mashed like potatoes. I quickly learn that manioc roots are not potatoes. They become a sticky mess when mashed — edible, though with difficulty. Tapioca is made from this root. I learn right away to just prepare it as the Amueshas do.

Groups of little girls surround Mary Ruth and me all the time. These curious, little kittens love to examine all we wear. While two are examining how the buttons work on the front side of my blouse, another one is at my backside lifting up my blouse to see what I have on underneath. Our watches are very fascinating to them. They ask us, *"Errpona't Yepapar?"* (How much is it our father?) which interpreted means "What time is it?" They call the sun "our father (god)." In the midst of all the scrutiny, we are learning new words. We learn to sit with them on the floor.

Shañe', my first, little thirteen-year-old friend, comes every day, taking it as her personal responsibility to continue teaching me new words. Today

33

when she comes, I try pronouncing a list of nouns that Pete has given us. I pronounce the first word *ma'yarr* (jaguar), reading from the written phonetic form on the paper. Her dark eyes look puzzled and troubled since she knows that she has not taught me that word yet. How could she know it just from looking at the paper? I read another word *ma'ñorr* (deer) and show her where it is written on the paper. Her dark eyes light up with great pleasure when she realizes her language can actually be written on paper!

We look at each other and revel in the realization that this is the first time ever these Amuesha words have been written. True, these same words have been spoken from ancient times, but this is the very first time they have been written down and read — history in the making! We recover from our great awakening as I read the next word.

As I pronounce each word, I want her to tell me if I am pronouncing it correctly. I learn that I can say *"Cohuena't?"* (Is it good?) after I pronounce each word. Just by adding the suffix -*a't* on the first word I learned — *cohuen* (good/pretty) — it becomes a question. If she thinks I have pronounced it well, she answers *"cohuenñačho'"* which I understand to mean "it's good, of course." Otherwise, she pronounces it again and I try until I get *"cohuenñačho'."*

I learn two new parts of words, suffixes, which have their own meanings (we call them morphemes in linguistics): -*a't* attached to a word to make it a question and -*ñačho'* attached to a word to make it mean "of course." Thus begins my journey to discover and remember all the 400 plus grammatical morphemes of this language in addition to its 10,000 or more lexical words. We start our "shoebox" files on 3" x 5" slips of paper for both the morphemes and the words.

Living with the people and learning their language — to speak as they do — is the best way of identifying[1] with them. You are accepted as one of them when you speak their language. This is especially true when their language is ridiculed by the people speaking the national or majority language of the country. We intend to stay as many years as necessary to learn their language well in order to make a good translation of the New Testament with their help. It is so fulfilling to be here identifying with the people. How did I ever get here?

I remember that day some years ago in Columbus, Ohio when I made that important decision to dedicate my life to whatever God might have for me to do.

*"I urge you . . . that you present your bodies a living sacrifice . . . unto God."* (Romans 12:1 NIV)

I couldn't get away from this verse that Sunday morning years ago, having just heard of it for the first time on the Charles E. Fuller radio broadcast. A sophomore in high school at the time, I was beginning to think of how I would spend my life. I had various possibilities in mind, but this verse struck me very forcefully. I knew that I could not be really happy and live with myself without making this surrender[2] of my life to God.

I was a new believer, but I had never considered giving my whole life to God to be used by Him as He might direct me. No one in my family or church had ever done such a thing. But I could not get away from this verse ". . . present your bodies."

Going directly to my bedroom, I knelt down and committed all of my life to God. It was so real. I knew at the time it would no doubt involve my entire life, full time in the future.

No one was home at the time, yet I wondered if I should tell my parents. I was afraid they would think I was a fanatic and try to talk me out of this decision I had made. Although we always went to church as a family, it was more of a social custom in the area where we lived rather than from individual devotion. We never read the Bible together in our home. So my lifetime commitment remained just between me and God, but was always real in my mind, and changed my manner of living and my life forever.

After finishing high school and realizing that my parents would not be able to send me to college, I took a job and started to save money so I could afford college.

Four years later, with what I had saved and what I presumed I would earn while working in college, I began to look for a school where I could prepare for whatever ministry the Lord might have in mind for me.

I still had not told my parents of my plans. In the meantime, I had become friends with a very likeable, young Christian guy. Early on, when I realized his thoughts leaned toward marriage, I told him of my future plans. He was very understanding and respected my thinking. However, he suggested that we continue dating until I left for college. Every time we were together he would ask me, "Have you told your parents of your plans yet?"

The day came when I decided I must tell my parents. I arrived home from work, sat down, and said nervously to my mother, "Mom, I've decided what I want to do. I want to be a missionary."

There was a moment of silence. I thought she didn't approve and didn't want to tell me. As soon as Mom recovered from her shock of thinking I was going to say, "I am getting married," she answered very sweetly, "If you are sure, Martha, that this is what God wants you to do, when Dad comes home tonight we will tell him, and then both of us will help you in any way we can." Her reply relieved all my anxieties.

I was not trying to be a "liberated woman" before my time, only seeking to do what I felt the Lord was leading me into.

I was determined not to consider a denominational college of my own church since I was aware that very liberal views of the Scriptures were being brought into our seminaries and colleges. At that time, I knew of no other conservative schools besides Moody Bible Institute. When I wrote to them, I received a reply that the school had no openings for new candidates in the coming years. Where could I study?

Mom came to my rescue, "Why don't we go talk to a friend of mine that I have known since we were children? Her family used to live next door, and I remember that they always had devotions together. She went to Moody and became a missionary."

My boyfriend drove us to the home of Ethel Thompson. She had experienced the same problem in deciding on the right school. Learning of my interest in missions, she immediately recommended Columbia Bible College (now Columbia International University).

While at CIU, I first heard of Wycliffe Bible Translators through Ethel Wallis who spoke in a chapel service. I never knew that so many indigenous groups of people still existed who had never heard any of God's Word. I too saw the great need.

As I neared the end of my senior year, my best friend suggested that we go to the University of Oklahoma for linguistic training. Although I thought this might be my weakest skill, I was sure the phonetic training would help me to learn a foreign language well wherever I would go. I was already corresponding with several missions but was undecided as to which one I should join. By this time, my vision was becoming focused on South America. I had been reading of the pioneer work of Sophia Mueller of the New Tribes Mission, which greatly impressed me.

As my studies at CIU ended, my money also ran out. Yet I went ahead and applied for studies at the Summer Institute of Linguistics (sister organization to Wycliffe Bible Translators) at the University of Oklahoma. Even before I graduated from CIU, money came from an anonymous person to pay for my entire course at SIL. This was the first time I ever had help with my expenses. I took this as an indication from the Lord that I should continue with my plans.

As I got into the studies of Phonetics, Phonology, Morphology, and Syntax, I realized I was making average and above average grades. I found the study of Literacy very enjoyable. Teaching people how to read in their own indigenous language, and learning how to compose the primer books to teach reading, was fun.

Many of the professors at SIL were Wycliffe members who had field experience. At the orientation sessions I began to think, what better thing could I do than to translate God's Word for people who have never had it before in their own language?

I applied for membership to Wycliffe Bible Translators, praying that God would not allow me to join if it were not where I was supposed to be. I was accepted and have never been sorry and never looked back. The work has been fascinating, challenging, fulfilling, and rewarding. God was so faithful in directing me to just the right place.

If I had my life to live over again, would I do the same thing? Yes! Yes! Yes!

"My God shall supply all your need according to his riches . . .
in Christ Jesus . . . "
— the Apostle Paul, (Philippians 4:19 KJV)


(God has provided — whether they be needs for shelter, food, and
clothing, or for wisdom to analyze and learn this complex language.
Thank you, Lord.)

# 5

# Reducing a Language to Writing

How do you write in a language that has never been written before?

Today Pete shows us his analysis of the sound system of the Amuesha language which he recently finished writing up and has published.[1] This is his great accomplishment from his first five years of work with the Amuesha. He and his wife, Mary, along with their two children, Audrey and Kenny, lived far downriver from here.

The Amueshas there are much more acculturated and speak more Spanish, which he was able to use.

As we study the paper with him, we see the twenty-nine phonemes in the Amuesha sound system — the smallest units of speech that serve to distinguish one utterance from another in a particular language. These phonemes will need to be represented by symbols (letters) in a practical alphabet in order to teach the people to read in their own language. (Phonemes represent only a fraction of all the phonetic sounds of the language and are all that are needed to distinguish one word from another.) Generally, our policy is to conform the indigenous alphabets we devise as closely as possible to the national language alphabet, which here in Peru is Spanish. In that way, the same (or nearly same) sound in each language will be written with the same letter symbol, thus simplifying learning to read in both languages.

It is interesting to note that of the large number of phonemes in Amuesha, only three are vowels and the rest are consonants, which means the consonants may include several complex symbols such as *ts, ch, čh, sh,* and *rr.* In addition, even the simple consonants *b, c, m, n, p,* and *t* have what we call palatalized counterparts (pronounced by raising the tongue to the palate). For example, the difference in the pronunciation of a plain *p* as opposed to the palatalized one is heard when comparing the following English words: "put" (a simple p) and "com<u>put</u>er" (a palatalized p). These palatalized consonants are also phonemic in Amuesha and need to be written in a specific way. For example, the pronoun *na* means "I"; the pronoun *ña* (palatalized n) means "he, she, it." Amuesha is certainly a consonant-heavy language.

We discuss and consider how best to write these palatalized consonants in the practical alphabet. Ordinarily, the letter y could be written following the palatalized letter (for example, ny, py). But in Amuesha, that same sequence of letters could occur at a morpheme break and would be confusing in reading. Spanish has the same problem but with only one palatalized consonant (n). In Spanish, it is handled by writing the palatalized letter with a tilde over it (ñ). To be consistent with Spanish, we decide to do the same with all the palatalized Amuesha consonants, $\tilde{b}$, $\tilde{c}$, $\tilde{m}$, $\tilde{n}$, $\tilde{p}$ and $\tilde{t}$.

We realize that in using this diacritical mark we are creating a printing problem for ourselves. However, the Amuesha people with whom we consult know some Spanish and like it this way since it corresponds well to Spanish. It is very important that we create an alphabet the people like so they can learn it easily and will be encouraged to read.

It is an awesome thing to realize you have the responsibility to form the alphabet of a language that will be used for years to come! One rewarding thing about this is to be able to write the same symbol (letter) for the same phonetic sound. Thus it is that we write the language just as it sounds, making spelling easy (unlike English).

"Write, therefore, what you have seen . . . Blessed is the one who reads the words . . ."
  – the Apostle John, (Revelation 1:19, 1:3 NIV)

"These (things) are written so that you may believe that Jesus is the Christ, the Son of God . . ."
  – the Apostle John, (John 20:31 NIV)

(Lord, help us to write this language in such a way that in the future when we translate your Word into it for the first time ever for the Amuesha people, they will delight to read it and come to know you as the only true God and your Son, Jesus Christ, as the only true Savior and Lord of their lives. Reducing this language to writing will be well worth the effort if it accomplishes this purpose. Thank you Lord.)

# 6

# *Cohuentena Arrorr*
# (The Moon Is Pretty)

"People pay big money for beautiful scenery like this," Mary Ruth and I say as we head off to the river to wash clothes.

Great puffy, white clouds frame the bright blue sky over the little clear-as-a-crystal Palcaso River. With the deep green foliage of the jungle on the other side of the water, it's a picture-postcard scene on a warm June morning. The early morning sun, the fresh, cool air, the clear, cold water are awaiting us. We can hardly wait to get started.

The children see us going and come running to accompany us. We choose a spot in the shallow rapids where we can sit right in the water and wash our clothes.

Quickly, the children peel off their dark tunics and head for the water, their little bronze-brown bodies being the only swimsuits they need. Anxious to cool off in the cold water, they want to show us all their swimming skills. Their greatest feat is to swim under water long distances. When they finally come up, they look to see if we are watching. We try to get our clothes washed by hand and watch them at the same time.

Suddenly, two boys come floating down the rapids with great shouts of glee, making sure we see them as their heads bob up and down in the swiftly flowing water. We wave to them.

"Isn't it great to have this nice, clear water to wash our clothes?" we remark to each other as we scrub away. We are in the foothills of the Andes Mountains, on the rainforest side, where the water coming from the higher elevations is clear and cold. In contrast, many of the rivers in the lower altitudes are muddy.

We choose to wash our own clothes so the people will realize that we can also work — sitting and doing our paperwork on the language analysis is not work to them. Also, we do not want them to think that we have come to make slaves of them as some of the early settlers did. Besides, we enjoy getting away from our language studies from time to time for exercise and fun with the people.

It's hard to believe that these very waters will eventually empty into the mighty Amazon far to the north of us, and then flow across the continent of South America to finally empty into the Atlantic Ocean. Like many of the headwaters of the Amazon, the rivers here flow north instead of south; so "up" and "down" can become a little confusing at times for two Southerners where "down" has always been south before.

We continue to learn new words even from the children, like *yapuena* (we bathe), *yetsama'tena* (we wash our clothes), *ye'potena* (we dive in the water), *yerranaserr* (we cool off again). It's really cool here in more ways than one.

We, also, take a little swim in the deeper water after finishing our wash. We need to practice swimming; we're not too good at it yet. As we do our sidestroke — the only one we learned to do fairly well in our jungle camp training in Mexico — the children watch us closely and try to do the same. It's great fun for them and for us as well. It's easy to bond[1] with the children here and important too, since they will be the responsible adults in the near future.

As we have seen the distended tummies of all the children today, Mary Ruth and I realize this means the children have many intestinal parasites, including worms. We decide to order worm treatments by radio from our clinic at the Yarinacocha Center for all who want them. They will be sent on the plane that will come to take Pete back to the center soon.

Since arriving here, each evening after supper the three of us have been singing Christian songs. We started in English primarily for our own enjoyment, but the people hear us singing and come to see what is going on, as well as to enjoy the light of our bright Coleman lantern. Squinting in the brightest man made light they have ever seen, they let us know they want to sing too! We teach them *Morrentenna Jesús* ("Jesus Loves Me"), which Pete has translated into Amuesha. We sing it many times so they can learn it well. The people learn tunes very easily and love singing.

On moonlit nights we play games with the older children and young adults on the open field in the center of the village. Even the young, married girls fourteen or fifteen years of age join in with their first babies swinging from their shoulders in the braided bands. We teach them Flying Dutchman and they teach us their traditional game of Buzzard Trot. They also like to run races with me. It is good exercise after a day of study on the language analysis.

We continue to learn new Amuesha words even as we play in the moon- light. I realize that the first word I learned, the adjective *cohuen* (good, pretty) can be verbalized (turned into a verb) just by adding the suffix *–t*, then the suffix *–en* (continuative/durative), and yet a third suffix *-a* (reflexive). We learn *cohuentena arrorr* (the moon is pretty). It surely is as it shines so brightly in the dark rainforest where there are no city lights.

". . . in thy presence is fullness of joy; at thy right hand there are pleasures for evermore."
— the Psalmist David, (Psalm 16:11 KJV)

(Thank you, Lord, for giving us this beautiful place to live and enjoy and serve you.)

# 7
# Shoeboxes and Morphemes

We stand on the river beach with all the people and realize this is it — we are alone in the middle of the jungle!

The JAARS plane with pilot Merrill Piper and Pete has just roared past at full speed for a takeoff from the water before reaching the next near rapids. We wave and yell when we see the plane is well in the air before the rapids, watching until it is out of sight.

We have so much appreciated Pete's help in getting us settled and acquainted with the Amuesha people. Now we know we are on our own — an awesome feeling, but so assuring to realize that God says, "I will never leave you nor forsake you."

We walk back up to the house with all the people around us. We truly are not alone. Looking over all the new things the plane has brought us (including the worm treatments), we first head for the mailbag. It's been twenty days without any mail. We can hardly wait. Twenty-four letters! Five are from my red-headed sister, "Ebbie," and three from my six-foot tall, football-hero brother, Calvin. I arrange them by date to get the news in the proper order. Some of the kids help me open the envelopes.

For something like two hours, Mary Ruth and I are both in another world, as we devour the news from our other "home," despite all the commotion around us. There is much good news, but it is disappointing to hear that Calvin's application to Wheaton College was too late to be considered. He now plans to go ahead with the football scholarship he was offered from New Mexico State. Later I manage to write him at the exact hour he said he would be graduating from high school. It's the next best thing to being there!

We try to get on a regular schedule of working with a language helper in not only learning the language but gathering new data in our notebooks, which we keep ready to record all the new words we hear. Shañe' becomes my teacher, coming daily to our house. Mary Ruth has gotten one of the young, married women, **Kosepa**, to teach her and goes to her house daily.

We study with our teachers in the afternoons from two to five since they both need to work in their gardens in the mornings, cleaning out grass and digging manioc for their daily meals. They return home about noon with large baskets of manioc strapped on their heads, often stopping to bathe in the river to cool off on their way back. Then they need to get the manioc peeled and cut up before putting it into large pots to boil over open fires. We smell it cooking, their "bread of life," as it permeates the whole village.

With the morning chores finished, Shañe' arrives at our hut for our afternoon language session. Mary Ruth leaves for Kosepa's house, which is just across the way. She will have a better atmosphere there for learning words in the natural surroundings of the Amuesha people.

Nouns are the easiest words to elicit in the beginning. When I point to something in our house, Shañe' knows I am asking its name. As I point to the floor she says *sotats*, to the corner post of the house, *quellpach*, to the doorway, *yetarr*. Chickens are always coming along, so I get *atollop*; then the rooster, *huareñtec*; then the little chicks, *tope'p̃*. The dog comes by and she says *ochec*.

We walk around to look at things outside. It gets a little tricky when I point to something like a tree and she says *tsach.* I don't know if she is telling me the specific name of that species of tree, the general name for "tree," or the word for the "bark" to which I am pointing. That's all right. I just write what she says and I'll learn the details later.

At times we look at the pictures in a *National Geographic* magazine. Shañe' tells me what is going on in a picture as she points to it:

*Matena.* (He is running.)

*Rrenet.* (They are eating.)

*Chope'chenet.* (They are walking.)

I see the common ending, *-et,* on the last two words and try to determine how the two words are alike in their translation: "they" (third-person, plural subject).

Then I stand up and walk and Shañe' says:

*Pechope'chen.* (You are walking.) She stands up and walks and says:

*Nechope'chen.* (I am walking.) I take her hand and we walk together and she says:

*Yechope'chen.* (We are walking.)

See what a good, little teacher I have? I am already learning the pronominal subject affixes (*ne-* I, *pe-* you, *ye-* we).

Then I find a picture in the magazine where only one person, a man, is walking and show it to her. She says:

*Chope'chen.* (He is walking.)

I find the picture of a woman walking and show her. She says the same thing:

*Chope'chen.* (She is walking.)

I think to myself, is there no different gender marker in the third-person singular pronominal subject to distinguish he and she? In fact, it has no affix at all as the other ones have. Is it possible that the default (zero) marks both genders in the third-person singular (he and she)? Also, it is strange that in the third-person plural (they) there is a suffix instead of a prefix as in all the other forms (*-et* they). It just goes to show that anything can happen in a language — or almost.

We prefer to work monolingually rather than through Spanish, the national language. In the first place, the Amuesha people don't know that much Spanish. In the second place, areas of meanings in the two different languages are not always the same. Furthermore, we want the Amueshas to know that we value their language and want to use it since it is often ridiculed by some of their neighbors who speak Spanish.

In the mornings we file the new words we have collected from the previous afternoon with our language teachers. Sometimes we are not certain of the meanings since we are working monolingually, but we can record a possibility or the occasion in which the term was used. Also with our data from the previous afternoon we try to identify morphemes (parts of words like suffixes and prefixes that are added to the root of a word) which have their own individual meanings. For example, from the above data with the word "to walk," I see that *ne-* marks "I," first-person singular pronominal subject; *pe-* marks "you," second-person singular subject; there is no suffix or prefix to mark "he, she, it," third-person singular subject; *ye-* marks "we," first-person plural subject; and *-et* marks "they," third-person plural subject.

Determining where one morpheme ends and another begins has to be considered, as well as the order in which the suffixes occur. When as many as ten suffixes can be attached both to noun and verb roots in this language, the order is very important. Then we try to identify the roots of the words. It is like working on a big, intriguing jigsaw puzzle as we continue to add to our "shoebox" files of both words and morphemes.

Our jaws become a little tired from trying to pronounce these difficult, new consonant sounds after about three hours of studying with our teachers. We take little breaks and trust our jaws will soon become accustomed to the complex sounds like *čh, rr, ts, ĩ, p̃,* and *m̃.*[1]

At the end of a week's work, we pay our teachers. Shañe' is so pleased to accept the first money she has ever earned that she can hardly wait to get home and show her father.

Sometimes on Saturdays or Sundays, when we need a break from hearing the language continually and striving to understand, analyze, and speak it more ourselves, we manage to escape and find our way to a beautiful spot upriver where no one lives and relax beside the clear, flowing waters. We read, have our devotions, sing InterVarsity Christian Fellowship songs, pray, read *Time* magazine, sunbathe, take a dip in the river, eat our picnic lunch, and return home refreshed and ready to start our language lessons again.

> "(Christ) in whom are hidden all the treasures of wisdom and knowledge."
> – the Apostle Paul, (Colossians 2:3 NIV)

(Thank you, Lord, that you become our wisdom as we seek to learn and analyze this language for your glory.)

# 8

# Pepe

The Amuesha people are fascinated when they see us writing their language and then reading it back to them. In fact, they are just now learning that their language can be written. While they have seen some things written in Spanish, they had no idea that their language could be written too.

We show them their Amuesha words written in a very simple, sight-reading primer book that Pete has made. Immediately some want to learn to read the words. We start with three students and more decide each day that they too want to learn to read. Before we are here hardly two weeks, fifteen want to learn to read, some children, some adults, including "Vicky's" bashful mother and Shañe's stepmother, **Shoncare'**.

Since they are not accustomed to coming together to be taught, I teach one or two of them at a time as they happen to come around. Their culture, in such situations is very individualistic; they like to proceed at their own pace. Each person remembers just where he or she left off in the reading book and starts there the next time.

Little Pepe is one of the most anxious of the children and the smallest. He stands at the table on the other side of me, his dark, sparkling eyes barely clearing the top of the table. His straight, shiny bangs stretch from ear to ear. Pepe has very little range from which to see his reading book, but those eager little eyes serve him well.

"*Apa*" (father), he reads, pointing to the word with great pride. Of course, the word being placed just under a drawing of an Amuesha father clothed in the typical man's tunic and crown helps Pepe to remember. The next day he will learn another word with its picture, and thus his confidence that he surely can learn to read grows.

Our practice of starting with sight reading of whole words rather than sounds of individual letters helps the pupil to realize that reading has meaning. As I am able, I talk to Pepe about *apa*.

"Where is *apa*?"

"*Ahuo' apa topo*" (Father went downriver.) is the answer, or

"*Ahuo' apa puetsaĩo*" (Father went to the woods.), depending upon where Pepe's father may have gone that particular day. I repeat the words after Pepe.

Thus I am learning to speak new words and Pepe is learning to read them. How cool! What fun!

Later in the reading book, Pepe will also learn to read that very sentence: *Ahuo' apa puetsaĩo*, thus reviewing his old word, *apa*, and learning two new words.

While the students continue learning more and more sight words, they have a tendency to forget the first ones they learned. In addition to the reviews that are found in the primers, I devise a game to review them. It's like Bingo, with the words written on playing cards in different orders. Each calling card has a different review word. As the caller reads a word, the players find the word on their cards and place a kernel of corn on it. The first one to get a lineup of words wins and calls out "*Ñempo!*" (their closest sounding word to Bingo) which means "branch minnow." "Let's play *Ñempo*" is their favorite request. Even the older people like to play it.

Still later, in more advanced books, we will also teach the sounds of syllables so that in time the students may become independent readers, able to read new words they have never seen before. Writing this language just the way it sounds makes for early, positive results.

With those advanced reading books, Pepe will be learning the sounds of the individual syllables contained in the sight words that he already knows: *a – pa*. Thus he will be able to read the new word *a-pa-pa'* (where is father?) without any help. As the number of syllables increases, I make another *Tempo* game. This new one will use syllables instead of words for review. Having learned the twenty-nine letters of his Amuesha language alphabet, Pepe will be able to read any word in his language, whether it be a little word like *ta* (he/she goes) or a big word like *omarrame'tampesyesnena* (various people are going downriver in a canoe, stopping often along the way as they go in the afternoon).

Older boys and girls, and even adults, can learn to recognize all of the letters of their own language very quickly. This kind of literacy work requires no equipment from the outside world.

Literacy is so important to indigenous work, where the people themselves become their own Christian leaders. This is the type of progress we encourage and the reason we start literacy training as soon as we start learning the language ourselves. We believe that teaching the people to read the translated Scriptures fluently is almost as important as having the translation itself. Christian indigenous leaders must be able to read and teach the Scriptures to their own people for them to be able to grow in their spiritual understanding and develop into strong, spiritual churches.[1]

Teaching and worship must be conducted in the native language and within the culture of the people for the most effective testimony. We agree with Dr. Ralph D. Winter, founder of the U.S. Center for World Mission, that this is "the really high-powered E-1 level" evangelism that will start a true church planting movement.[2]

We also agree with *Mission Frontiers* (magazine of the U.S. Center for World Mission) in their "Ten Common Factors" (of Church Planting Movements) where they state: "Worship in the common heart language keeps it accessible and within reach of all members of the community and allows everyone to participate in the new church's formation. Missionaries who identify and embrace the heart language of the people they are trying to reach are well-positioned to stimulate a Church Planting Movement. Nothing reveals a people group's world view as much as an intimate knowledge of their heart language. Missionaries who choose to work through a trade language begin their ministry with a curtain between themselves and the hearts of the people they are seeking to reach."[3]

Learning to read in one's own heart language instead of the trade language opens the curtain to the development of indigenous Christian leaders who will read God's translated Word not only for themselves but for their own people.

"Blessed is the one who reads the words of this prophecy . . ."

— the Apostle John, (Revelation 1:3 NIV)

(Thank you, Lord, for the positive response of the people here in learning to read in their language. May there be many readers ready for your Word as it will be translated in the future.)

# 9

# Child Witches

It was in the quiet, midmorning hours one day that a child's scream suddenly rang out through the village.

Startled from our language work, Mary Ruth and I look at each other in fear of what might have happened. Jumping up, we exclaim, "A child must be injured."

Running to the door, we check to see if there is someone we can ask. No one is anywhere in sight. Meanwhile, the screams continue. No one is in our house either, which is quite unusual since ordinarily several people are here reading the primers, looking at pictures, or listening to the recordings.

The screams not only continue, they become louder. We don't know what to do. We have tried to not get involved in family affairs, or in some cultural things we don't yet understand, but the bloodcurdling screams continue.

We decide that surely a child has been hurt and must be in great distress. So we head out the door and hurry down the field toward the source of the screams. As we rush along, we think it strange that we don't see anyone else rushing to investigate. In fact, we see no one anywhere.

As we arrive at the end of the field, we can tell the screams are coming from a large, old deserted-looking building. We can now hear a great commotion of angry people inside the house, along with the continued screams.

As we near the building and are about to enter the door, we hear the rapid shuffle of bare feet on the dirt floor, with the sound moving away from us and going toward the back door of the house. Entering the room, we see only a small boy of about five or six, lying limply on the dirt floor and appearing to be in great distress. He has stopped screaming, but is sobbing uncontrollably. His tattered little tunic is scarcely hanging on his small, thin shoulders.

We sit down on the ground with the child to take a look at his injury, but we see no open wound. What could possibly have happened? Has this child been beaten? Could that be? Even if we could understand him, he is not able to talk because of his sobbing.

We feel desperate as to how we can help this child. Mary Ruth remembers a little shirt she has that we can give him. It's evident that he can use some clothes, and maybe this will cheer him up a little. And it does. When she returns with the shirt, the boy grabs it and holds it to himself as if this is his only possession in the world, and it probably is. His sobs lessen a bit.

It will be a long time before we find out what really happened that day. As our ability to understand more of what is being said grows, Mary Ruth's teacher, Kosepa, mentions that the situation we ran into is a common practice.[1] A small, orphaned child may be accused of bewitching another person and causing the person to become sick or even die. They say the child does this by secretly burying fish bones in the ground, which can effect this bewitchment. The remedy is for several adults to beat the child with sticks, sometimes even to death.

We have come with the intent of working within the culture of these people. We have studied anthropology and realize the importance of learning the culture and beliefs of the people. That's why we consider it very important to learn the language of the people which reflects their true culture. Without mastering the people's language, it would be difficult for anyone to accurately determine the cultural beliefs.

We have been led to believe that all aspects of a culture are good and beneficial to the members of that cultural group. Could we be wrong? We are realizing that this "unspoiled jungle" is not a Garden of Eden to all its inhabitants as some teach — not to a small, orphaned child — or even to some of its adult population.

Among the Amarakaeri, another of the indigenous language groups, as witnessed by linguists working there, sometimes grown women are considered to be witches. Four women of the village had been declared witches. They were beaten and machete hacked, and thrown into the river for dead. One of the women survived to tell the story. Another neighboring group, which is of the same language family as Amuesha, has the same cultural practice of beating child witches and is said to have continued this practice until recently.

What do the Amuesha people themselves think of all this? It is revealing that those who beat the child did not want to come face to face with us on this particular day, hence the rapid exodus from the other side of the house as we approached. Were their own consciences condemning them?

Ordinarily, Amuesha families do take care of orphaned children, but when sickness and death occur, especially of respected members of the group, everyone can suspect a certain orphan. As our hearts ache for the defenseless orphan, we realize anew the desperate need for God's Word here.

We are happy that no further incidents of this practice take place while we are here. Maybe the orphan's new, little red shirt is a reminder of God's love for this child.


"You shall not afflict any . . . fatherless child."
  – Moses, as given by God, (Exodus 22:22 KJV)


"Be not overcome by evil, but overcome evil with good."
  – the Apostle Paul, (Romans 12:21 NIV)


(Thank you, Lord, that the little child was not killed. Show us what is our responsibility in matters of moral standards and cultural practices among the Amuesha people.)

# 10

# Worms, Lice and Bonding

How can you refer to someone when he or she doesn't seem to be called by a name?

Finding names which Mary Ruth and I can use in referring to individuals we want to talk about to each other has been difficult. In the first place, some people here don't seem to have given names. When the people talk among themselves, they use kinship references rather than given names as they refer to and address one another. For example: "My sister" *nomo'nerr* (female speaker), "my brother-in-law" *norrar* (female speaker), or "my sister-in-law" (male speaker).

Of course, this leaves us not knowing how to refer to individuals as we talk about them. Between us, we develop our own nicknames to refer to them.

"City Woman" gets her name when she first comes to meet us with white talcum powder rubbed all over her bronze-brown face. This is to make sure we understand that she had once been out to a city somewhere. "Rag Doll" gets her name because her little tunic is so tattered and torn up from the bottom. "Vicky's" older brother is always playing jokes on others, so why shouldn't we refer to him as "Playboy"? "Pretty Woman" gets her name because that's what she is — beautiful.

The people are also at a loss in knowing how to refer to us. Since we are still in our 20s, they don't know whether to call us their children or their sisters. For lack of a better word and wanting to be respectful, they use a Spanish term they know — "Señorita." As we become acquainted, they start to "possess" us by calling us "our Señoritas." And as they get to know us better, they begin to refer to us as "sister" *noch* (male speaker) *nomo'nerr* (female speaker). We, in turn, call them "sister" and "brother" in their language. It is a good way to bond even more with them.[1]

Suddenly, Mary Ruth gets a strange pain in her scalp. I look at it to see what it might be, but can see nothing that looks unusual. The pain continues and becomes worse day by day. Still I see nothing unusual, no infection. Maybe a small bump.

We talk to our doctor at the Center by radio. He only suggests the possibility of a boil, but we know that's not it since there is no infection.

We have not shown it to the local people yet for fear of what treatment they might suggest — sterile or not. Since the pain continues to increase, we decide to show it to some of them. The women take one look at it and say, "It's a worm; we know how to treat it."

Before we can stop them, they go home and heat some **caucho** (raw rubber) to make liquid rubber and are soon back with the warm liquid. They apply it to the spot and tell us not to take it off until they come back in a day or so. We pray and hope for the best.

They return at the right time and very carefully pull up the solidified rubber. The group gathers around Mary Ruth to see what is happening. Up with the rubber comes a very tiny, white worm, which they quickly squash.

Turnabout is fair play. We have been treating the people with our medicines; now they are treating us with theirs. Bonding comes in more ways than one!

Then it's my turn. All the time that I'm thinking it won't happen to me, it does. I have head lice!

I thought that if one washes her hair every week she could not get lice. Even though I know the people all have lice in their hair, I think that it is because they don't wash their hair regularly. In fact, their head lice don't even seem to bother them. Rather, it is a very pleasant pastime for the women as they relax with friends to look in each other's hair for lice. When a number of the women are relaxing, as they often do at our house, it is common to see them line up, each one sitting in front of the other, tandem fashion, looking through the hair of the one ahead of her. Great social conversation goes on in the meantime as they exchange favors with a neighbor.

This is such an enjoyable activity for these women that when we hear about a related group in which outsiders came in and eradicated all the lice, we wonder what will happen to the social pastime there. Believe it or not, we learn later that the women send someone to a neighboring village to bring back a few lice to restart their pastime.

Now that the women realize I also have lice, I am really "in." "City Woman," Amo (her daughter) and "Spook" are all inspecting my hair at the same time. As their long hair falls down over mine while they look, I know I am getting ten times more new lice from them than what they are finding. Since they are so happy to have me "in," I don't want to disappoint them by trying to squirm away. Besides, I think a kerosene treatment will get rid of what remains.

Bonding does come in more ways than one!


"I have become all things to all men [people] . . ."
    – the Apostle Paul, (I Corinthians 9:22 NIV)

# 11

# Is There a Doctor in the House?

*"Atsna'ten ach,"* (Mother is sick) Pepe comes to tell us one morning and give us some venison his father brought home.

We understand this word *atsna'ten* easily, because we have heard it many times. Sickness is very common among these people and we have been kept busy treating those who are ill. Pepe's mother is Kosepa, Mary Ruth's language teacher.

We hurry over to see what the problem is. We find that Kosepa has a high fever and many body aches. Others in her extended family, living in the same house, seem to be sick in the same manner. They are lying all around on the ground, some near the fire. We decide this must be a flu or pneumonia since so many have the same symptoms. These people often have pneumonia because their lungs are in a weakened condition from intestinal parasites. It can easily be fatal for them.

We have not yet learned to give penicillin shots, but we do have sulfa pills that we know will help. We start all the sick ones with fevers on the sulfa pills and tell them as best we can how to continue to take them: at *ahuatecma* (early morn), and *pocto'tsen* (midday), pointing to the sun for each time, and again at *elleroneĩ* (evening) and *tsapo* (night), and to continue *tsapaĩ* (tomorrow) and everyday until they have taken all the pills.

They are not accustomed to taking medicines consistently. We decide one of us must go back each time to make sure they take their medicines correctly. In fact, these are the first medicines they have ever had.

Other members of this extended family continue to come down with the sickness until there are thirteen sick at the same time in Kosepa's family. Other families are becoming sick also — a pneumonia epidemic!

This keeps both Mary Ruth and me busy. We divide up the families between us so we can continue checking to make sure that all of them are taking their medicines correctly. We just hope and pray that our sulfa supply does not run out. Pneumonia epidemics have killed off large numbers of the Amueshas in the past, we have learned.

The people are so happy to find the medicine is helping them recover. They begin to realize that our medicines are *atarr cohuen* (very good). Happily, everyone does recover in this epidemic. Thank you, Lord.

The mothers start coming to request *shachoperetspar* (medicine for worms) for their children. They know we now have a new supply of these treatments. Each morning a different group of children is brought to us by their mothers. This turns out to be more work than even the pneumonia epidemic.

We decide to take turns in the early mornings. One of us gives the treatments at our front door while the other prepares breakfast. We soon find out that these treatments turn into a time of "weeping, and wailing, and gnashing of teeth." Most children do not want to take the pills as much as their mothers want them to. I find the best way is to put the pill far back in the child's mouth and then push it down quickly with my thumb before the child realizes what is happening. It's true I have gotten a few bites, but no blood was drawn.

Little Pepe becomes one of the most resistant. Even with his mother's threats and my big thumb, Pepe does swallow his worm pills, but not without a hassle.

After the pills come the Epsom salts later in the day. This is even worse for the children to swallow. We feel so bad for these kids, but they really do become stronger and more resistant to the frequently occurring pneumonia that has killed so many of them in the past.

Later we learn from our Center doctor that we will need to repeat the entire deworming process. Some worms are as resistant as the children! Even our hardtack candy rewards have run out.

Along with the daily routine, we treat the people for sore eyes, skin problems, malaria, headaches, stomach aches, ear aches, fungus, machete cuts, and tuberculosis. We soon realize that we are the only doctors in the house.[1] We are doing more business than the shaman. People are coming for treatment from far away villages. I see the need for learning to give shots of penicillin.

As our medical work increases and people visit us more and more, our language studies become more strenuous. We realize we are more exhausted by the end of the day. Then it is our turn to listen to the one Gospel Recording record we have in English — "He Giveth More Strength as the Labors Increase."

"And Jesus went about ... healing all manner of sickness ... "
— the Apostle Matthew, (Matthew 4:23 KJV)

" ... I was sick and you visited me ... "
— Jesus, (Matthew 25:36 KJV)

(Thank you, Lord, that we can relieve some of the suffering of these dear people.)

[Who would ever think that someday little Pepe would become the first sanitario (health promoter) of his own people at Stingray village? I would! Who would ever think our medical help would influence the desire of the people in the distant future to have copies of God's Word that we would translate? As one of them would say, "You were the ones who gave us medicines when we were sick; that's why we want God's Word which you have translated for us."]

# 12

# Cherry Pie
# in the Jungle?

"Rag Doll" comes to see if we want to go with her and her brother, Gaspar.

*"Semneña't o'ch sociay; o'ch ye'nena' cocllom̃?"* (Do you want to go with us to look for *cocllom̃*?)

*"Yemneñca'ye."* (We want to, yes.) *"Eso't ñeñ̃ cocllom̃?"* (What are *cocllom̃*?)

*"Atarr puetsarr pue'mer, tsamaietoll."* (Very sweet, little, red fruits.)

Sounds good to us, like cherries maybe. Besides, it is a chance for a trip in the canoe. We have scarcely been away from here since arriving some five months ago.

Others want to go also when they hear of the trip. Even Grandma Santos, the oldest woman in Stingray village, wants to join in as well as a young man named José.

We cross the river in their canoe and head up another tributary, a small, clear stream. Pristine beauty unfolds ahead of us like a giant, color TV — beautiful scenes one after another as we round each bend. No roads, no houses, no people, just dark green jungle foliage mingled with lovely, purple flowering trees. We hear no sounds except the soft lapping of the canoe paddles and the calls from beautifully colored birds along the riverbanks. It's like a fresh, new world where no one has ever ventured before us.

As we paddle close to the shore, lost in the panoramic beauty, Grandma Santos begins telling us the names of each of the trees and plants we see along the way. She, no doubt, knows the names of over a thousand trees and plants that cover this vast Amazon rainforest. (Little do I know that in the not-to-distant future, Amuesha school children will be writing these never-before-written names of the myriad of jungle foliage for the very first time.)

We dock on the shore and leave the canoe to start up a very sharp incline from the river. At times it is so steep we have to pull ourselves up by the bushes and small trees along the way. The fellows take the lead, showing us the way since there seems to be no path. I wonder how Grandma Santos is taking this energetic walk. As I look back at her, she is doing as well as the rest of us — especially me.

As we reach the top of this incline, they point out the big *cocllom̃* trees along the ridge, their red berries shining brightly in the sunlight. The fellows quickly climb the tall trees with tree-climber vines (*a 'tapačh*) tied around their ankles. With his machete, José begins to cut off whole branches with their berries and drop them down to the ground. We women pick up all the berries that fall off in the drop.

Mary Ruth and I both examine them. They do look a lot like cherries but have a rougher surface. All of us delight in the sweet *cocllom̃* cherries — we for the first time, and the Amueshas for the first time this *cocllom̃* season. We load up the canoe and head back home.

As we glide back downriver, "visions of cherry pies dance in Mary Ruth's head." She has already decided to make a *cocllom̃* cherry pie, which she does as soon as we get home. Cherry pie in the jungle! What a treat!

"He has made everything beautiful in its time. He has also set
eternity in the hearts of men (people)."
— Solomon, (Ecclesiastes 3:11 NIV)


(Thank you, Lord, that the people want to share with us their
good things even as we want to share with them our good
things.)

# 13

# Photo Op

Whoever heard of taking a picture without a smile?

"Now don't a one of you smile," the newly arrived Amuesha father sternly charges his many children as he lines them all up for me to take their picture.

He has not only heard in his village far upriver about our having good medicine, but he has also heard that we have a machine that will make pictures of people.

I invite his two wives, who are sisters, to join in the picture along with their husband. I hear the younger one with a baby say to the older one, "They want a picture of us with our husband (*yerrollar*)." These words, "our husband," sound so strange, but this is Amuesha culture. A man often takes sisters as wives in succession. As the first one gets older, he takes her younger sister also. The children call both of the sisters *ach* (mother).

I take the picture as they want it — no smiles. Amueshas feel that a smile is more like a grimace and not to be desired in a picture.

You may think this should be one big, happy family, but that's often not the case as I later discover. An older wife comes and tells me her husband is

planning to take her younger sister as a wife also. The older sister is definitely
not happy about this. Amuesha men have often taken young girls as wives
even before they reach puberty. The very young girls are often not happy as
wives.

Trying to use the few words I know to make conversation with the
visitors, I say to the younger woman, "Do you know who Jesus is?"

"No, I don't know. Maybe if I knew who his mother is, I would know who
he is." It is quite evident that these visitors have never heard of Jesus.

They soon leave to go back upriver. When will they learn about Jesus?
Again I realize how much God's Word is needed throughout Amueshaland.
It is another incentive to keep plugging away at learning this language.

We are happy that the children here in Stingray village are learning
something about Jesus. We trust they will soon be sharing what they know
with their neighbors upriver. They love to sing "Jesus Loves Me" with us. The
young fellows are also becoming interested and join the children in singing.
I even hear someone from the Santos household playing "Jesus Loves Me" on
his reed flute. What a beautiful sight to have Daniel (another of the young
men), Sabella (Shañe's little sister), "Rag Doll," her older brother, Gaspar,
and "Playboy" all joining around us in singing "Jesus Loves Me" this evening.
The older men are helping us to get the wording to fit the music better.

We show them some of the very early preliminary translation that Pete
has worked on and read it to them. Some of the older people also are
interested and listen in.

"Is this our father's message to us in our own language?" they ask us in astonishment. They call the sun "our father" (god). We try to explain to them that the true "our Father" is the one who made the sun and that we want to write this true "our Father's" words in their language, and we want them to help us.

They become more and more interested as we stand there under the thatched roof eave of our house. We are so involved in talking about the possibility of having the true "our Father's" Word written in their language that we are all unaware of the threatening storm and of the rain that begins to drip down on our heads. I am completely unaware that Mary Ruth has been calling me to help get things covered up that are getting rained on. It is worth getting wet to see the real interest of the Amuesha people in having God's Word in their language.

"City Woman" is showing a great interest in knowing about the true "our Father" and his Son, Jesus. Because of our lack of ability in the Amuesha language, we can only tell her that Jesus died for her and if she believes, she will go to live with Him. We trust the Holy Spirit to work in her heart and help her to understand what we can't tell her yet.

The young men are now also starting to come to us for reading classes, joining the children and women. They learn quickly and are already learning that the syllable is the basic sound block from which any word may be read phonetically. They learn the letter symbols with their sounds right away and are soon able to read new words they have never seen before. Ever so often I hear a chuckle as one is able to read a new, long word all on his own. It's gratifying to see the young men becoming interested in reading because they will soon be the mature leaders of the village.

We now play the Bingo game using the syllables of the language instead of the words for the younger children since everyone is reaching the same point in their reading. The game is a very useful tool for reviewing the many syllables and fixing them firmly in the pupils' minds so they can be read easily. Everyone likes to play — young and old alike. "*Tempo!*" rings out every few minutes as the first one recognizes all the called out syllables and wins the game.

Four of the mothers are now among the students. "Vicky" is not quite old enough yet, but he comes along with his mother and Shañe's stepmother for their reading class. Today "Vicky" spends all his time during the reading class searching for his *ma'ñorr pa'clle'* ("deer's eye" marbles) which were being hidden beneath the long tunics of the women.

Shañe' is doing the best of all the readers and is already able to read new words in Amuesha. Of course, she gets more practice with me in our study times together. She is also attempting to read some of the preliminary translated Scripture. Her father, Cruz, who is one of the leading men of the village, comes today to hear her read some of the Scripture. "The true 'our Father's' Word can be written in our language!" he marvels.[1]

The literacy work is going well, but we are both a little discouraged in our grammar analysis of this language. I have been working on the accent in the words, and Mary Ruth has been working on the morphology — identification of morphemes (meaningful parts of the words). We both realize we have not begun to solve all the puzzles of this very complex language and that there is a long road ahead yet. A verse that has encouraged me in daily devotions is this one where David said:

"I will not sacrifice to the Lord . . . offerings that cost me nothing."

      – the Psalmist David, (II Samuel 24:24 NIV)

(Thank you, Lord, that the people do show great interest in having your Word in their language and a great interest in learning to read.)

# 14

# Our First
# Six-Month Break

Six months in Stingray village!

We can hardly believe it. The time has gone so quickly; we have been so busy.

They tell us on the radio that the plane might be coming for us tomorrow, and then they say it might be a week from tomorrow. With many flights scheduled for the pilots throughout the jungle and the uncertainty of weather conditions, they are not sure they can make the flights as scheduled.

Since tomorrow is a possibility, we'd better get ready for it. We spend the day scrubbing pots to pack away, washing clothes and mosquito nets, some to go and some to leave here.

Today they tell us by radio to have our things ready to go by ten o'clock tomorrow, the plan being to take only our equipment first, then us. We really have to get busy. The people hear about us leaving, and many come to see us.

The pilot, Merrill Piper, makes a perfect landing to pick up our baggage to go to Yarinacocha. We load it on quickly since the pilot is scheduled to pick up more equipment downriver for Pete and then head back to Yarinacocha for another flight elsewhere today.

We were expecting the plane would be back for us the following afternoon, but even before lunchtime we hear the sound of the plane. Plans have changed again, and they want the plane back at Yarinacocha for an afternoon flight. We work like mad to get all the last-minute things done and pack ourselves a lunch to eat on the way to Yarinacocha. It has only taken us thirty-five minutes to get ready from the time we heard the plane was coming sooner.

All the Amueshas are gathered around to see us off. People we didn't even know existed six months ago are now good friends. Leaving is not easy. I say good-bye to each one individually. They follow us right to the plane doors, not the least bit afraid of the plane like they were when we arrived.

Shañe' is standing right by the door so she will be the last one to say good-bye. I see the tears in her eyes and my tears start too. We have grown to love each other as sisters. I have learned much of their language, life, and culture; and yet have much more to learn. God has been faithful in every way.

It is with much emotion that we leave Stingray village and the new world we have come to know, and head back to Yarinacocha for our old world, so completely different. *Will we fit in there now?* One thing is certain we will never be the same again after our six months with the Amueshas.

We eat our lunch on the plane just after takeoff. Soon we are landing on the lake at Yarinacocha at 3:25 p.m. Many of our folks who work full time at Yarinacocha are down at the dock to meet us and welcome us back. We feel almost as strange back in this world as we did when we first arrived in Stingray village. Yet we soon "shift gears" and feel right at home again.

Elaine Townsend invites us to have dinner with her family to hear about our life with the Amueshas. Viola Galenzoski (Escobar) asks us to have breakfast with her the next day. Pete and Mary Fast invite us for dinner the next day.

As we get around to talking to our director, he assures us that he wants us to remain with the Amueshas. Pete Fast is being given more and more group duties.

Since I went to the Amueshas so soon after arriving in Peru from the U.S., I have not had time to study any Spanish, the national language of Peru. I am thinking of studying Spanish for a short time and will be going into Lima, Peru's capital, to live with a Spanish-speaking family and be immersed in that language. It's good to know some Spanish for all the negotiations that have to be done on a national level. There, again, I will need to learn to adjust to another culture so different from Amuesha, and also different from our American culture. The Amuesha language is not at all like Spanish since the Amerindian languages were being spoken long before the Spanish conquerors arrived in Peru.

I am learning that I must be able to adapt quickly from one language and culture[1] to another. God does enable us as we commit our way to Him.

"Commit your way unto the Lord; trust also in him; and he shall bring it to pass."
— the Psalmist David, (Psalm 37:5 KJV)

(Thank you, Lord, for the good six months you have given us among the Amuesha people. Thank you for them receiving us into their lives, and for their desire to know more of your Word in their own language.)

# 15

# Going Back to Stingray Village

What does "going to the tribe" mean?

Our dear friends at the Center have been giving us farewell parties all this week. Bad weather has been holding us up, but this morning we get the word to "load up," although it is still a little cloudy. Several of them come down to the plane ramp to see us off, including our present director, Jim Wroughton, who leads us in a prayer for our trip and time out with the Amuesha people. After my short course in Spanish in Lima, we are on our way to "the tribe" again.

After the last hugs and good-byes, we board the little Aeronca float-plane.

Since we are heavily loaded, Mary Ruth and I both sit as far forward in the plane as possible for a quicker takeoff from the lake. There is always that anxious thrill of finally leaving the water and waving good-bye to our friends still standing on the ramp. Thus, we continue on to the beginning of our second year with the Amuesha work.

It's fun to be in the air again. In the little Aeronca, it seems just like you are riding through the air on a broom. It's a windy day and right away the plane starts bouncing — first sideways and then up and down. That funny feeling in your stomach (partly from the excitement of returning to the village, and partly from the breakfast you just had) all but knocks you out. Thankfully, we manage to keep our breakfast down.

Leo Lance, one of the newest to arrive in Peru, is our pilot. Over the roar of the motor, he points out in his husky Oklahoma voice that Tournavista[1] is to our left as we pass it. The weather wasn't very good when we started and it is now getting worse. We are having to cross some ridges with low clouds over them. As we follow the general course of the Pachitea River, it is always a welcome sight to see the water beneath us. It can always become a forced landing field. (In fact, Leo tells us later that he did look seriously for possible landing sites.) As we continue on, the weather becomes beautiful on the other side of the ridge.

As I look down over the never-ending, green rainforest below, and the snake-like river that we cross repeatedly as we follow it, I begin to think: Here I am going out again as a missionary; I can hardly believe it is true. I marvel that God is allowing me to do this — me with all my inabilities and shortcomings. Thank you, Lord.

As we near Stingray village, I have mixed feelings of fear and anxiety once more. We get to where we see our old landing spot on the river. Leo starts to set the plane down, and I think he is going to land in the rapids instead of the pool above. I quickly proceed to tell him and he answers, "I know." Leo makes a perfect landing, and I later ask him if he can ever forgive backseat driving in a plane.

The Amueshas are standing on the bank just like when we first arrived. Right away I recognize "Rag Doll," Sabella, (Shañe's little sister), and others. The kids have grown so much in the few months we have been away. I do not see Shañe' and ask right away, "Where is Shañe'?"

"She is sick," they answer. I wonder what this will mean.

We unload the plane quickly and Leo takes off to do some shuttling with the plane downriver. We start up the bank to the village but to our surprise and dismay the village is not there! Only a few poles of the houses are still standing, including the house where we once lived. Our hearts sink.

"What has happened?" we ask, fearing to even know.

They tell us that the headman of the village died. Fearing the spirit of the dead one, the whole village moved to a new site.

It looks so sad. All of the houses are torn down, with just a few poles showing the place where they stood. The grass has grown high on the field where we had played.

They lead us on toward the old trail to Domingo's house, where we used to go through the jungle. We go on over the trail, cross logs fallen across gorges, up and down hills, and over downed logs and stumps from the newly-cleared ground for the village. In each of the houses we come to, we find some of our old friends. We stop, greet and talk with them as much as we can.

We come to Cruz's house and there I see Shañe' sitting. I don't recognize her at first; she is so thin and feeble looking. I can't help but put my arms around her. She almost cries, and so do I. Holding back my tears, I try to find out what happened to her. She says her knees and elbows became very swollen and stayed that way for three months. Then her left leg became stiff and now she can only walk with the help of sticks. This explains why she didn't come down to the plane to meet us. We aren't sure what Shañe' contracted — maybe polio. I ask her if she still wants to help me. Without any hesitation, she says she does.

We don't know where we will live and the villagers don't seem to know either. We will just wait and see what happens. Finally we get on to a little house where no one is living, and which happens to be built with parts from the little house in which we used to live. We are told we can spend the night here and then move to another place in the morning.

This new village site is downriver on a high plateau overlooking the bend of the river below — a beautiful sight, even if it is hard to reach. Some of the men, including Shañe's father, Cruz, brought our baggage downriver by canoe and up another trail from the river.

We don't try to organize anything. We just greet and talk with the people as they come. Kosepa, Mary Ruth's teacher, has the cutest little baby girl. She tells Mary Ruth after everyone is gone that she has named the baby after her. Mary Ruth is delighted. However, Kosepa calls the baby by her baby name, Shecac, (a little land toad).

Happily, we do have our sleeping bags with us, so we are in the sack by 7:30 p.m. after such a full day. The next day, we find some kerosene that we had left and strain it for our little Primus one-burner stove to boil some water for drinking as we haven't found the coffee yet. We eat some of the food we brought with us. We talk with the people all morning. Shañe' comes hobbling over. I almost cry again when I see her so disabled. After most of the people leave, I show Shañe' pictures I had taken of us working together. She is so pleased.

As we talk, Shañe' tells me her father cried when she became so sick. "He thought I was going to die," she says. *"Camprropano campa'n."* (He gave me the steam treatment.) This is a treatment where they heat stones and put them in a pot of hot water together with certain medicinal leaves. The steam comes up from the hot pot that they place under the wide tunic they wear and thus steam treat the body.

Later the people tell us we can live in Domingo's little house since he has another one he can use. It only has a floor and roof, but that's okay. They want us to come over and try it out for height. Since we are taller than most of them, sure enough, we can't stand up straight without hitting our heads on the rafters. They quickly lower the floor — no problem.

We are happy to have a place to call "home." We proceed to put up our big mosquito net, which completely covers all the floor space, thus forming our only walls. There is room inside for both our cots and a footlocker that will be our eating table as we sit cross-legged on the floor. Our cooking place will be outside the net on the ground next to the edge of the floor. Not bad for a quick home. In my morning devotion time, I remember the words of our graduation song at Columbia Bible College — "Thy tents shall be our home."

Seated at our footlocker table, with the net rolled up, we have a breath-taking view. From our high plateau we look across the river and on to the forest and foothills of the Andes beyond. The sunsets are so beautiful!

We are now living right in the midst of the people. Llollo (grandmother) lives alone on one side of us with her dog, "Lobo." She and Lobo get along fine until he wakes up in the middle of the night and gets into the warm ashes of her fire or into her food. In the darkness of the night, Lobo gets a loud tongue-lashing, which we can't escape either. It's part of our 24/7 language training.

Llollo is the mother of the main men of the village — Lopez, Domingo, Martin, Cesar, Ahuash, and **Ashaï** — six brothers. She is also Shañe's grandmother. Every morning, some or all of Llollo's sons come to her house to talk with her about what they will do that day. She is a very important figure in the family.

Domingo, the second son, and his wife, Margarita, live about twenty steps away on the other side of us. Martin has recently taken Margarita's sister, Rosa, as his wife and they live nearby also. Lopez is the husband of Mary Ruth's teacher, Kosepa. Cesar, Ahuash, and **Ashaï** are not married yet. Ahuash is a great help to us in carrying things we find too heavy. He is kind; we appreciate him so much.

As the people come to visit us, they want to hear the record in their language again. We also sing with them *"Morrentenna Jesús"* ("Jesus Loves Me").

 For fun, we show them pictures of our relatives. When we try to tell them the relationship each one is to us, we soon discover that in this language, there are two sets of kinship relationships — one for men speakers and one for women speakers. We need to learn double sets of words for all the kinship terms. For example, when a male says "my father," he says *nompor*. When a woman says "my father," she says *nepapar*. This difference between men and women's speech is found in all the kinship terms except a few, which are the same for both sexes. One of our chief mistakes is to use the men's word for some of our relatives. Their raucous laughter shows us our bad mistake. We realize we will have to be very careful in the future Scripture translation to know which is speaking — male or female — in order to use the right kinship term.

After finally getting all our things together and arranged in our mosquito net house, we work on our linguistic files again, together deciding what to call the words grammatically and how to classify them. We decide to create only one file between us to reduce the weight of the paper on the plane.

With things cleared away, we go over to talk to Cruz, Shañe's father, about possibly building us a house in the future. He is very busy, as are all the men, clearing the new ground, setting up new homes, and hunting and fishing for food. We understand the situation and decide we will not mention it again until they do. We probably will be in our makeshift house longer than we thought, but it is not all that bad.

The little, portable oven works well over the one-burner stove. Our appetites are running wild with all the energy we use going up and down to the river, to our water spring, and up and down from our house. I bake an eggless chocolate cake for extra energy. We also make biscuits in our little oven. They taste so good in the wilderness.

Many people come to visit us today, including some from the neighboring group called Campa (Asheninka). Their language is of the same family as Amuesha. However, the two languages are mutually unintelligible. We do not understand them, but we try to be friendly with them too. This whole family of languages is called Arawakan. Other members of this Arawakan family include varieties of Asheninka (such as Pajonal Asheninca, Ashaninca), Machiguenga, and Piro. Wycliffe translators are working in these languages also. The New Testament in the Piro language is almost finished in draft and many believers have resulted from it.

"From one man he made every nation of men, that they should inhabit the whole earth; and he determined the times set for them and the exact places where they should live."
— the Apostle Paul , (Acts 17:26 NIV)

"The Lord will watch over your coming and going both now and forevermore."
— the Psalmist David, (Psalm 121:8 NIV)

"...for I have learned in whatever state I am, to be content. I know how to be abased (live humbly) and I know how to abound (live with prosperity)."
— the Apostle Paul, (Philippians. 4:11-12 KJV)

(Thank you, Lord, that the people have received us well again and given us a place to live.)

# 16

# Starting to Analyze the Grammar of This Language

Snakes alive!

*"Shecheṗ!"* (snake) Shañe' suddenly yells out in the midst of our study time.

I know this word already and look up to see a snake of about five feet in length. With all this newly cleared ground, we'll have to watch out for snakes.

It rains while we are working, and then the sun comes out and a beautiful double rainbow appears. I am thinking how pretty it is, but not Shañe'. In her culture, they are afraid of rainbows. They say if a child is sick and looks at a rainbow he or she will surely die. So no one walks outside when it is in view. How can the rainbow mean such different things to the two of us? Of course, Shañe' has never heard that God put the rainbow in the sky as a good sign. I try to explain, but I lack the words yet to make clear what God's Word says.

After our study time, the teenager "Spook" arrives from downriver. She has been gone some time and wants to hear the record in their language again. After hearing the record, Mary Ruth asks her, "Who made the world and all the people?"

"Our father, the sun, made the world and the people." Again we realize how much God's Word is needed here.

As I write in my diary, I realize that today is June 4th — Dad's birthday. "Baked you a banana cake today, Dad. Wish you could eat it with us. Mixed it sitting on the floor." (The quote is taken from my diary.)

Shañe' tries going down the steep hill to the river today with her sticks. This is the first time she has tried since becoming sick. We go along with her to help if she needs it. She makes it okay and is happy to be able to bathe normally and wash her tunic and hair.

We find a new place for washing clothes where the water pours through the rocks and into a natural rock basin. We soap up our sheets and hold them by the tips while the water whirls them around in the basin. Who said you couldn't have a washing machine in the jungle!

Today we work on getting our grammar file in better condition. We recopy the verb suffixes and prefixes, changing them from the old phonetic script to the new orthography (alphabet) we are now using to simplify writing. We already have found over fifty of the verb affix morphemes (parts of words that have their own meanings), not counting the allomorphs (variant forms) of many of them. We have not identified all of these yet, nor do we know all their meanings.

It's interesting that our language helpers cannot tell us the meanings of these morphemes since the affixes are a part of the word and cannot be isolated and talked about by native speakers. We try to determine the meanings of the affixes by comparing a simple form of a verb with a form that has the affix in question and then comparing their meanings. For example, notice the change in the meaning of the following words using the simplest form of the word *ent* (he/she sees).

| | |
|---|---|
| *ent* | he/she sees |
| *ent-nom* | he/she sees on passing |
| *ent-os* | he/she sees upon arrival |
| *ent-a'muen* | he/she sees in the morning |
| *ent-nen* | he/she sees in the afternoon |
| *ent-err* | he/she sees again |
| *ent-yes* | he/she sees various (things) |

> *ent-an*   he/she sees (a 3rd person object)
>
> *n-ent*   I see

We can determine meanings of each word and the morphemes of each word in the particular context of a story, which helps us to know the meaning. For instance, we find that the *-nom* suffix means "action completed in movement," *-os* means "action completed upon arrival."

If more than one of these morphemes can occur on any one word at a time, then you see that our next task is to deal with the sequential order of the morphemes. Thus, this becomes our next project. Consider this word, for example:

> *ent-yes-os-a'muen-err-an*
>
> (he/she sees again various third-person objects upon arrival in the morning)

When you see there are something like four hundred of these different morphemes on all the different word classes, you realize this is a big puzzle that can keep us busy for a long time. No wonder we needed our studies at the Summer Institute of Linguistics to know how to do it.

People come every day wanting to hear the record in their language. Today Domingo and Martin are here and they explain more to the people after the record has finished. Kosepa's sister and her family come from downriver. "City Woman," her mother, brings them to hear the record. Cruz, Shañe's father, also brings his visiting relatives to hear it. We are happy that the record is a testimony even though it is a slightly different dialect from the one here, and we are not sure how much they are understanding.

Kosepa comes back from her morning work with some *chonta* palm hearts. She gives us some of them and are they ever good. They are eaten raw like salad, just as they come out of the heart of the *chonta* palm. We let her know we really liked them. We don't get any fresh vegetables here; the people don't have them and don't like them. They consider green vegetables to be food for the ducks and geese. Since we don't get fresh vegetables, the raw *chonta* tastes good. I understand that palm hearts are considered a delicacy in nicer hotels throughout the world. Who said the Lord couldn't give us His best here?

Tonight Llollo and her daughter-in-law, Margarita, are burning out a big stump very near their house and ours. They are sitting in the moonlight doing their cooking at this burning stump. We go over to sit with them and visit. They give us new words and then ask us to tell them what our word is in English for that particular word. It is funny hearing them try to pronounce our words. Now they can sympathize with us.

The stars are already coming out as we return home from Llollo's. They seem to be brighter here than anywhere else — no electric lights to dim them. We take our cups of after-supper coffee out to star gaze. With the mountains in the background, we are thinking how beautiful it is just to live in this place where the Lord has put us. "Everything is wonderful when we are in his place for us." (a quote from my diary, June 7th).

Domingo tells us tonight that he would like to build a house for us. This is great news since we had said nothing more about a house to anyone. He thinks he can have it finished in a month and a half, working with another friend. He is happy with the price we have offered him. Thank you, Lord.

"Delight yourself in the Lord and he will give you the desires of your heart."
    — the Psalmist David, (Psalm 37:4 NIV)

# 17

# The Fish Bash

A letter all the way from the jungle to the U.S.A.?

We have been in the new village a month now. We want to send a letter home to our folks to assure them that we are okay; so we read a letter we have written to our families on the radio today. Luke, the operator, takes it down and sends it to our folks. We didn't even need a postage stamp. We appreciate you, Luke. Thanks.

We finish recopying our morpheme file using the new orthography. It looks good! It looks more like a real language now and is much more easily read.

I go to Shañe's house today for our study time together. She tells me what the members of her family are doing. Her father is mending his spear with which he spears fish. The old man Ťo' and his daughter, "Rag Doll," are staying with them. Ťo' is dyeing his tunic and his *poshac* (man's carrying bag) in a pot of boiling water with a bark dye. I record these new verbs as we see all the action going on around us.

Shañe' is gaining ability in getting around. I think working with me again has given her a new interest. She is also gaining weight. She is even able to get into the swift rapids in the river again. I was a little fearful for her since the rapids here are much swifter than those at the old place. But she is doing well even with her paralyzed leg.

The people gather and want to have a big fish catch with a poisonous vine. They dam off a branch of the river so less water comes through. When everything is ready, they pound the vine with rocks in a canoe to get the juice out and mix it with more water.

Then they take the canoe out into the shallow branch of the river and turn it over, making all the water turn white. In just a few minutes "the fish become drunk," as they say, with the poison and start jumping up out of the water.

The sport is to shoot the fish with arrows or spear them. What great fun! They gather the fish they have gotten into baskets. The women and children help to round up the little sucker fish that come out to the water's edge. Mary Ruth and I accompany them in all their happy activity.[1] However, we see some things coming out to the edge of the water that we don't like too much — stingrays. They didn't name this place Stingray for nothing. Yet it is good to get some of them cleared out of the way with this poisonous vine. A stingray wound in the flesh is very painful and is extremely difficult to heal. Mary Ruth knows because she got one once, and healing it took a long time.

The people go back with baskets full of fish. As we return home by way of Shañe's place, we see all the little sucker fish (*meshet*) strung up for smoking and drying. They look like necklaces the women wear. When I mentioned that similarity, the people were amused and laughed, not seeing any likeness. The Amueshas will smoke the majority of the fish in order to be able to keep them longer. We are given our share of the fish too.

Shañe', "Rag Doll," and Sabella come all overjoyed as though going on a picnic. They want to go with us to the river for bathing and swimming, anxious to show us how they can go down the rapids, which are much swifter in this new place.

The little boys are at the river too. They get their small canoes to show us how they can handle them in these swift rapids. One tiny guy who looks to be not over four years old has his own canoe and purposely turns over in the rapids just for extra fun. We wish we had their abilities in the water. It is just a natural part of their cultural education.

Mary Ruth and I are still afraid to try the rapids since we are not the good swimmers the Amueshas are. Yet, we do practice our swimming in a deep spot where the water empties into a gorge and is very still. The Indians tell us they have not found the bottom in this spot. We gain confidence in knowing that this "swimming hole" is very deep. Ability and confidence are important since we may need to travel more on the river in the future.

The radio operator told us today that the plane will be coming out to our place tomorrow. The news gets out and all the people come around. They are as excited as we are. We decide to take someone down to a possible new landing spot nearer to the new village to check the depth of the water. Cruz and Domingo go with us and find the water plenty deep for the plane to land. We pass the word on to Dave, the radio operator.

I bake a cake in our little oven just in case the pilot will have time to eat with us. Before we are scarcely ready, we hear the motor of the plane in the distance. We take off for the river and are joined by all the people. Even before we get down the steep hill, the plane has already landed. Leo is the pilot again. He says he has his lunch, but it didn't take much persuading for him to come up and have lunch with us. Leo likes our *sachapapa* French fries. He eats quickly and is off again.

The people are happy to get the fish hooks and line, thread, combs, and other things they had ordered. We are happy to get mail after five weeks and some fresh vegetables along with other supplies we ordered. There's a good, long letter from my best college friend, Beulah Stapf (Kruhmin), and letters from family members, donors, and prayer partners. There is even a letter from my college professor, Miss McClarty. All are a joy and encouragement to us.

Shañe' and I are studying together today when suddenly we hear a great commotion at Llollo's house next door. Llollo has come home from her field work and found that Lobo, her dog, has eaten her cooked manioc. We hear the tongue-scolding that Lobo often gets. He just drops his tail and slowly walks over to our house and lies down. Before the tongue-lashing stops, he is sound asleep.

Shañe' is telling me how fellows and girls become mates. She says the fellow says to the girl, *neyorap̃* (I take you as wife).

"Has anyone told you that?" I ask her jokingly.

She laughs and says to me, "Has anyone told you that?" Turnabout is fair play.

"Why don't you marry Ahuash? He is so nice," I say.

"I can't marry Ahuash; he is my brother."

Actually, Ahuash is her mother's sister's son . . . evidently not a marriageable possibility.

Lobo sleeps on peacefully in his adopted home as we finish our study time.


" . . . Follow me and I will make you fishers of men."

– Jesus, (Matthew. 4:19 KJV)

# 18

# Jungle Celebrities

A reporter from a U.S. magazine is coming out?

They tell us on the radio this morning that a reporter from a U.S. magazine would like to come out and interview us for a story.

"Would you be willing for this visit and interview?"

What can we say but okay. We think we can crowd another person under our mosquito net in our makeshift house. We learn that the reporter is a woman whose name is Mary but wants to be called Gary.

Great news today! Domingo and his helper have the corner posts placed in the ground for our new house. They are floating the long roof poles down from upriver. We can hardly wait!

"Rag Doll" and Sabella have become great friends since "Rag Doll" and her old father, Ťo', have been staying with Sabella and Shañe's family. The two girls are about ten years old. They hear all the news of the village and pass it on to us. Today "Rag Doll" tells me her sister is going to have a baby, and they know who the father is. They don't realize the older folks don't tell us all they know. Anyway, it's good practice for me to learn to talk with them. I feel less conscious of the mistakes I make.

(July 16th happy birthday, Mom! I baked you a cake — banana upside-down cake. Mary Ruth and I sang "happy birthday" to you at lunch today.)

I continue to have my study time with Shañe' at her house. Today old To' is baking a fish wrapped in a leaf in the coals of an open fire. This is a very common way of cooking one fish at a time, so I learn the words used to describe it. Shañe' also gives me a little text telling about how she first became sick. She is very good in slowing down her talk so I can write it. I get new words as well as verb forms that I analyze later for all the morphemes.

After study time, Mary Ruth and I battle a big, round-bodied spider, creating excitement for all the people. She is on the outside of the mosquito net and I am on the inside when the spider appears. She gets after him outside the net and scares him, causing him to run inside. I try to get him on the inside, but chase him back to the outside. This goes on for some time until Mary Ruth finds the hammer, and when the spider next appears on the outside, she lets him have it. Spider juice splashes up on her arm. She lets out a bloodcurdling scream that brings people running to see what terrible thing has happened. Has she been attacked by a jaguar? When they see the demolished spider, they get a big laugh. Although we are embarrassed, at least we get rid of the spider.

We invite the young people to come in the evening and help us translate a Christian song into Amuesha. We are encouraged in our first try, but we need to do a lot more with it. The long Amuesha words make it hard to fit the notes of the music with the lyrics. One place where we just couldn't get the right word to fit, Llollo sings it for us as she thinks it will work. She just adds enough notes of her own to make it fit. We are happy to see their interest in having more Christian songs in the Amuesha language. We hope to find tunes in their native culture to which we can put Christian words. We haven't found any yet. When I tell Shañe' that we plan to write a lot of songs in their language and also to translate God's Word in their language, she is very happy.

Today, the ridgepole for our house has been erected, along with all the supporting roof poles going up to it. They are all tied together with vines. The palm leaves for the thatched roof are being brought from downriver. Some people are coming to help fold the palm leaves and tie them onto short slats that will then be tied to the support poles. We join the other women, including Llollo, in folding leaves. It's a lot of work.

We also start drawing floor plans for our new house. It will have only two rooms, with a large porch that will cover half of the total floor space. This will give us much more space for receiving people. Between the two rooms, there will be a small space for storage. We can hardly wait — the first home of our own in the jungle! We wish we could have it finished before the reporter arrives, but there is no chance of that.

We write letters to send back on the plane that will bring the reporter. We clean our makeshift house and trust the reporter is of the kind that can rough it since our accommodations are rather limited.

On the radio today they tell us the reporter is coming and will arrive around noontime. We get a meal all ready and call back in at 11:30 to find out if the plane is on time, only to learn they did not get off as soon as they had planned and would arrive about one o'clock. The people are all around, waiting for the latest word from the radio. We wonder what this reporter will be like.

Finally, we hear the motor of the plane in the distance and take off down the hill to the river along with all the people. Ahuash gets a canoe ready to take us down to meet the plane. It has already landed when we get there. We see the reporter appear and take our picture as we arrive in the canoe. We do not realize this will be the picture we will later see when it appears in a magazine in the U.S.[1]

Gary is a true reporter; she never lets go of her camera. We meet and greet her in the midst of her picture taking and help her transfer all her cameras and equipment into Ahuash's canoe, hoping none of it will get wet in the rapids. The Indians are all eyes, seeing a woman dressed in slacks for the first time. We have not worn slacks in order to identify with their culture. They realize she is different from us.

Happily, we make it through the rapids without too much water coming into the canoe. Getting another sleeping bag under our mosquito net is quite a stretch! Gary is very talkative, and despite her early complaints of bug bites, I am really enjoying her company. Our city guest soon asks for our medical supplies and dressings for her many bug bites.

As she treats her bites, and amidst all the other commotion, we suddenly find "Rag Doll" behind our house with a bad nose bleed. It is hard for her to keep her head back since the blood keeps strangling her. There is blood all over the place. With all the medical supplies Gary has out, it looks like a hospital here. Finally, the bleeding stops enough that we can carry "Rag Doll" home.

Gary has brought trinkets of beads, combs, mirrors, etc., which she wants to trade with the people for their artifacts. After explaining this as best as we can to the people, old Llollo takes it to heart and soon comes back with a woven fire fan to trade. She takes a mirror in exchange. She is so pleased she runs home with the mirror and combs her hair very nicely. She then brings out pretty, red seed ornaments to trade and takes sewing needles in exchange this time. Of course, Gary is getting her pictures in the meantime, including one of Llollo at her burning tree stump. She and Gary become friends. She even allows Gary to accompany her to her manioc patch for pictures.

Shañe' finishes making a native tunic for me. Kosepa has been working on one for Mary Ruth. Shañe' comes to tell us that they are planning to dye the tunics today in the bark dye. We, along with Gary and her camera, follow Shañe' to see the process.

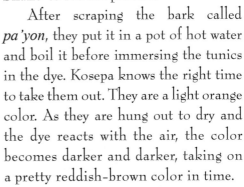

After scraping the bark called *pa'yon*, they put it in a pot of hot water and boil it before immersing the tunics in the dye. Kosepa knows the right time to take them out. They are a light orange color. As they are hung out to dry and the dye reacts with the air, the color becomes darker and darker, taking on a pretty reddish-brown color in time.

We are delighted to have our new tunics just like the Amuesha. I have already acquired deer toenails, monkey teeth, and a little ocelot tail, along with clusters of pretty seed ornaments and beautiful bird feathers to attach to the shoulder seams of my tunic, just as they do. With the perfectly woven *tse'llamets* (woven straw bands Kosepa made for us) over our shoulders, the people say we look just like a *po'napnora* (a grown-up girl at her puberty rites). The people like to see us wear our new tunics.[2] Gary gets more pictures.

Mary Ruth wakes up today with a fever. Gary and I convince her that she should stay in bed for the day. Gary wants to take pictures across the river in a more pristine jungle area. "Playboy," a young girl named Petrona, and friends get a canoe to take us across the river and up a tributary to where Petrona's family lives.

We find Petrona's old father over there, sitting in his little thatched roof shelter. When I tell him Gary wants to take pictures of him just like he lives, he gets the idea to act naturally. Hollywood would not have done it any better.

Gary says to me, "Tell him to look in the far distance."

When I tell him this, right away he gets this far away look in his eyes and Gary responds, "That's perfect."

Coming back in the canoe, we get stuck on the rocks several times. "Playboy" throws off his tunic quickly and into the water he goes to push us off the rocks. His young, brown, nude body furnishes Gary with more pictures from behind.

Gary packs her equipment to have it ready to leave tomorrow. Mary Ruth and I try to write quick answers to letters we received when Gary arrived.

When the plane comes today, we try to get Gary and her equipment through the rapids again without getting wet. Leo loads her things up and they are off.

We realize we have taken a good bit of time from our language work to help the reporter. We trust it will serve a good purpose. More letters arrive on this plane, including two letters from Mom and a letter from Miss Wood, the librarian at Columbia Bible College I worked for during my college days. Miss Wood has taken on some of my financial support for my field work. Thanks, Miss Wood.

"Be not forgetful to entertain strangers . . . " (even journalists in the jungle)
 (Hebrews 13:2 KJV)

# 19

# Our First New Home
# in the Rainforest

A hot dog stand in the jungle?

Only the inside walls are lacking on our new house. We mark the floor with charcoal where they are to be, having decided to have just half-walls in order to let in more light and air. The half-walls around our kitchen, I must say, make it look just like a hot dog stand. So what! The people here have never seen a hot dog stand anyway.

We pay Domingo and Huancho, his helper, for all their work. Then we get as busy as ants building the kitchen shelves. Shañe', Mary Ruth, and I form an assembly line to make the shelf frames — Mary Ruth measuring and cutting the poles, Shañe' scraping off the bark, and I nailing the poles in place. (I always knew learning to drive nails as a kid while helping my dad would come in handy someday.) We carry a thermos of coffee over and sit down in the middle of our building mess for a coffee break on a cool, cloudy morning.

Becoming experts at building shelves, we go on to make another set on our big porch for the radio, record player, books, and all the things we use when the Amueshas visit. With our bright Coleman lantern, they like to come over at night.

We carry all our things to our new house, including the big tables and chairs we were not able to use in the makeshift house. How nice it is to be eating at a table again.

Huancho comes by again and this time makes a round thatched roof on the end of our house near the kitchen. Here we can have an open fire on the ground where we will roast our manioc and bananas like they do. We will also be burning out some stumps and logs around our house just like Llollo does.

Shañe' tells me in study time today that Shoncare', her stepmother, is making *po'cashe'mañollesha'* (its little clothes) for a new baby she is expecting. Shañe' also tells me how girls are chosen by their husbands, something about giving them a leaf treatment, which I don't fully understand. I'll have to work further on this sometime soon.

Ahuash kills a deer today. All of us go to see him bring it in. Young man that he is, Ahuash tries not to show how proud he is of himself. But a deer is a good find for any hunter, providing meat for the entire village. Ahuash starts cutting up the deer as Shoncare' shows him where to divide the meat for all the people. The Amueshas are very generous and share their food with everyone in the village. We watch as Shoncare' slits open the deer's abdomen.

*"Ačhomen!"* (it's pregnant) they all exclaim as we see a little baby deer in its womb. Sabella gets so excited. It's just like a gift from Santa's bag. She can hardly wait to receive it. Shoncare' takes it from the bag, pulls off its cord, and hands it to Sabella who holds it up with the same delight as a little girl with her first doll.

Llollo starts carrying pieces of meat around to everyone. Ahuash brings us a nice piece of the leg, so we have deer steaks for supper. Steaks in the hot dog stand!

We have a strange night. Martin, who lives next door to us, wakes us up about three in the morning yelling *"choyeshe'mats!"* (bad spirits or ghosts). In a voice filled with fear, he is shouting, "The spirits are shrieking." He tries to wake up his wife, Rosa. Then he starts making loud sounds and building up his fire in an effort to drive the spirits away.

Martin is the most acculturated of the people. He has been out to where the Spanish-speaking settlers have moved in, and has worked for the coffee plantation owners and learned some Spanish. Even so, he is still bound by his fear of evil spirits. Again we realize how much God's Word is needed here.

For a break from our concentrated study on language analysis, Mary Ruth and I decide to make a table with shelves underneath for our clothes in the bedroom. So far we have just been keeping them on the floor in plastic bags. We start off with a bang after our great success with the other shelves, but the more we work, the harder it becomes to keep the pieces together. Maybe it is because I got the idea to use large, heavy poles for the four corners to keep it from turning over on the springy bark floor, yet it doesn't keep it from looking like a monster. We just have to sit down and laugh at our "monster in the bedroom." However, it fits in with the rest of our house — very crude and funny looking — but it's convenient and serves the purpose, so we are happy.

After a bath in the cold river, we sit in the sun and have ourselves a little hymn sing on the rock ledge by the river.

" . . . for I have learned in whatsoever state I am, therewith to be content."
– the Apostle Paul, (Philippians 4:11 KJV)

(Thank you, Lord, for keeping us happy in whatever circumstance we find ourselves because we know that we are in the center of your will for us.)

# 20

# Catalina and Storying

Who is the master storyteller of Stingray village?

The master storyteller turns out to be Catalina, "City Woman's" sister. Catalina is one of the older women and is in an advanced stage of tuberculosis. She is anxious to tell us all the stories she knows, so we get out the tape recorder and start the generator.

Catalina seems quite sure of herself without a note of any kind. Her black hair falls around her shoulders and onto her dark tunic that is decorated at the shoulder seams with adornments of every kind — deer toenails, a string of monkey teeth, clusters of shiny seed ornaments of many kinds. Wearing this beautiful blend of natural colors, Catalina is a lovely picture of the typical Amuesha woman. With her *tse'llamets* (woven bands) over her shoulder, she is completely poised and ready to start relaying her tribal legends — legends that from the ancient past have been

passed on orally from one generation to the next, now to be recorded and transcribed for the first time!

Many people come running when they hear the generator and stay to see how this machine that "grabs our words" works. They also enjoy hearing their legends retold since there have been no books in their language yet except the very beginning primers. People of an unwritten language seem to develop tremendous memory capabilities as this is their only way of remembering things.

We show Catalina how to hold the microphone and talk into it. Mary Ruth runs the recorder and I seat myself opposite Catalina along with the others listening spellbound to her stories.

"*Ahuaĩ Encpa' yoran yachor Palla; c̈hota'tan yachor . . .* " Catalina begins her story. (A long time ago, the Inca took our mother Palla [as a wife]. Very much he beat our mother . . .)[1]

Catalina relives the legend as she tells it. Her gestures with her hands and intonations of her voice make the story come alive for her listeners. Her eyes light up as she recounts the events.

Her second legend is about "our father, the sun (god) who made the earth and all the people." Of course, we understand very little of what Catalina is saying at the time, but we keep listening to encourage her to tell us more. While she is very animated, she does have to stop from time to time to cough because of her tuberculosis. She wants to keep going, and we record several legends before stopping.

Every language group has its legends that reflect its own cultural beliefs and customs. We need to be aware of these, not only for us to fit in well with the culture of the people, but for translation purposes later on. For a good, meaningful translation of God's Word into the language of these Amuesha people, we need to learn to think in their thought patterns, to understand their world view, and their belief systems.[2] We must get to know their fears and problems, and their presuppositions, which are often different from ours and those found in the Scripture.

Legends incorporate much of the culture of the people about which we need to learn. They also incorporate some of their history. It is very likely that the Inca Empire dominated the Amuesha people at some point in the past. Their extreme disdain for the Inca, as expressed in the legend, probably indicates some kind of domination by the Inca. There are also scores of words in the Amuesha language that have been borrowed from Quechua, the language of the Incas.[3] This too indicates some kind of close contact.

At the same time, the narrative texts of these legends provide us with larger chunks of the grammatical structure of the language that we need to study in order to analyze its various parts. Legends also give us new and useful vocabulary that we can begin using.

The hard part will be to get the legends transcribed into written form, so I go to get Shañe' to help me. I tell her just what I want her to do:

"We will listen to the story just a little bit, then we will stop the machine and I want you to repeat for me exactly what Catalina said, but you need to speak slowly so that I can write it down. Catalina talks so fast I can't write it down that quickly. You will have to tell me word by word what she is saying."

Shañe' agrees to do just that. I start the recorder not knowing just how this is going to work out, or if Shañe' can really do this. We listen to the first part of a sentence and stop the recorder. Shañe' is great; she can tell me word by word just by hearing the recording once. *Thank you, Lord.* She can also slow it down almost syllable by syllable. I write like mad. Then we go back to the recorder and start with the beginning of the sentence again and go on through to its end. Sometimes when Catalina is caught up in the flow of her story, I can hardly tell where one sentence ends and another begins. Shañe' is a big help, giving me even the hesitation words and stutters that Catalina speaks as she relays her tale. At first I am not even sure what is a word and what is a stutter, but I learn as I go along. This legend is now written for the very first time!

After we finish one legend, we go back to the beginning and I read to Shañe' what I have written. Now we work on the meanings of the individual words I don't understand, which are many. Legends are much harder to understand than conversation, and a lot of detail is omitted in the telling since everyone is expected to already know it. If the word I don't know is in a context of words I do know, it is easier to determine the meaning of the new word. Since this is not often the case, I try my best to get the meaning from Shañe'.

Here again, Shañe' is very good. If it is an action verb, she can often act it out for me. If it is a noun, she can describe it to me in words that she knows I already have learned. It's amazing how she seems to keep a record in her head of all the words I know. If it is some abstract term, it is harder for her, but she can most often get me to understand.

Today as we work on new words, and I ask her what the word *tsetatstosa* means, Shañe' is at a loss to tell me. I think whatever in the world can this word mean that Shañe' can't describe or show me its action. I have to know this mysterious word. While we are talking, Catalina happens to come by, so I ask Catalina, "What does this word *tsetatstosa* mean?" Catalina makes no attempt to describe it. Instead, she jumps up in the air and comes down on her bottom on the floor. "That's what that word means," she casually replies. I realize why Shañe', with her lame leg, could not show me this action. Catalina probably should not have tried it either. I hope she didn't break anything.

Then I come to the next word I don't know — *eñmatena*. Shañe' has to think and think about how to explain this one. In fact, we have to continue on it the next day because I just cannot understand it from her explanations. The next day, as we start on it again, Shañe' has thought of a good explanation, "It's like when you are very, very thirsty, but there is no water to drink, you are not *eñmatena*." I get it right away — "satisfied." See what a good teacher Shañe' is? Could you have explained an abstract term that well?

"A word fitly spoken is like apples of gold in pictures of silver."

— Solomon, (Proverbs 25:11 KJV)

(Lord, help us to learn all the words we need to know to "fitly" translate your Word into this beautiful Amuesha language.)

# 21

# Writing Our First Linguistic Papers

What's involved in writing a linguistic paper?

I continue to work with Shañe' to transcribe Catalina's legends. I seek not only to know the meanings of all the words I don't know, but to try and determine the meanings of the parts of words (morphemes functioning as suffixes and prefixes occurring with the root of the word, which is called morphology). For example, in the words *yoran yachor* (he, Inca, took our mother) and *ĕhota'tan yachor* (he beat our mother) I see the common suffix *–an* on the end of these first two verbs. I think it might possibly indicate that the following word (*yachor*) is the direct object of the action of the verbs "to take" and "to beat." I make a mental note to check all further third-person subjects occurring with third-person objects to see if they carry the suffix *-an*. Thus I can determine where the root of the word ends and where the suffix begins, and the probable meaning of *-an*.

I plan to write a syntactic analysis of Catalina's Inca legend for the linguistic paper which we each need to write to show the progress of our language analysis. A syntactic analysis is done on the sentence level of the text. I will identify each word of the sentence as to its function in the sentence, such as subject, object, predicate, locative, temporal, etc. Then I will identify the word class filling that function, whether it is a noun, a pronoun, a verb, or an adverb.

As I work on the 197 sentences of this text, I am learning much concerning the grammar of the Amuesha language. It is extremely important to know it well as I start to translate God's Word into Amuesha so that I will know if the translation wording conforms to all the rules of the grammar. If not, there will not be a clear understanding of the message.

Of course, I am also learning and using the new words from the legends. The people delight in hearing us talking more and more in their language. This greatly strengthens the bond between us.

Mary Ruth chooses to write her paper on the meanings of morpheme suffixes and prefixes. This is called morphology and will consist of identifying the morphemes and their order and meanings.

In the midst of getting our papers typed, Mary Ruth accidentally drops her typewriter. Now we will both have to use the same typewriter. This puts a little more stress on both of us since we are running short of time. We'd like to take our papers completely finished when we return to the Center.

On the day I start to type up my paper, I tell Shañe' that I will not be able to study with her this day. Even so, in the late afternoon she comes to see if I have finished. I've been typing all day and have barely finished. I show her where her name appears in my paper as my language teacher. She is happy to have this part in it. I do not know at the time that this paper will soon be published in the *International Journal of American Linguistics*, with the title "A syntactical analysis of an Amuesha (Arawak) text," Vol. 23, 1957, pp.171-178.[1]

Mary Ruth also finishes her paper on time. Since we have been concentrating on these papers for the last several weeks, we decide to bake a chocolate cake to celebrate and have a little picnic up at our favorite spot on the river. We finish evening devotions together with special thanks to God for His faithfulness in enabling us to complete our first linguistic papers. These are only the beginning of many more papers we will write on the various aspects of the Amuesha grammar and related subjects, including a book of the complete grammar and a large dictionary that I write at the end of my work with the Amueshas, (*Diccionario Yanesha'-Amuesha – Castellano*, Serie Lingüística Peruana, No. 47 and *Gramática del Idioma Yanesha'-Amuesha*, Serie Lingüística Peruana, No. 43).[2] We have been so preoccupied with writing our papers that the work of filing new words and morphemes has piled up. Now it's time to get caught up with the many new words we have learned from the legends. The morphology file keeps us both busy too.

Adding to the difficulty of studying the morphemes is the fact that in Amuesha any one morpheme may change its form slightly as it appears in different words. For example, the morpheme meaning "second-person singular pronominal object" ("you") is found to occur in four different forms: *-ap̃, -ep̃, -p̃, -p*. Why the difference if they all mean the same thing?

Our big puzzle broadens as we get more into the language and look for rules that may govern the use of the variations of the morphemes that are called allomorphs. We learn like children to say the words as the people say them, but for our complete write-up of the grammar in the future, we will need to know the grammatical rules that govern the use of one or the other form of the allomorphs.

Within the complexity of a total language many such perplexities exist. The struggle to solve the grammar problems has become our biggest "jaguar" so far in the language learning process. What a challenge! We love it and commit ourselves to it each day, knowing God will enable us as He has promised. What a thrill to find the answers, one at a time, and to know that the more we understand the rules of the grammar, the more meaningful the translation of God's Word in Amuesha will be.

"If any of you lack wisdom let him ask of God . . . and it shall be given him."

— the Apostle James, (James 1:5 KJV)

(Thank you, Lord, that as we commit our problems in the language to you, you do enable us to find the answers. We look forward to the day when your Word will be translated in the Amuesha language conforming to all the rules of grammar you have made known to us. May it bring glory to you.)

# 22

# Vacation Time

Do Wycliffe missionaries ever have any vacations while on the field?

Yes, we do. Mary Ruth and I take our vacation in the month of December since November is usually the end of our stay in the village for the year. However, this year we are planning to return in January after our December vacation and stay until April, when our yearly conference takes place at Yarinacocha. We are now finishing our second six-month period of living with the Amuesha.

We often hear our best friends Millie Larson and Jeanne Grover reporting in on their radio from their location among the Aguarunas in northern Peru. They usually take their vacation in December like we do. As we are nearing that time, Millie asks to have a talk with us by radio. They ask us if we'd like to go into Lima and see our new Guest House that is just being finished and vacation together there in the big city. Wow! Can we adjust to city living? We decide we can and make our plans accordingly.

It will be fun having our vacation with Millie and Jeanne because we spend most of our time sharing our experiences among the Amueshas and Aguarunas. Whatever unusual stories we tell, they can always top it with one bigger and better. We laugh and relax together. We are looking forward to it. We will also spend Christmas there.

We are enjoying the luxury of our new house. How elegant it feels to be able to walk from one room to another, and especially to have so much space for guests. The people come often to listen to the record in their language and they bring newcomers who are visiting them. They arrive almost every evening and want to sing the Christian songs in their language. Some come to continue their reading lessons, some just to look at the old *National Geographics* we have out and see people of other cultures. It's a special time for them when we pop big bowls of popcorn for everyone. They have never had popcorn before, but now think it is the best stuff they've tasted yet.

It's corn season now. Rosa and others bring us roasted corn — yummy. Shañe' brings a good roasted manioc. We are now using a fire out under our open thatched roof for cooking. I am beginning to try my hand at roasting in the open fire as the Amueshas do. Roasted foods are much more delicious than stove cooked foods. I've learned how to thump the manioc root to know if it is done in the middle. We also like roasted plantain (cooking bananas). The children like to come and join us around our open fire. It's a great place to socialize. Our jungle camp training in Mexico in how to build a good fire is coming in handy.

Llollo has not been feeling well lately. Today as I go down to get water from the pool in the stream, I see the rocks have been pulled out and the stream opened up. When I ask about it, someone tells me, "The water is mad at Llollo; that's what is making her sick." A cultural belief of the Amueshas is that various items of nature can become angry at a person and make him or her sick. It can be water, a certain rock, a termite nest up on a tree, or whatever. As they say, "It becomes angry and aims at us and makes us sick." We can see the possibility of contaminated water making a person sick, so we urge the people to boil the water they drink.

"Keep away" and "dodge ball" have become favorite games to play with the young people and children on moonlit nights. The girls like my "jacks" game also. At first we didn't have a small ball to toss up while the "jacks" are picked up, but Shañe' made us one out of crude rubber that she heated, cooled, and shaped. "Jump rope" is another new game the kids enjoy.

"City Woman" comes today all upset, tears falling like raindrops from her eyes as she tries to tell us that her daughter Elena's little baby is very sick. It is such a tiny thing and has never seemed to grow. Secretly, we doubt that the baby will live. Sometimes we feel so helpless when there seems to be nothing we can do except pray. "City Woman" tells us that Elena does not have enough milk for the baby. For lack of anything else, we decide to give her some oatmeal to cook in hopes the baby may be able to swallow it. We learn to pray for the babies even more so when we can't help in any other way.

By the time "City Woman" leaves she is feeling much better about the situation, having more faith in the oatmeal than we do; or maybe it was just sharing her sorrow with us. Maybe it was her faith in the true God she has been hearing about and wants to believe in. About two weeks later, they come to tell us that the baby is much better. They are so happy they bring us two big, fresh pineapples.

"Rag Doll" arrives and is talking to me over our half-wall where I am working at the kitchen table. She tells me with fear in her voice, "We saw a devil (*oneñeñĩ*) last night over at our house (next door to ours). It had four eyes, two extra in the back of its head. To' (her old father) was seeing it well." He used to be a practicing shaman. We pray for him a lot because he is very old and can hardly see or hear. We don't know if he has heard enough of the gospel record to understand and believe.

We work on our order to place over the radio for things to come on the plane that will take us out. These are supplies that we will need for the three months after we return from vacation. It's important that we plan well ahead of time in order to utilize the plane both coming and going.

As we go down to the river for our bath today, all the kids and young people are having their usual fun in the river. The young fellows take a canoe up to the head of the rapids and come down through the swiftest part, purposely allowing the boat to sink in the water and then pulling it out and emptying it — all as they float through the rapids. They are very good at their water tricks.

Shañc' persuades me to try the rapids, but not the swiftest ones. I finally get up my nerve and find it to be great fun. Who knows? I may need the experience and ability some day.

Starting to prepare for our leave, we take our room-size mosquito net to the river to wash. It is so big that Mary Ruth starts washing one end of it while I start on the other end. Some of the women happen by and get a good laugh from our "double-duty washing machine."

Today I write in my diary: "November 21, Sunday. A very blessed time during our devotions this morning. Under the Lord's convictions, we confessed our faults to each other — apologies and forgiveness we needed from each other." How blessed such times can be in bringing us closer to Him.

Shañe' comes after supper with her little *llamparen* (kerosene lamp made from a tin can) and asks if we can sing the Christian songs. She says Cesar wants to sing since it is the last night before we leave. We all gather around Shañe's little *llamparen* and sing and sing. I refill Shañe's can with kerosene since it is very precious to the people here. Shañe' is reluctant to leave. She does not want us to go and talks about going with me.

But today is the day we must leave. Even before we finish breakfast, the people have come by to see and hear the latest. They want to know just what is being said on the radio:

"Has the plane left Yarinacocha yet?" "Who is the pilot?" "How far has the plane gotten?" "When will it arrive here?"

"Not before noontime," we answer. We manage to get our final packing done in the midst of much chatter and excitement, making sure our linguistic papers are in the things to go with us.

By eleven o'clock we have everything packed away, and Ahuash takes us down the river in his canoe to the place where the plane lands. Most of the people take their canoes and follow us. Shañe' is sad she can't go all the way to the plane, so I hug her and tell her good-bye on the beach. She knows we will be coming back soon.

The plane zooms in on the river right on schedule. Leo is the pilot again. The people are happy; they know him now. He is in a hurry, as usual, with some stops to make downriver. We bid the people good-bye.

Leo is afraid we are a little heavy for the takeoff from the short water strip here, so Mary Ruth and I both sit as closely as possible to the instrument board. We start off with a great roar, holding our breath as we keep plowing through the water and the distance to the rapids becomes shorter. What a relief when we feel the plane leave the water before we reach the rapids. Thank you, Lord, for another good six months with the Amuesha people.

Several of our friends are there at the ramp in Yarinacocha to meet us as we glide down on the big lake — mission completed for this time.

"To the weak I became weak, to win the weak. I have become all things to all men so that by all possible means I might save some."

— the Apostle Paul, (I Corinthians 9:22 NIV)

(Thank you, Lord, for another opportunity to live with the Amuesha people and to share some of their sorrows and also some of their joys. Thanks for them helping us to learn more of their language and its grammar. We look forward to the day when we will be able to give them your Word in their language.)

# 23

# Spiders in Our Soup

Will our home in the jungle still be there when we return this time?

Vacation time is now over, and we are anxious to get back out to Amueshaland. From the city to the village in just a few days! George Insley is our pilot. It is the first time George is flying us out to Stingray village. As we near the village and circle around, we point out the exact landing spot to George. We can see the Amueshas running to the river to meet us. George makes a good landing.

Ahuash is there with his canoe to pick us up. Shañe' is waiting on the beach, without any walking sticks. She is walking with just a slight limp. She has gained back all her lost weight. How good it is to see her well again. But Llollo is sick again, with malaria we think. We rejoice to find our house in good condition and our things still here. Ahuash has even built a little thatched roof house for our generator.

George stays to fix the bad connection to our radio and our Coleman lantern. We get out our packed up things and prepare supper. It is too late for George to get back to Yarinacocha; so he stretches out his mosquito net next door.

The people come by after supper to visit. Shañe' informs us that we have been gone five weeks and that they want to hear the record in their language again and sing. After everyone has left and we are already in bed, Elena comes with her little boy, who has a bad burn. I dress the wound and then go back to sleep.

After George leaves in the morning, we decide to do a little more work on our kitchen before settling into study. A spider dropped down on our kitchen table last night and we want to make a cloth ceiling to fasten to the cross poles in our kitchen. Great success! The white ceiling makes our kitchen lighter, and we'll have no more spiders dropping in our soup!

From my diary today: "January 8th — happy birthday! — my 30th one. I can't believe it and don't feel like it, but that's what the numbers say." Early this morning, after having been out on the porch talking to the people, I come back into the bedroom to find a present on my bed from Mary Ruth. She also makes my favorite chocolate cake with nuts and a white frosting, and even candles."

The people visit us all afternoon. We give them little candies and tell them it is my birthday. They don't know anything about birthdays. Since they have never had calendars or kept records, no one knows when his birthday is or how old he is. A pretty good way to live, don't you think?

The linguistic papers we turned in resulted in permission for Mary Ruth and me both to work on some preliminary translation. She can hardly wait to get started, and asks Cruz to help her start translating the Gospel of Mark. He knows some Spanish, so they can start using Spanish. I choose to work some more on legends before starting translation in order to be able to produce a more idiomatic translation. Then I plan to begin translating some Old Testament stories.

Catalina and her sister, "City Woman," both tell us more legends on tape. I work with Shañe' in transcribing them. I do not know at the time that a few years later, when we have the first literate Amuesha writers, one of them, Julio Gaspar, will write one of these legends on his own — the first time a legend has been written by an Amuesha.

With Ahuash, Cruz, and Cesar we write more Christian songs. They love singing and want to have more songs in their language. We are now translating

"Jesus Is the Way to Our Father's House" and "I Have Decided to Follow Jesus." While we work on the words, we tell them what we are able about Jesus, who is God's Son and who died for our sins. It is amazing how much of the Gospel we are expressing in the songs even before we start real translation.

Llollo is getting better after her treatment for malaria. Although we are treating Catalina for tuberculosis, she is not improving and is now spitting up blood. We wonder if there is anything more we can do for her since her disease was so far advanced when we first met.

I go over to visit Catalina and find her setting up all the threads for weaving material to make a tunic. It looks very complicated with so many threads that have to be woven together. A species of cotton grows here on a large bush. It is spun into thread with a hand spindle.

Catalina is incredibly creative. Using the Italian ceramic beads we brought in at their request, she has already made bracelets using traditional Amuesha designs. There are a number of these native geometric designs that I want to learn about in the future.

Today when Shañe' comes to work with me she explodes in tears when she starts to tell me what has happened. She says her father, Cruz, beat her with the broad side of a machete. Her stepmother, she says, told him to do it; she accused Shañe' of causing her little sisters to run around. Shañe' and her father have always had such love for each other since Shañe's mother died that I'm sure this is a great blow to her emotionally as well as physically. I sympathize with her, hoping I can take the place of her mother in a small way. I hate to see Shañe' hurt so. I cry with her.

Shañe' wants to write a letter to her older brother who is away somewhere working. She thinks she will have to find someone who knows Spanish who can write it. They have never realized a letter could be written in their own language.

"Why don't we write the letter in your own language?" I suggest to Shañe'.

"I don't know how to do it," she answers sadly.

"I will write it for you. Just tell me what you want to say to your brother and I will write it just that way."

"I can really write a letter to my brother in our language?"

"Yes, let's get started. Just tell me what you want to say."

Thus, the first letter ever written in Amuesha is now history. There have been many more written since then.

I keep identifying and filing the many noun and verb phrases I find when transcribing the legends with Shañe. Knowing how to use these different grammatical constructions will be essential as I start translation. I am also starting to write my paper on these grammatical constructions of the Amuesha syntax.

Mary Ruth, with Cruz's help, continues working from Spanish on some preliminary translation of the Gospel of Mark. Having difficulty finding words for "Lord," "repentance," and "forgiveness," she is a little discouraged. Do these concepts even exist in this culture and language? We have a lot more to learn.

" ... The Lord your God has given you the land."

[Amueshaland] ... Do not be afraid; do not be discouraged."

— Moses (from God), (Deuteronomy 1:21 NIV)

(Lord, thank you for the Amuesha people who live in this jungleland. We want to claim these people in this land for you and your Word. Help us not to become discouraged as we struggle with the language and spiritual concepts, because we do have your promise of victory.)

# 24

# Puberty Party

What is a puberty party?

We heard that one of the young girls who lives downriver is having her puberty rites celebration soon.[1] *O'ch čha'nerr po'napnora.* "The grown-up girl will come out," as they say in Amuesha. It really is a literal "coming-out party" since the grown-up girl has been shut in a dark, thatched room for two months after having her first menstrual period. She is not allowed to talk to anyone except her mother, who brings her food of limited amounts with no salt. She is supposed to spend her time learning to spin cotton thread. It is a time for her to learn to be a grown-up woman and not be lazy.

Since we had already heard of this cultural practice, we want to see it. José volunteers to take us and others downriver in his canoe. In fact, there are eleven people in one small canoe, but the river water is low and we have a smooth, safe trip.

"Rag Doll," who has been here for several days already, meets us as we arrive and tells me they have deer meat to eat. It is the obligation of the father of the grown-up girl to provide plenty of meat for the occasion. The girl's mother is just coming in with a big basket of manioc. "Rag Doll's" older sister is getting the meat cut up and into pots to cook.

Soon after we arrive we are served some boiled manioc and boiled deer liver. The women get busy preparing all the meats for smoking and boiling. Besides the deer, there are wild pigs, large jungle birds about the size of turkeys, several kinds of fish, and three monkeys hanging high over the fire, already smoked. The father has done a fine job.

The grown-up girl is still in her thatched room and will not come out until early tomorrow morning. This ceremony always takes place on the full moon, but tonight the moon is not shining since it has become very cloudy and rainy.

As it gets dark, all the fellows take off for the river with a great hoopla and holler. We hear the big splashes as they hit the water. This is all a part of the ceremonies, the women tell us. As the men return, the women head for the river. We go with them to watch.

We eat again, this time manioc and fish. Then the talking begins. The men are over on one side of the house talking continuously, and all of them at the same time. They have already started drinking their fermented drink called *co'nes*. It too is made from manioc root that has been boiled, mashed, and mixed with masticated sweet potatoes, then left for several days to ferment. For a big party like this, they have made great quantities of *co'nes*. It is stored in large, wooden, canoe-like containers — the largest containers they have. Before it is served, the *co'nes* is strained and mixed with more water.

As the night draws on, people just lie down in their clothes on the floor, the men on one side, the women on the other. The entire floor space is covered with visitors. However, there is very little sleeping, if any, since someone is always talking. About every hour, whoever wakes up gives a yell and wakes everyone up, and the talking starts all over again. Around 1:30 in the morning I see the women down by the fire peeling more manioc, getting it ready to cook.

When we can barely see in the morning light yet, the women get all the prepuberal girls together. The girls walk in a single file, each one holding the hand of the girl behind her. They go to the thatched enclosure where the grown-up girl has been living for two months and escort her out to the public as a *po'napnora*—a mature woman and a full member of the society.

She is adorned in a new tunic in a bright orange color freshly dyed with *pa'yon* bark. The shoulders are adorned with many seed ornaments, deer toenails, monkey teeth, and every color of bird feathers. Across her shoulder are newly made *tse'llamets* (woven straw bands) and strands of beautiful red and black seeds. Over her recently closely-shorn hair she wears a black scarf that covers not only her head but much of her face. The ceremony seems to mark only the physical maturing of the woman since some girls are given in marriage even before reaching puberty.

The grown-up girl seems a little embarrassed, but she knows what is expected of her. To show that she is not lazy, she starts immediately to serve. First to the men she serves the fermented drink, *co'nes.* Then she serves the men food, followed by the women and children. She is supposed to keep serving, and with the large number of people, it keeps her busy.

The morning turns out to be an almost continual feast with the many kinds of meat to eat. The pots are kept full of manioc cooking. Sticks line the fires for roasting meat. The air is filled with scent of roasting meat and boiled manioc, along with smoke from the open fires. But the strong odor of the fermented drink overcomes all other smells. Between six and twelve o'clock we eat four times. The deer's head seems to be the favorite. Several people crowd around it and dig out the meat from every crack and crevice with their fingers.

The men's gab sessions continue all morning while the women continue preparing food. One man works on changing the skin on his drum so it will have optimum sound for the ceremonies to follow in the evening.

Since it is a rainy morning and no sun is shining to tell the hour of the day, someone is constantly asking us what time it is. At noon, the *po'napnora* is supposed to go out and dig more manioc, which she does, but not before changing into an old tunic because of the rain. After digging up the manioc to show she is not lazy, the *po'napnora* is supposed to cut grass. She hardly gets to doing so before it is time for the nettling process. The *po'napnora* must take off her clothes and allow everyone to nettle her with long, thorny plants. We can see the welts coming out on her body.

In the evening, the dances start. One of the dances, Catalina tells us, is called the Old Man's Dance. Those taking part have headgear made from the whitish tassel of a river cane that hangs down long and resembles long, gray hair. They also have placed a bundle on their backs under their tunics to make them appear humped as an old man. For this dance, the drummer stays in the middle, while two others shuffle back and forth past the drummer with a certain rhythm.

Next the reed panpiper comes out. He doesn't make much music but keeps the rhythm with the drummer. The women join in, each holding the hand of the one behind her. They too keep the same rhythm and sing a kind of chant that has loud wailing sounds that fade out. These activities go on and off all night long; they dance and drink their fermented beverage. We now know what a puberty party is all about.

It is still raining in the morning when José says we will leave to go back home. We don't know yet what trying to travel upstream on a swollen river is like. The water is up over the scrubby bushes along either bank. José tries easing along the sides to keep out of the swift current in the middle of the river. We have to hold up the bushes and ease under them, which almost drags us from the canoe at times. In a very swift place, the canoe gets hung in the scrubby bushes. The water comes rushing through. We have to get out and hold onto the bushes to keep from being swept downstream while the fellows get the canoe out. Catalina has a basket with one duck and two chickens. "Pretty Woman" has her little sister and a boy, along with the two fellows. We are all a pretty sad sight, soaked to the bone and dirty from being caught up under the bushes.

José says we should try the other side of the river; maybe the current is not as swift over there. We plunge out into the middle of the river only to be carried far back downstream with the current. The other side is obviously no better. We plunge out into the middle, once more, to return to the side we were originally on, only to be carried back to where we had started. José says we will have to trek through the jungle to get back home, so we climb out and hit the muddy trail. After about two hours of fast walking up and down gorges with creeks at the bottom, we finally arrive at our village. Home never looked so good!

Now that we are back home again, the people come often to learn the new Christian songs we have written and to listen to the record in their language. Mary Ruth and I resume our language work.

I get my syntax paper all typed up to take back to Yarina while Mary Ruth and Cruz translate the story of the Prodigal Son from Spanish. Our three months have gone by so quickly.

"To those not having the law (of God's Word) I became like one not having the law . . . so as to win those not having the law."
– the Apostle Paul, (I Corinthians 9:21 NIV)

". . . with your blood you purchased men for God from every tribe and language and people and nation."
– the Apostle John, (Revelation 5:9 NIV)

(Thank you, Lord, that you have promised to save those from all language and cultural groups of people in the world.)

# 25

# Singing Water Village

Where is Singing Water village?

After our annual conference at Yarina Center, we are headed back to the village. We gather with our housemates Millie, Jeanne, and Vi along with Pete and visiting pastors to form a circle at the ramp for prayer as we prepare to leave for another six months among the Amuesha people.

Following a last-minute pickup of our repaired air mattresses from the hangar, we board the plane. Leo is our pilot again. We make a quick stop at Tournavista on our way to get a better check on the weather. But we soon arrive at Stingray village. We notice from the air how nice and clean it appears around our house. (We later find out that Llollo and Shañe' have recently cleaned there for our anticipated arrival.)

As I leave the plane and look for Shañe' I don't see her. They tell me that just yesterday she went downriver with her father. All the others gather around to greet us. It is so good to see them and be welcomed back. I am happy to find Catalina somewhat better despite her advanced tuberculosis.

Later in the day as we are getting our house set up, Shañe', Sabella, and "Rag Doll," just arriving from their trip downriver, come bouncing up onto our porch. Just beaming Shañe' says, "We saw your plane go over while we were downriver. We knew it was you; we shouted to you. If we had known you were coming today we would not have gone downriver." How she does love us! How we do love her!

A few days later, Shañe' tells me that her younger sister, Sabella, has been taken by a man and is now living at his house. *Oh dear,* I think. Sabella is only about ten years old. Cruz, their father, has given her to this man. I wondered why I had not been seeing her around. Shañe' says she is very sad and wants to come home. She is ashamed to come here to our house.

As always, many people continue to visit us to hear the record that "talks our language" and to sing the new Christian songs that they like so much. We take much time with them, renewing acquaintances and making new ones.

Petrona's mother tells us about the village of *Eñenas* (Singing Water), which is far upriver and higher in the foothills of the Andes. With great pride she says, "*Eñenas* is where I was born. That's where the real Amueshas are who really know our customs and culture."

This is the very first time we have heard of more Amueshas elsewhere. We take note and think maybe this is where we also need to go. We gather all the facts we can about Singing Water village, which turns out to be in another province called Junin. This is the general area where Villa Rica, La Merced, San Ramon, and Tarma are located. It is also called Yurinaqui in the Asheninca language.

The next time we talk by radio with Pete in Yarina about the new set of primers he is making, we also tell him about this place which he has not heard of yet. We mention that we would like to go there and perhaps even live among the people.

I have many work projects in mind that I want to accomplish during this next six months. They include translating some Old Testament stories like the lives of David and Joseph[1] to start with. I need to get some more advanced reading books made that can lead our students into further independent reading. And I would like to write another syntax paper on the language. (I've had good reports on my first two linguistic papers.) In addition, Mary Ruth and I together want to study the rhythm patterns in the words of this language, which involves modified vowels, intonation, and stress.

Although Amuesha has only three phonemic vowels, each of the three short vowels may be modified in three ways: by lengthening, by aspiration (with a little puff of air), and by glottalization (a cutoff of the vowel sound in the glottis of the throat). For example, the three following words show the contrast:

*aap* (lengthened vowel) – a certain vegetable (*caigua*)

*ahp* (aspirated vowel) – a certain fruit seed (*guaba, pacae*)

*a'p* (glottalized vowel) – to remain, become accustomed

Since I hear the intonation and stress best with my helper, and Mary Ruth hears the modified vowels best from hers, we each can work on our special rhythm patterns. It requires us to list many words in which to compare and contrast these various features.

Literacy is very important in order to have readers as we translate, so I choose to start with preparing the more advanced reading materials. I show "City Woman" a book I have of many of the animals in this area. She recognizes each one, and being the great conversationalist that she is, she starts talking with much enthusiasm about each of them. I get it all recorded on tape, "It's an anteater. Wherever the anteater sees an ant nest, he digs it out. He sticks out his long tongue and pulls it back in eating all the little ants . . ."

We will later transcribe all these animal stories and make them into a book with pictures of each one. (Animals are the Amuesha's favorite subject.) This kind of familiar writing makes good practice reading for students who have learned the basic sounds of the letters. It is highly predictable reading since the students already know the features of the animals. Thus they gain fluency in reading through easy, familiar subjects, which encourages them to continue.

Today on the radio, out of the blue, we are told that another visitor would like to come to the village. We don't know him, but find out that he is the famous converted wiretapper now associated with the Billy Graham Los Angeles Campaign. Cecil Hawkins, radio operator at the time, warned us jokingly that we might need to enlarge our doorway for this visitor. We didn't know what he meant until our guest appeared — all six feet, five inches, and three hundred pounds of him. No joking.

We send a canoe to bring him from the plane. As we watch him approach on the river, it looks like the canoe sides are barely clearing the top of the water — his body hanging over the sides of the little canoe. When he steps from the canoe onto the beach where we are standing, the Indians start backing away. They are all so short and he looks like a giant in our midst. Margarita, standing near me, says in a whisper, "We just never have seen a man of such a size."

We have our lunch ready, so I invite our guest to just step up from the ground to the closest table seat (so he will not have to walk across our palm bark floor). He chuckles as he does so and says, "I know why you gave me this seat."

"Yes, that's why," I answer. He likes to joke about his size. It's a nice change to have a joker around for a while.

We rejoice with him in his newfound faith in Christ. Even so, the people keep their distance, fearful that he might breathe a little heavily and blow them all away, but he understands. He loves hearing them sing Christian songs with us in their language. They will long remember the *atarrpe'n* (big mountain).

Pete sends us two more choruses he has written in Amuesha — "Our Father Takes Care of Us" and "God Loves Me." With the songs and choruses Mary Ruth and I are writing, we now have a total of ten Christian songs.

We usually sing a song in English before eating our supper. Old To' happens to be coming along and hums along with us. He has recently told us about his shaman practices. He says there is a certain bark that he can bury in the ground if he wants to kill someone, and that person will die. He says he has ten spirits that will come and help him if he gets sick. He comes to hear the Gospel record in his language, and we can tell he is hearing well enough to understand something of what is being said.

I check out the examples from my syntax paper with Catalina and Llollo and get it typed up to be ready to send back to Yarina when the next plane comes.

We notice that Sabella is back at her home again. The people tell us she was so sad she wouldn't eat at her husband's house, so he just sent her back home. She and "Rag Doll" were around again, laughing and playing as they always did. Then we hear that the people had a meeting and decided Sabella should go back to her husband. Later tonight we hear little Sabella screaming and crying and someone beating her, evidently trying to make her go back to her husband. Our hearts ache, but what should we do? We pray.

After I finish my syntax paper, Shañe' asks me when are we going to work together again. We barely get started when Shañe' comes to tell me she can't work with me anymore because her father has given her to a man who has asked for her. This man has much work for her in his manioc patch, so she will not have time to help me. I ask if she wants to marry this man, but she will not say yes or no. She only says her father wants her to and he would beat her if she didn't. To make matters worse, this man has already had various women as wives, but the father says who will be his daughter's husband. Again, we pray.

The young man, Ahuash, wants to come in the evenings to learn all our new songs. Many others arrive as well and we spend the evenings teaching them the songs. We decide to get the songs typed up, and although the people can't read that well yet, it will be a great incentive for them to learn. Ahuash is also taking great interest in having God's Word in his language. He told Shañe' he would like to help us translate. This is a real answer to my prayer, for I am wanting to start translation of some Old Testament stories. I feel that stories are the best place to start for people who have had nothing of God's Word. We start with the story of David.

Ahuash knows a little Spanish from being out a few times working where Spanish-speaking people live. When he comes to work on translation with me, I read him the story aloud in Spanish. He does not fully understand the Spanish, so in my limited Amuesha I am able to help him understand what is being said. Then he repeats the story to me in good Amuesha which I write down.

I am frightened when I begin my first translation of God's Word. As I get into it further, however, it is awesome to realize that God is enabling me to have a part in spreading His Word to a whole group of people in their very own language. Wow!

Martin, another of Llollo's sons, has agreed to help Mary Ruth in translating the Gospel of Mark. They are starting with Mark, chapter seven, which is where they left off the last time we were out here. Mary Ruth and I both realize we have much to learn, but what a joy it is to be doing our first preliminary translation of God's Word in Amuesha!

" . . . Go and make disciples[2] of all nations . . . teaching them to obey everything I have commanded you . . . and surely I am with you . . ."

— Jesus Christ, (Matt. 28:19-20 NIV)

(Thank you, Lord, that we can go and take your Word to people who have never had it before, that they may become your disciples also.)

# 26

## Jungle Jewels

What do you call a giant when you have never seen one?

Ahuash and I continue with our translation of the story of David. We get to the part about the giant, Goliath. Small people that they are, the Amueshas had never seen a very large person until our recent visitor. We heard them referring to him as the *atarrpe'n* (literally, *atarr* — "big;" *-pe'n* — "mountain"). I now have my word for giant — "the big mountain."

Since Ahuash's knowledge of Spanish is so limited, we first just talk about the text in Amuesha. What does it say; what does it mean? I often write out a very preliminary version in my limited Amuesha, which helps him to understand the text more than he does in Spanish. Then he helps me compose it into proper Amuesha.

After finishing with Ahuash, I go to the master storyteller, Catalina. She understands what we have translated but she helps me improve my storytelling technique and with other difficult concepts. As we work on the verse "God does not look on our outward appearance but on our hearts," I trust it speaks to Catalina's heart. We are making progress, and I move on to translating the story of Joseph with Ahuash.

Singing the chorus "I'm So Happy" to myself today, the words in Amuesha just come to me and I write them down. With a little more thought to iron out the bugs, we have another new song. When the people come to sing again I share my new song with them. All of them want to learn it right away.

Mary Ruth reads her translation of the Prodigal Son to Llollo. She seems to understand and asks good questions about it. We never know just how much they understand the spiritual concepts of our translation, but we pray they will be receiving the truth of God's Word.

Many visitors arrive from upriver. They have not heard the Christian songs, and the people here like to teach them. One of the wives of the man looks so puzzled as she tries to understand what the words mean. Llollo starts explaining the song we are singing, how you have to believe in Jesus if you want to go where He is. As Llollo talks about Christ, the young wife asks, "Who was his father?"

"God, our Father, who made the earth," Llollo answers.

Llollo is doing a good job of witnessing, and it seems to me that she really believes. Then I tell the young wife as best I can about God who is the true "our Father" and who loves us greatly. He sent His Son, Jesus Christ, to this earth many years ago, and He died upon a cross of wood to pay for our sins. If we believe in Him and follow Him, we will go to where Jesus is when we die. The girl shows great interest, but it all seems a mystery to her. I hope I can talk to her again later.

I don't see much of Shañe' anymore. Her husband has taken her downriver. How I miss her! I continue to work with Catalina on checking out the stories of David and Joseph. We are now on the story of Joseph, where the sons of Jacob try to "console" their father. I have learned a new word *emya'teñets* from Ahuash for the word "console." I ask Catalina, "What does *emya'teñets* mean?" She starts to pat my face and says softly, "*Amach peyahuatsto*" (don't cry). With that good illustration, I'm sure we have the right word.

When we get to the "twelve sons of Jacob" we have to say "ten with two left over." I read back all the story of Joseph to Catalina, checking for meaning as we go along by asking her pertinent questions that will enable me to know whether she is understanding the correct meaning. When I get to the part where the brothers relate to their father how they told the ruler of Egypt that they had another brother at home and their father said to them, "Why did you tell him that you had another brother?" Catalina laughs understandingly, which helps me to realize that she has been getting the point all along.

She thinks it is unusual when Joseph cries upon revealing himself to his brothers. She says, "We are always happy when we see our loved ones again." She makes the comment at the end of the story, showing great insight: "It was really God who sent Joseph to Egypt."

We have been experiencing some very hot summer days. At midday we have been going to the river to cool off and relax. I've also been swimming in the deep part of the river to increase my confidence. I even swam up and down our branch of the river without stopping. I feel the need to become more at ease in the water just in case we turn over in a canoe some day.

In the evening, Pepe and his little brother, Sholle, come bearing gifts. They have brought Mary Ruth and me a large lightning bug, one for each of us. What could be more precious after a hard day's work? These are no ordinary lightning bugs; they have two lights on the front of their heads just like little cars with headlights. We thank Pepe and Sholle for sharing their best treasures with us.

We have started reading some of our Scripture stories to any individuals or groups that come to visit and may be interested. Mary Ruth reads one of her translated stories to Cruz's wife and two other fellows. With a few questions along the way, we can generally tell how well they are understanding it.

I have begun using flannelgraph pictures for one of the Scripture stories. I tried it out on Cruz's wife first. She was so delighted in seeing the pictures that illustrate the story that she went to get her husband and others and asked me to show it all over again. With fear and trembling, I tell the story to this larger audience. I mispronounce some of the more difficult words I had even studied beforehand, but you have to start somewhere. And my audience likes the pictures with the story.

Teresa, who is "City Woman" and Catalina's sister arrives to visit them from far upriver. They haven't seen her for a long time, so in true Amuesha fashion, Catalina and her newly-arrived sister start the ceremonial greetings.

"City Woman," thinking we would want to hear about this cultural event, comes running to invite us to join them. This formal ceremony goes on for several minutes. It's a kind of prayer chant to "our father god (the sun)" including thanks to the sun for "making our manioc and corn grow, and for giving us light and warmth." Amueshas have always seemed to be a "religious" people within their own culture.

Later in the day, they bring their sister to visit us and hear our songs and stories. "City Woman" plans to go back with her sister upriver and she wants to learn all our new songs before she leaves since she won't be back for a long time.

Teresa comes back the next morning and tells us she too wants to learn the songs. She returns again in the afternoon. We explain the words of the songs to her and read her some of our translated Scriptures. We instruct her about Jesus. She is very interested and  says she wants to believe in Him. We tell her how to pray and ask Jesus to enter her heart. She prays very simply: "Jesus, I know I am a sinner. I ask for forgiveness with my whole heart. I want to believe in you and obey you."

We read some more verses with her and sing. As she leaves she tells us, "I am going to tell my people at home when I get back that I now believe in Jesus and I will live with Him when I die." What a great pleasure to be leading our first "jungle jewels" to Jesus!

We have just gotten back from our late afternoon bath at the river when Cruz comes puffing up to the house to inform us that Pete Fast has just arrived. We have had no communication with him and are totally surprised. Pete is just finishing his survey upriver in the higher altitudes where more Amueshas live, including *Eñenas* (Singing Water), the new village we had told Pete about. He entered that area from the other end of Amuesha territory, back in the mountains from San Ramon. He has been walking twelve days through some of the most remote and difficult-to-travel areas with help from the Amueshas all along the way.

We are anxious to hear about Singing Water village. Pete informs us that the chief and the Amuesha people there accepted him and were very friendly. He sang some of our Amuesha songs with them and read from our newly-translated Scriptures in their language. They were delighted and said that is just what they want, to have things in their own language so they can better understand. He told them of the prospects of having a school built there for the children. They have never had a school and were happy to hear this good news. As far as Pete can say, the majority of the people want to have God's Word and believe. We talk until midnight. Pete shares all his experiences with us. Then comes a time of prayer together. Mary Ruth and I decide immediately that God would have us go there our next time out.

The next day, Pete writes out a report several pages long regarding his trip and I type it up for him. We also talk to him about some phonemic data in the language and how best to interpret it and write it orthographically.

Pete finds two fellows who are willing to take him downriver where he has helped the Ministry of Education start an Amuesha school. One of our JAARS planes will pick him up downriver after he finishes the rest of his trip.

The people come again in the evening, wanting to sing. We are happy to see that Ahuash has memorized all the songs, although he appreciates having a printed copy of them. Following the words on the printed copy also helps him in learning to read. Not only has he become a better reader, but he is even helping others to learn now. How happy we are to see this and encourage him in it. This is the way an indigenous ministry begins.

Even little three-year-old Llemllem, Shañe's little sister, likes to sit on my lap and sing. When I remark to her mother how well she knows the songs, her mother informs me that she goes around the house singing:

"Our Father takes care of *ema'* (baby);

Our Father takes care of *apa* (father);

Our Father takes care of *acheñ* (people)," (thus adding her own words).

I finish the translation of the David and Joseph stories with Ahuash and Catalina and type a copy for Ahuash to support his reading progress. He looks with pride at the work he has helped to accomplish. Since he knows the stories well, it will be easier for him to read them. To keep the momentum with our reading program, we often play the syllable game *Ñempo*.

Shañe' finally comes back from downriver. She informs us that her husband has left her. She doesn't seem to be sad. She says that he has already had twelve different wives. She is embarrassed because he has left her, and at first she doesn't want to come  visit us when others are present .

Catalina visits us today too. As I try to make conversation with her, Mary Ruth comes up from the stream with a bucket of water. She sees this little *ɨempo* (branch minnow) in the water and flips it out onto the ground before taking the water into our house. The tiny fish starts flopping around. Just for something to do, I pick up the little fish and put it in a clear glass of water. I mention to Catalina that I will take the fish back to the stream when we go for more water.

"Then he will tell all his *pamo'ts* (buddies) what happened to him," she replies.

Thus she starts relating a story as if the little fish could talk to his buddies:

"An *oc* (outsider) came and dipped me up in her bucket. Then she threw me out on the ground, and I almost died. Another *oc* had pity on me and picked me up and put me in a glass of water. If she hadn't picked me up and put me in water, I would have died." I am thinking, what a cute story, and it could even have a spiritual application. I am also thinking that I will soon be getting into schoolwork, and I want to gather some good stories for the children.

After I have taken *ɨempo* back to the stream, I let Catalina know what I have done. I also ask her to repeat the story slowly so I can write it down. She does just that, and now knowing the ending of the story she adds more:

"If the lover had not picked me up, we would not be seeing each other again" *ɨempo* continues to his buddies in the stream.

This little "*Ɨempo* Story" will later become the favorite story of the Amuesha children as they learn to read.[1] Even Catalina now wants to learn to read. As the author of the first children's story in Amuesha, she wants to read it for herself. I will have to get a copy made for her.

This story was also my first introduction to the "contrary-to-fact" mode in the Amuesha language that is expressed by the morpheme *-Vñ/-ñ*. *Amach ateɨ perrnetañepa' amach yabchannerrañe.* (If she, the lover, had not picked me up, we wouldn't be seeing each other again.) Now I know how to say, "If Jesus had not died for us, we could not be saved."

I work on a new song with Catalina — "For God So Loved the World" (people of the world). When the people come to sing again today, we will have it ready for them. It's amazing how much of the Gospel we are getting into the songs and how much the people love them. Catalina is not able to do physical work, so it's really great that she can work with me so much. She is happy to be making some money also.

Getting up this morning, I am wondering which of my ten projects to start on. I want to finish them all. Before we get our morning devotions finished, visitors come from downriver. Mary Ruth reads some stories to the older woman from her Mark translation, her ongoing project. These new visitors have heard about our singing and they want to sing.

In the middle of the afternoon, the wind starts to blow hard. It blows harder and harder, and off comes the top row of thatched leaves over our bedroom. We spread our plastic raincoats over our beds, but the rain comes in so hard our beds become pools of water. Kosepa comes running over in the wind and rain looking for Pepe. He is nowhere to be found. The wind and rain continue and off comes the top row of leaves over our kitchen. Kosepa is not able to get back home in the storm. Now the rain pours into our kitchen. The two of us, with Kosepa, crawl under our kitchen table and stay there till the storm blows over — our only dry place!

Cruz is coming again to work with Mary Ruth on translating the book of Mark. She also writes another song — "Into My Heart." With each new song that we write, the people are eager to learn them. One day, when we are singing with old Juana, Shañe' and Margarita arrive in time to sing the last song in the book with us. Shañe' says, "That's the end of the songs." She suggests we complete the one we began some time ago and didn't complete — "Everyday with Jesus." She and Margarita enjoy working on new songs. Catalina comes by and offers a suggestion of how to say "everyday" and make it fit the music, which solves the last problem. The ones there sing it over and over. The Amueshas here don't know any of their native tunes, so we are not able to use them yet.

Mary Ruth works with Kosepa again to check on her translation of Mark, expecting to finish the first rough draft soon. I read some of the Mark translation to Catalina, beginning with the story of Christ's crucifixion and resurrection. We long to see her come to know the Lord before we leave, fearing she might not be here when we return. And she seems so interested, but hesitates.

Today while I am having my morning devotions, I just feel this will be the day when Catalina will come to know and accept the Lord. At our breakfast blessing I pray, "Lord, may this day count for eternity." At our noon blessing, Mary Ruth prays, "Lord, may this be the afternoon Catalina will be saved." My faith grows that this will be true. When I go to work with Catalina in the afternoon, after first reading to her the story of Jesus walking on the water and the triumphal entry into Jerusalem, I read her some verses on salvation. Catalina says sadly, "I am paying for my own sins with my sickness. I have had ten 'husbands,'" counting off each one with all her ten fingers.

"You don't have to pay for your own sins. That's why Jesus died, to pay for your sins and mine and everyone's sins," I joyfully tell her.

Then I read again where the Scripture says: "Believe on the Lord Jesus Christ and you will be saved."

"Do you want to believe?"

"Yes."

"Then just tell Jesus that."

She prays very simply, "I know I am a sinner, Jesus, but I now know that you died for my sins. I believe!"[2]

Catalina comes home with me to tell Mary Ruth about her decision, "Now I believe in Jesus! He came to this earth to pay for my sins. Now when I die I will go to live with Him." She seems so happy. Tears begin to fill our eyes. We know that many people's prayers have been answered. Thank you, Lord.

Mary Ruth finishes the first rough draft of the Gospel of Mark! It's a great day for us. Thank you again, Lord.

Knowing the power of story and Catalina's unusual abilities, I start working with her on the translation of a children's story called "Snowflake." There will soon be more schools among the Amueshas where this story can be used. It's the story of a little, white lamb that disobeys his shepherd and gets lost. Amueshas are not acquainted with domesticated sheep. They have not had sheep like the high Andes people. Looking toward future translation where sheep are very prominent — the story of the lost sheep, the lamb as a sacrifice in the Old Testament, the symbolism of the "Lamb of God," in

Revelation — we will need to use these terms in relation to sheep.[3] Therefore, if we introduce sheep early in story form, showing the characteristics of sheep and their use in sacrifices, the people can become acquainted with them.

The flannelgraph pictures to go with this story will help Catalina know what sheep look like and their characteristics. The first problem is a name for this very white, little lamb. "Snowflake" won't do in Amuesha since there are never any snowflakes in this hot climate. We'll just have to give him another name. As I show Catalina a picture of the little lamb, I ask her, "What would we call a cute, little, woolly animal like this which is very white?"

She thinks and answers. "*Os*" (cloud). Then she asks Llollo who is watching also.

Llollo thinks and exclaims, "*Besllom̃!*" (cotton ball). We know immediately that "Snowflake's" new name will be *Besllom̃*.

A preliminary rough draft translation of the story is done in my limited Amuesha. I read it to Catalina, showing her the pictures that accompany the story. Using the pictures, she easily gets the drift and then puts the prose into correct Amuesha with all the morphemes to bring it to life. She even adds her own interesting details to the story. We tell the lamb's story in the first person just like Catalina did with the little fish story. Her clever addition in one place was to have the little lamb remarking, "I taste the grass as so very sweet; I can hardly wait to get to it."

The story shows the characteristic of the lamb to go astray — to go out on its own and get lost, thus causing his loving master to endanger his life to search for him. The correlation can be made to Christ, who is our Good Shepherd; we are the sheep who go astray. I run the story by Shañe'. She is delighted to be working with me again, and is getting over her embarrassment.

We later translate another story about a mother hen that stays on her nest in the open field to save her newly hatched chicks when a fire races over the field. She dies in the fire, but in so doing saves her chicks as she covers them in the nest. The chick story, too, becomes a favorite with the children and the adults. Such stories help prepare the people to understand how Christ died to save us.[4]

Our time is drawing near to leave once again. All the people want us to sing before we go. As we finish the song "I'm So Happy," we hear Catalina giving testimony. "That's how Jesus makes us happy," she says. "He forgives our sins when we believe and receive Him, and then we go to be with Him." It's a joy to hear this coming from Catalina! We do not know at this time that when we return to the village, Catalina will already be with Jesus — another jungle jewel for Jesus!

"Now therefore go, and I will be with thy mouth, and teach thee what thou shalt say."
   – the Lord God, (Exodus 4:12 KJV)

"... Ye shall be witnesses unto me ... unto the uttermost part of the earth."
   – the Lord Jesus, (Acts 1:8 KJV)

(Thank you, Lord, for enabling us to share your Word with our sister, Catalina, in her language so she can really understand and receive you.)

# 27
# A Man Called Peter

Is the sun really "our Father (God)"?

"Like all my Amuesha people, I prayed to the sun, even when I was still a child. We called the sun, 'our father god.' But at times when I looked up at the sun, I would think, Is the sun really our father god or is there another one who is the true our Father? I remember one time when I was still a child, I prayed to the sun, 'If you are not the true our Father, may someone come someday who will tell us who the true our Father is.'" The young, energetic Amuesha man, Pedro (Peter) Lopez, tells how he doubted that the sun was the true "our Father," even from childhood.

Pedro's prayer was answered just a few years later when he heard portions of the newly translated Gospel of Mark being read in his own Amuesha language in a nearby village. He had come to play soccer with his buddies at Chispa. In fact, they were waiting for him to arrive so they could start the game. They yelled for him to hurry, but Pedro says, "I knew as soon as I came up and heard the reading in my language that this must be something about the true our Father for whom I had been searching." Then Pedro yelled to his soccer mates, "Go ahead and play without me; I want to hear what is being read here."

Pedro didn't understand everything at the time Pete Fast was visiting and reading from the newly translated Mark, but he did make his decision to follow this true "our Father" and His Son, Jesus, and to gain more knowledge of His Word. Pedro also learned from Pete that he could study to become a schoolteacher among his own Amuesha people. Very interested in seeing the Amueshas have schools for their children and their adults, Pedro made plans with Pete to study at the Yarina Center and take the Teacher Training Course sponsored by the Ministry of Education the following January-March period.

We are now on our way to the area where Pedro and his wife live to follow through as was planned. Our JAARS plane has already transported us from Stingray village far downriver to where Amuesha teacher, Santiago Pashco, has already started teaching in an Amuesha school. Santiago will take us by trail from his school over to the Chispa area where Pedro lives, and from there to another Amuesha teacher candidate, Graciela, and her husband who are also expected to attend the Teacher Training Course in Yarina.

The three men plan to make a large balsa raft there high up on the Omaiz River for the three couples and us to go downriver since JAARS planes cannot land on the small Omaiz River. It will be a ten-day trip downriver to Pucallpa (the main jungle city near the Yarina Center).

Since we are just now becoming acquainted with the new Amuesha teacher candidates, we want to go with them for the first five days to get to know them better, and for the adventure of white water rafting. We are just hearing about this fad in the U.S., and here we can experience it in our daily work — free! The small, fast moving streams here in the foothills of the Andes are ideal for this.

At the end of the first five days, we should be far downriver at the mouth of the Pichis River, where Pete and Mary Fast are clearing out the house they lived in among the Amueshas. Pete has been reassigned to our Lima office staff, so they are leaving the Amuesha work. They have requested that the large Norseman floatplane take them back to Yarina. We will join them on the Pichis River and all go back to Yarina together. At the point where the Pichis River flows into the Pachitea River it creates a very large river, which is needed for the Norseman landing.

We have now left Santiago's place with him leading us on the four-hour hike through the jungle to the area where we will meet Pedro and his wife, and Graciela and her husband. We leave early in the morning, hoping to get to the river we must ford on the way before more rain falls. If the river floods, we will not be able to ford it.

Happily, we ford the river in time and continue on over fallen tree trunks and along the jungle floor of matted tree roots and vines. This is our first experience of a long hike through the rainforest, and we must admit, our legs are giving out by the time we reach our destination. Santiago is a good guide; he knows the area well.

Soon after we reach our meeting place, we see Pedro and his wife, Petita, who have come from their more remote village. This is our first introduction to this "man called Peter," who has been searching for the true "our Father." Pedro is so friendly and likeable, and has a ready smile all the time. We couldn't help but like him and his young wife, Petita. They did not bring along their little two-year-old girl, thinking of the dangerous raft trip ahead. We look forward to getting to know them better. Pedro quickly goes on to help Santiago and the others build the large, balsa raft that will carry all of us downriver.

How could we know at this time the great plans God has for this man called Peter, the man we have just met, as he rushes on to help the other raft makers? As it turns out, God's plan for him is to finish the Teacher Training Course at Yarina, then be faced with a call to the distant upriver village of Singing Water to start a school there to be schoolteacher for his own Amuesha people, most of whom he has never seen before. At first, however, he will be hesitant, saying, "I know my own people. Sometimes they are slow to accept even a fellow Amuesha when he comes from another village."

Pedro grows so much in his faith when he meets with fellow Amuesha trainees to study God's Word in his own language in daily devotional times at Yarina during the Teacher Training Course. As he reconsiders, he quickly continues, "If the true our Father wants me to go there and help my own people come to know the true God, then I will go there." There is no further doubt in Pedro's mind that this is God's will for him.

He and Petita make plans to leave their downriver village where they have lived all their lives and go to the distant upriver village of Singing Water, which they have never seen. This is a great step of faith for Pedro.

How happy Pedro and Petita are after they make the long journey to Singing Water village and find that the chief and all the people there take them in as family. They give them land to live on and extra land for growing coffee. They help him get his school started, and all the children eagerly enroll. It is the first school they have ever had.

Just as soon as Pedro starts teaching the children in school, he also starts teaching all the people about the true "our Father" he has come to know, and about His Son, Jesus, who loves them and died for them. He invites the people to come in the late afternoons after they have finished their day's work to join together and learn the new Christian songs he has learned and to listen to the newly translated Word of God that he has so recently come to know. How happy we are, after finishing various projects, to go to Singing Water village to live and find Pedro already teaching his own people what he knows of God's Word — the first missionary evangelist among his own Amuesha people!

The Amuesha people in this area where we presently have gathered for the raft building have heard about our singing at Stingray village. They come to greet us and ask us to sing here also. At first they are astonished to hear us speaking their language. They tell us no one else from the outside has ever learned their language. We sing all our Christian songs. They are delighted and want to learn them right away. Since we have to wait for the raft to be finished, we have plenty of time to sing with all who come. We also read to them some of our translated Scriptures and tell them about the true "our Father," the one who made the sun, and about His Son, Jesus, who loves us, and died for us, and rose again. Many are very interested, and we pray with various ones who want to really believe.

"... You are my witnesses, declares the Lord, that I am God. . ."

> – the Lord God to Isaiah, (Isaiah 43:12 NIV)

"I will praise you, O Lord, among the nations; I will sing of you among the peoples."

> – the Psalmist David, (Psalm 108:3 NIV)

(Thank you, our Father, that you are the true God, and that many here are hearing your true Word for the first time. Thank you, that many as they hear are believing. Thank you for more jungle jewels.)

# 28

# White Water Rafting in the Headwaters of the Amazon

White water rafting in the jungle?

Before long, the fellows come and tell us that the raft is ready and we are to go over to the river. As we are leaving, the head man of the area presents us with a large, red rooster as a gift for us to eat along the way on our five-day raft trip. We are at a loss as to how to hold on to this big bird on a raft. We do want to be appreciative, so we duly thank him. Struggling to get this monster's feet tied, we begin our "odyssey with the old, red rooster." We follow the trail to the Omaiz River where the raft is awaiting us.

The raft is big, about ten-feet wide by twenty-four-feet long, the balsa logs tied together with vines. There will be ten or more of us after we pick up Santiago's wife on the way. The Indians load on bananas, chickens, and other foodstuffs. They even make a palm bark flooring for sitting on and cargo. We set off about mid-afternoon when everything is ready.

Mary Ruth and I have never been on a raft before. We're looking forward to this trip, and getting to know and bond with these new Amuesha teacher-trainees. The river is low — not to our advantage since more rocks will be showing than in high-water time. But the water is so clear, and it's a beautiful day. Floating down the river is delightful as we admire the lovely, flowering trees on either side while we slowly glide along.

Not far into our trip, they decide to stop and throw out dynamite in order to get a catch of fish for supper, even though we have considerable food on the raft. The dynamite goes off and fish come to the surface everywhere. We help pick them up. The wives start cleaning them even as we continue on down the river.

We approach a very narrow rapid where there is hardly enough room for our big raft. They tell us to take our shoes off before we go through a bad spot — just in case we need to swim. As we are going through another stretch of rapids, someone happens to look back and see that our rooster has floated off and is up in the rapids flapping his wings. We think, is this the end of our big, old rooster? No, in a flash, Pedro is off the raft and heading up into the rapids. He catches the flapping rooster with his legs still tied and comes swimming back with our rooster under one arm.

Next we come to where the Omaiz River flows into the Comprechmas River, or Chuchuras, as it is called from this point on. Just after entering this river there is a very rough stretch of water. Santiago is able to keep us to one side of it and we come through okay, keeping our shoes off as we move into yet another rapid. We get well into a sharp drop and the water narrows. I notice a big rock over to the left side. As we start the descent, I observe the back left side of the raft swinging over toward the big rock. At first I think we are going to clear it, but the very last six inches of the raft hit with a great cracking sound, and I see the logs knocked off and rising up into the air. Then I see the whole raft rising up into the air from that side, and I realize the raft is turning over. I am sitting on the back right side, so I quickly decide to jump far out into the water to the right to prevent the raft from coming down on me and pinning me underneath. As I hit the water, nothing but white water surrounds me and I feel chocked by it splashing all around. Pedro jumps too, so the two of us swim to the right while the others manage to swim out from under the overturned raft and stay with it.

I get to shore and look for Mary Ruth. The Amueshas are good at taking care of themselves in water, but I don't know about Mary Ruth. Looking toward the overturned raft, I see her head come up on the other side and I breathe a sigh of relief, knowing she can hold onto it. Pedro and I see all the others on or around the raft and we thank the Lord. We are told later that Mary Ruth and one of the other women had to be pulled from under the raft.

Safe and sound on shore, I have to think of the Lord's faithfulness and timing. Barely a week ago I gained confidence in white water up at Stingray village, and here I'm having to use this newly acquired skill already. God is certainly faithful in his timing and enabling! All of us on the raft had just been singing "God Cares for You."

After they finally get the upside-down raft over to the shore and we join them down the river, it gets dark. The fellows manage to rescue our bags from the water since the rubberized bags floated for some time, but our shoes that were not in the bags are  lost. We are shoeless for the rest of the trip. Mary Ruth did manage to hold onto a plastic bag in which she carried a camera and our diaries. Despite being under water, she held the bag so tightly that the pictures in the camera were fine and our diaries still legible. Our clothes and sleeping gear are all wet. All the chickens that were on the back of the raft are nowhere to be seen. We think, with some pleasure, that this is surely the end of the old, red rooster.

We find a deserted-looking house nearby, and finally some people arrive. They help us look for some wood so we can start a fire to dry out our wet clothes and warm up in the chill of the evening. We huddle around the fire to get warm.

The fellows inform us we will have to spend the night here so they can repair the raft in the morning. We lost all our food, including the recent catch of fish, along with the cooking pots. The people who live here have some chickens, so we buy one from them and borrow a pot. After we all start to dry out, have some hot, boiled chicken, and warm up, we feel much better.

Someone finds part of an old blanket in the house and offers it to Mary Ruth and me. It's not big enough for both of us, but we try to cover our toes and foreheads to keep the bats from biting us.

We wake up to rain in the morning, but the fellows begin repairing the raft. Another young Amuesha man named Guillermo finds us and joins us. He wants to go study at Yarina to be a schoolteacher among his people. He is so knowledgeable and helpful, we decide he would be a good candidate and invite him to go with us.

The fellows work all morning repairing the raft. In the meantime, some of our party goes back upriver where our raft flipped over and what do you know — they find our old, red rooster alive and well on the shore. Of all the chickens, he manages to make it to shore, much to our consternation. With great joy they return, bringing him back to us!

As the rain continues to fall, the river begins to rise. The rivers can rise very quickly at this altitude. Although the river is high and much more forceful than when we first started, the advantage is that more of the rocks will be covered and we will float faster. We take off again about noon. We seem to be zooming down the river now, gliding along on the fast moving water.

In the late afternoon we reach Santiago's place, where his wife is waiting to be picked up. Santiago has many things to do here. Mary Ruth and I leave the raft and find a small, clear stream where we can bathe and wash a change of clothing. Santiago's wife cooks up a big pot of rice to fill our empty tummies. We share our little can of instant Nescafé coffee. They are not used to drinking coffee, so it is a treat for them.

Our sleeping bags have not dried out yet from their swim in the river and all the rain, but Santiago's wife offers us a thin sheet. Thankfully, we are getting down to a somewhat warmer climate. We also have a rubberized tarp we bought while upriver. Despite getting a bit cold at night, we are able to get some sleep.

Early the next morning the fellows work to put a thatched roof over the raft. Nobody knows how long the rains will continue since we are well into the rainy season. We take off again about ten o'clock.

We stop at a German landowner's hacienda. (German colonists have been in this area for some time.) We buy some metal plates and spoons to replace what was lost when the raft overturned. We also would have bought them pots to replace theirs, but there were none for sale. We can get them farther on downriver.

As evening comes, we stop along the river for the night. We tell the women they can have our rooster for the evening meal, thinking that would be a good way to get rid of him and that they have lost so many of their own chickens in the turnover. Instead, just before dark, the fellows go out to the river and throw dynamite, and come back with loads of fish. We help the women clean them all. Then the fellows carry them up to a house where some early settlers live, get the fish cooked, and bring them back for every-one to enjoy. It is pouring rain by this time, but under our newly made roof we keep dry and have a good fish supper.

All of us sleep on the raft this night. Tight quarters! The tarp we bought along the way serves us well since our sleeping bags still have not dried. As we all bed down, Pedro and Petita start singing some of their native songs. We encourage them, because up until now we have not heard any of their native tunes. They finish one song and then they say, "This is another pretty song" and start singing again. We tell them we like them too and want to learn them. We are so happy to be hearing some of their native tunes that we can also use with Christian words. Then we sing some of our songs, and finally we all go to sleep.

We get up early since we have a long way to go to meet the plane down near the mouth of this river, the Palcaso, where it flows into the big Pachitea River. We push out from the bank while it is still dark. It's a little scary going down the river in the dark, but dawn soon breaks. The river rises even more as the rain continues. Before very long we stop at another house along the way and cook some more of the fish.

While we are at this place, a fellow arrives from downriver. He tells us that we should not try going on downriver today. He says there are giant whirlpools down there that could tear our raft apart, so we decide to spend the day tied up where we're at and wait for the water to go down. I start catching up on my diary; Mary Ruth starts sunning some of her clothes.

All of a sudden Santiago says, "Let's just go on down to the mouth of the Pososo (Salt River) and see how it is there." We are leery of going on after what this other man said, but Santiago wants to continue. As we arrive at the mouth of the Pososo, Santiago takes a careful look and says, "It's all right, let's go." We must admit that we were scared, but we get through the mouth without any mishaps.

The fellows tell us there is another dangerous spot a short distance ahead, but if we get through it, we'll be all right. We do survive that one okay also, yet there is still another. If Mary Ruth and I had had our way, we surely wouldn't have gone on this swollen river, but the Lord is taking care of us. There are vicious whirlpools in some parts of the river going around and around like a mad racetrack. If we are drawn into one of them, we will not escape as we did when the raft overturned. Happily, Santiago knows this river well. Every time we come to another whirlpool, he starts telling us how many people have drowned here before. This doesn't exactly encourage us, and we only hope he will try to row harder to keep us from getting caught in one.

The farther downriver we go, the bigger and smoother the river becomes. Toward late afternoon (record time because the river is so high) we arrive at the mouth of this river at Puerto Victoria where it flows into the Pachitea. Just a little further on, we arrive at the mouth of the Pichis River, our final destination. We ease into the calm Pichis to keep from being swept on downriver. It feels good to have our old raft tied up here, away from the swift, swirling water.

We don't see anything of the plane that is scheduled to pick us up. We think maybe the weather has been too bad for the plane to come. We find out that Pete and Mary are up the Pichis River a little way, where they are finishing clearing out their old house.

We visit with some Amueshas here and find a fellow who will take us in his canoe on up the river to where Pete and Mary are. We "donate" our old, red rooster to our fellow rafters who have five more days' journey to Yarina. Thus ends our odyssey with the old, red rooster. We say good-bye as we head upriver to the Fasts' house and arrive there at dusk. They are surprised to see us at this late hour. We eat and relate all our experiences.

It is still raining in the morning. Just as we decide it is too rainy for the plane to come as planned, we hear it in the distance and rush to get everything ready. In an hour's flying time we are landing at Yarina in the JAARS

Norseman plane. Many of the folks are down at the ramp to meet us. Do we ever get razzed for arriving barefoot. Dr. Kenneth Pike, our chief linguist and president of the Summer Institute of Linguistics,[1] is there to meet us also. We will shortly be involved in the Linguistic Workshop that he has come to the Center to conduct for on-the-field training. Everyone wants to hear all about our experiences.

Thus ends our third eventful and profitable stay with our Amuesha friends — some twenty-one months in all.

"When you pass through the waters, I will be with you; and when you pass through the rivers, they will not sweep over you."

— the Lord through Isaiah, (Isaiah 43:2 NIV)

(Thank you, Lord, for your great faithfulness to keep us safe when we are in danger. Thank you for allowing us to become acquainted with the Amuesha teacher-trainees I will be working with soon. Thank you for another profitable tribal stay and seeing a number of new believers — more jungle jewels.)

# 29
# Bilingual Teacher Training Course

What is a bilingual teacher?

At the end of their ten-day raft trip, Pedro and his fellow raft buddies arrive at our Yarina Center and enroll in the upcoming session of the Bilingual Teacher Training Course for indigenous peoples of the jungle. Pedro is hoping he knows enough Spanish to understand the Spanish-speaking Peruvian professors assisted by our SIL staff, who will be teaching the basic primary education courses in reading, writing, and arithmetic. These are the very same courses he will later be teaching Amuesha children in their own language. Thus, the "bilingual teacher" (one who speaks two languages) will be bridging the education gap between his own native world and the outside world as his own people will be learning to read first in their mother-tongue and later in Spanish.

In 1945 a contract was signed between the Peruvian government's Ministry of Education and William Cameron Townsend (founder of the Summer Institute of Linguistics and Wycliffe Bible Translators). In 1952 a later resolution was signed to establish a government-sponsored bilingual education program for Peru's ethnic minorities with the cooperation of SIL.[1]

This is now the third year for this Bilingual Teacher Training Course to function.

Pedro learns that the first teacher-training program started in 1953 with fifteen candidates from seven minority language groups of the jungle: Aguaruna, Amuesha, Cashibo, Huitoto, Machiguenga, Piro, and Yagua. In the second year of the training course, more candidates from other language groups joined the first ones. This year, still more candidates come from other language groups, including Pedro and his fellow rafters of the Amuesha language group. What a wonderful way God has provided for all the language groups of the jungle to learn to read His Word in their own individual languages. Thank you, Lord.

Pedro is fascinated by seeing these fellow candidates from all the other language groups. With each group speaking its own language, Pedro seeks in his own way to get better acquainted with them. He carries a notebook in which he has a list of words in Spanish (the national language), and with each new language speaker he finds, he asks them how they say those words in their language. Outgoing person that he is, Pedro makes many new friends by learning how to say some words in their languages since Spanish is new to most of them.

By this time, the Ministry of Education and SIL have built new thatched roof classrooms overlooking Yarinacocha Lake where the trainees are learning the new concepts of reading, writing, and arithmetic. Several of us linguists sit in on these classes to become familiar with what is being taught each day in Spanish so we can help candidates from the language group we work with in the evening study hours.

Another part of their daily scheduled hours is a thirty-minute time of devotion, each language group with its own linguist, after the evening study hours. I join Pedro, Guillermo, and the other Amuesha trainees. We sing the Christian songs which all of them are learning. It's a very informal discussion time as the best reader reads the translated Scripture aloud and the others follow along, reading from their own copies. Together we talk about it. They make their own comments and ask questions. As we study together the first translated Gospels of Mark and John, they learn of the true "our Father" and of his Son, Jesus Christ who loves us, died for our sins, and rose again.

Almost all of them decide that this is the true "our Father's" Word and want to follow Him. As the teacher-trainees continue to meet for evening devotions, they are the first ones of their language group to hear God's Word in their own language.

It's a good time for me to test the translation and find out which parts are not easily understood and revise them accordingly. In addition to the new truths they are learning, it's excellent practice for them to learn to read in their own language. This is the first time many of the Amuesha trainees have seen their own language in writing. Often, Pedro chuckles out loud as he recognizes a new word in Amuesha, "This is how *Yompor* (our Father) looks in writing!" The majority of them soon believe and carry back the first translated books of the Bible to read to the people in their own communities, as well as to their students in their schools.

The closing exercises of each Teacher Training Course are often attended by the Minister of Education or his representative. This is a festive time when each of the different language groups demonstrates some of its native dances and other cultural arts, such as the shooting of bows and arrows or blowguns.

Many of those who have completed the training are named bilingual teachers, with a salary from the Ministry of Education. They rush back home after the course to get their thatched roof schools built to begin classes by the first of April.

We do not realize in these early beginnings how soon the Amuesha nation will become literate, with schools and teachers in all the communities. Candidates for teacher training continue to come in each year to take advantage of this government-sponsored program for their people, and the literacy rate becomes seventy percent in a relatively short time with some thirty bilingual schools throughout Amuesha territory.

Who would ever guess that the number of churches the people themselves would establish, teaching and preaching from their own translated Scriptures, would in time grow to forty-five and cover all Amuesha areas!

Although we should have expected it, how would we know that this man called Peter (Pedro) would become one of the greatest of these preachers and teachers, carrying God's Word and evangelizing many areas where Amueshas live? With great joy and love for his people, Pedro would share with them God's Word, the true "our Father" he had been searching for. How would we know that Valerio, one of the earliest teacher-trainees, would in a short time teach many Amuesha young people in a Bible School using the newly translated Scriptures! How would we know that from the students of these teacher-trainees would come forth preachers, teachers, health promoters, school supervisors, writers, evangelists, and Bible translators?

"I am the Lord your God who teaches you what is best for you ..."

(Isaiah 48:17 NIV)

"Go ... and teach all nations (peoples) ..."

– Jesus, (Matthew 28:19 KJV)

(Thank you, Lord, that many of the Amuesha teachers want to be able to teach their own people not only reading, but want to teach them your Word.)

# 30

# Our First Trip to Singing Water Village

What will we find in this more remote village in the deep jungle?

At last we are on our way to live in Singing Water village, having finished the Teacher Training Course and our annual conference in Yarina. Singing Water village is higher in the Andes Mountains (about 4,500 feet). We are not able to use our JAARS floatplane since the streams are not large enough to land on at that altitude. Wheel planes must be used to fly to the nearest landing strip at the Peruvian town of San Ramon. From there we will work our way back as far as the road goes into the mountainous area where the Amueshas live. Then we will have to go on foot.

Soon we are looking down at mountain tops below us, and when we see a large mountain close to the side of the plane we know we are descending between the mountains to the landing strip at San Ramon. We know that no one will be here to meet us because we are still in a Spanish-speaking area.

We unload our baggage and look around for some way to get to nearby San Ramon or La Merced, where there are places to spend the night which Pete Fast has told us about. A little, old man with a vehicle that has to be cranked by hand comes to our rescue. We get to La Merced and find a small backwoods hotel with a tiny room barely big enough for the two of us and our baggage.

It is still not too late, so we venture into town to buy flour, sugar, and other supplies we will be needing for our stay of several months in Singing Water village. This is necessary since we will not be getting supply flights as we did in Stingray village. The Peruvian Spanish-speaking people stare at us — two young, foreign women in this frontier town. We get a good night's sleep despite our "rock-hard" pillows and someone waking us up at four o'clock in the morning.

For our coffee in the morning, we are brought cups of hot water and coffee in the form of a concentrated syrup which we add to the hot water to make it the strength we desire. It's really quite delicious. We are in the coffee growing area in Peru, and these two towns are the markets for the coffee grown in this mountainous region.

About eleven in the morning, we are told there is a vehicle going about half way to our destination. We think we had better take it since there are very few vehicles going back into the mountains to Villa Rica. We make arrangements with the driver. We get to sit in front with him as the rest of the vehicle is already full.

We run into landslides all along the route, but he just makes his way over or around them and continues on. At one point, we run into two Amueshas — Agosto and Hua'yoll — that we know from Stingray village. They update us with news from their home and tell that many Amueshas pick coffee up here in this mountainous area for plantation owners.

After switching to another vehicle midway, we keep climbing higher into the mountains. We pass a different style of houses where the German colonists settled and have their large coffee plantations. We end up at a house on the top of the mountain. This is as far as the driver will go.

We are pleasantly surprised to see two blonde, young girls dressed in jeans coming out to greet us. They are very friendly and take us right in. We find out that they are the daughters of the plantation owner here. They are flabbergasted to find out what we are doing — going out alone to live with the Indians!

These beautiful girls, Erika and her younger sister, whose mother tongue is German (but they also know Spanish), want us to speak English with them, which we are happy to do.

Their house is very much European style — various levels, with little staircases going up to higher levels.

Erika is evidently her tall, German father's "right-hand man" as she hurries to help him get his tractor motor started, then starts another motor to churn the butter — very masculine-like behavior, but also very femininely pretty. She asks us if we'd like to go with her on another tractor to pick up the sacks of coffee the workers have picked that day. We agree, and stand on each side of her on the tractor as she dashes through the green coffee plants with their red berries. Once the workers load the sacks on the tractor, we move on to the next batch of coffee sacks. What a pleasant, enjoyable change for us.

In the evening, the girls share some of their homemade bread, butter, and cheese. After eating, Erika plays some of her American records. They are glad to have the fellowship of Americans. We talk for some time, explaining our mission to the Amueshas, before retiring in a neat little room.

About nine the next morning, we hear a truck grinding up the mountain and rush out to see if we can get a ride to Villa Rica. Happily, the driver says okay, loads up our stuff, and allows us to sit in front along with another passenger.

Winding up the curvy road we finally come to its end in Villa Rica, the most remote of the frontier towns. It's a quaint, little place, looking just like a wild west frontier town — a saloon being the main building and the streets muddy ruts.

Since the saloon seems to be the only public building, we go in. All the bearded men stare at us. We ask the man in charge where we can rent mules to take us into Amuesha country. He says he will contact a mule owner for us. We bring in all our belongings, and a room off the barroom is quickly arranged for us.

When the men in the barroom realize we are going in to live with the Amueshas, they can't believe it. We tell them we already know some of the Amuesha language. Soon after, someone brings in two boys they say are Amueshas. When we start to talk with them in Amuesha, all eyes are on us. An old man tells us the Amueshas live on the other side of this big mountain. "No one has ever learned their language," he tells us.

It becomes dark and the owner gives us a candle for our room. He even serves us some food later in the evening. He tells us we are to leave early the next day. We go to bed and sleep soundly despite there being no lock on our door.

In the morning he serves us crackers and coffee for breakfast. We wonder if we can walk the twenty kilometers (twelve miles) on such a meager breakfast, so I eat plenty of crackers. The mule driver finally comes and starts to load our things. There is one mule extra for us to ride. Mary Ruth says to me, "You take your turn in the morning and I'll take mine in the afternoon." I agree, although I think I would rather walk.

As we get further from the Spanish-speaking people, the young mule driver admits he is Amuesha and starts talking to us in Amuesha, which we appreciate. Before long, we find out that the trail is every bit as bad as the men back in the saloon told us — mud up to our knees! The mule trail runs all through the jungle, and with frequent rains, it never dries out. The small feet of the mules keep the trail a quagmire with them constantly carrying heavy sacks of coffee out to market. The frequent, sharp ascents and descents of the trail keep me continually trying not to slide off the back of the mule or over its head. On one steep climb in the slippery mud, one of the mules loaded with our baggage rolls over backward, rolling down the hill with it all. That's where our pot handles get broken off. The mule jumps up ready to go again.

The mule driver helps the one of us who is walking. He has a unique sense of humor. One place where the trail is very narrow and slick on a cliff that goes down and down, I remark just to make conversation, "If I fall off here, I will surely die."

"We'll just bury you by the trail," he answers casually.

I ride the mule until noontime. Then Mary Ruth takes her turn. As I dismount, I feel numb in my legs and topple over backwards in the mud. All of us have a good laugh, including me. In some places where we step, the water is deep in the holes, and a spray of water comes up like a geyser sending muddy water all the way up into our hair.

We finally arrive about four in the afternoon. We come right out of the bush at the little school and there is Pedro teaching the children — so good to see him with his school already going. He asks us what time it is. His clock says 2:30. He has all the kids in the school shake hands with us. He tells us that the chief has been sick and has not finished our house. We see a little loft up over his provisional school and ask if we can live there in the meantime. After a much-needed bath in the creek we get our bedding set up, but are too tired to blow up our air mattresses.

Not only does Pedro have his school started and going well when we arrive, but he also tells us that he has those who want to sing and hear about the true "our Father" to come in the late afternoons to his house and he is teaching them. How our hearts rejoice to hear this. This is the way we want it to be with Pedro himself sharing God's Word with his own people. We realize that this is the most effective E-1 testimony that can be given.[1] Pedro invites us to join them if we like.

We go on up the hill to where the chief and Pedro and Petita live, greeting the people as we go along. The chief's wife is very friendly and gives us a boiled egg and manioc — tastes so good after our twelve-mile hike through the jungle. Going on up to Pedro and Petita's house, Petita gives us some fried bananas and coffee.

After eating when Pedro says, "Let's sing," all the kids go scampering off to find their songbooks. As he calls out the numbers they search eagerly to find the numbers — numbers they are just now learning in their school. Then they sing so heartily you would think that they are reading the words, but I don't think they have learned to read that much in the short time the school has been functioning. They have already memorized the songs.

Then Pedro speaks on some of the Bible verses in the book and prays. We rejoice again in what Pedro is already doing here and he himself such a recent believer — the start of a real indigenous work.

As we leave to go back to our "loft apartment" they teasingly tell us not to fall off. We are right under the thatched roof. I tell Mary Ruth, "We'd better keep our mouths closed as we sleep, in case a spider drops down from the roof." We are so tired and sore from our mule trip, we think nothing more of spiders and sleep soundly.

"... Sing to the Lord a new song, his praise from the end of the earth."

(Isaiah 42:10 NIV)

"Endure hardness, as a good soldier of Jesus Christ."

– the Apostle Paul, (II Timothy 2:3 KJV)

(Thank you, Lord, for the good, indigenous work Pedro is already doing here. Thank you for keeping us in "all our ways" of travel.)

# 31

# Bilingual Teachers Become Spiritual Leaders

Early the next morning, we are startled at the rustling coming from the jungle path. Suddenly, they appear — Amuesha men adorned with crowns, feathers, red achiote face paint, seeds, and beads, and wearing their rustic, dark tunics. Our fears are relieved as they greet us,

*"Puetare' nočhaneshacha'; yehuapa'muena o'ch yemo'ta'muenes."*

(Good morning, my sisters; we come this morning to visit you.)

We realize these are Amuesha men (including the chief) who were not here when we arrived late yesterday afternoon. They have come to officially meet and greet us, wearing their best adornments. We are pleased to meet the chief of this area. His twinkling, light brown eyes let us know he is happy to have us come and live with his people. They are extremely surprised, yet happy to hear us talk to them in their own language. We don't know it at the time, but they are beginning to call us, among themselves, "the daughters of 'our father,' the sun," since we are speaking their language. That really makes us one of them.

Soon the kids and Pedro come to begin their regular school day, with their morning exercises of lineup and roll call. We have not had time yet to unpack our things. We start a little fire out away from the school where we can boil some water for drinking and make some coffee. The people keep giving us boiled eggs and manioc, which help a lot until we can get organized.

We need to find and set up our radio and call in to Yarina Center as it has now been six days since we left there, and they no doubt are wondering where we are. The men are very helpful in setting up the antenna poles. "Yes, we have now arrived at Singing Water village" we tell them. The radio works fine, despite all the jolts from the rough roads and mule trail. The people "ooh" and "ah" at this talking machine.

Very gradually we get our things unpacked, taking lots of time to talk to all the people who come to visit. After all, that's what we are here for — the people.

Living directly over the school classroom, we hear much of what goes on. The children are enthusiastic about having a school for the first time. At times I hear Pedro telling the kids to go outside at recess, but they don't want to; they would rather keep learning to read and write. Once I hear little Ballentin, pleased with his learning, remarking " 'Our father' (the sun) is helping us so well." It is true — they are already reading way ahead of their scheduled program. Of course, Pedro is teaching them seven hours a day when only five are required by the Bilingual School system.

Mary Ruth does not like schoolwork, but I love it. We decide between us that the schoolwork will be a part of my responsibilities. When I told Pedro I had brought his pay from the Ministry of Education, he did not want to take it. He felt he was doing his work for the Lord and only consented to take it when I helped him realize he will not have time for other work where he would be paid, or even to make a field to grow food.

One day, as Mary Ruth comes up the ladder to our "loft apartment," she sees Pedro's writing on the blackboard for the children to copy. Quickly, she says to me, "Go down right away. Pedro has his Ss all written backwards on the blackboard for the kids to copy." I choose not to do it immediately, lest the children lose confidence in their teacher, and also so I won't embarrass Pedro in front of his students. I talk to him later, after the children are gone. It's true that Pedro is not the most qualified teacher, but his wonderful enthusiasm far outweighs his deficiencies. He truly inspires his students.

We continue to meet with Pedro as he leads his people in daily evening devotions. We are happy it was his idea[1] to help his people know about the true "our Father God" and His love for them. He later comments to me, "I lack so much, but I just want my people to believe and follow Jesus." We marvel and praise God for the way He has prepared Pedro for this work, not only as a schoolteacher, but as a spiritual leader, and for the way He brought us in contact with Pedro.

Mary Ruth talked to one of the women we have noticed who has come to the devotions every evening. She told Mary Ruth, "We've been wanting to know these things about the true 'our Father.' Our forefathers wanted to know too, but they have now died without knowing." We return to our loft in the evenings enthralled, amazed, and rejoicing at the way God has brought all things together — preparing the hearts of the people and preparing this man called Peter to minister to them.

With "Flag Day" coming up as one of the school observances, I work with Pedro in planning a little program so we can invite the parents to see what their children are learning. Being new at this, Pedro is a little nervous at first, but he does well with his patriotic speech as the chief and the people sit on logs, listening and giving their approval to all that goes on.

We have each of the children demonstrate something they have learned. Pedro has the first two students write the word that he dictates on the board. The parents look on with great admiration. When he has one at a time read from his or her Primer book, the parents can hardly wait for their own child to read. We hear them saying, *"Na'cñeter* (my little one) has not read yet." As each child performs, his parents smile with pride. Parents seem to respond in the same manner the world over. Pedro too was smiling with pride at his pupils. Even little Poso'mer (the "Tail End"), the smallest student and cutest, performed well. The parents here and elsewhere have already told us that they do not want to learn to read, but they surely want their children to learn.

As we talk with the chief after the program, he tells us he wants to make a fiesta for us so we can see how the Amueshas perform their dances. Not knowing that they are calling us "the daughters of 'our father,' the sun" we give our consent. Many of the people have not yet seen our "loft apartment," so they climb the ladder and Mary Ruth entertains them there. We have to be careful so that too many people are not in the loft at one time since the floor  could collapse and all of us wind up in the schoolroom below.

The chief comes to tell us that his baby is sick. He has two wives and seems to care for each of them equally, and all the children as well. We go with him up the hill to see the baby. The baby doesn't seem to be too sick, but the chief says the child has not slept all night. We tell him we will check on the baby again later in the day.

In the meantime, we find our way to the small stream at a distance for a bath. This is where we will come to wash our clothes too. We even find a place where we can take a little swim.

We have an early supper so we can go far up on the mountain where the chief lives to see the baby again before heading back for the evening devotions with Pedro and all the people. The chief and his family are still concerned about the child, but we can see nothing wrong. We talk to them about trusting the true "our Father," and Mary Ruth prays for the baby before we leave.

This Saturday morning, while Pedro has the children doing their weekly school cleaning, Guillermo (whom we first met on the raft trip) and his school children who are from a nearby area where he is appointed to teach, arrive for a visit. As we talk, Guillermo asks us when we will go to see their school. He assures us that he will prepare a nice room for us. We assure him we will be coming soon. Guillermo is so young; he hardly looks older than some of his oldest students.

Before long, the students of both schools and their teachers are engaged in the new sport that is gaining popularity — soccer. Later, I talk with

Guillermo about the progress of his school. He gives me a list of all the names of his students, neatly written out. All on his own he says he talks to the people there about the true God's Word. He asks us if he can copy the Christian songs we have so he can teach them to his people.

On Sunday, we go up on the hill to meet with Pedro and the rest of the villagers to sing and read the Word. He had told us they meet about nine o'clock. We find Pedro spreading mats on the ground for everyone to sit on. We are surprised and pleased to see the large number of people who attend Sunday services. They love to sing the new Christian songs that Pedro has already taught them.

When it comes time for the message from the Word, Pedro has Guillermo stand up with him before the people. Pedro reads some of the Scripture verses and has Guillermo talk about them. Then Pedro has Guillermo read more of the verses and Pedro talks on them. What a neat way to share the teaching of God's Word. Our devotional times together during the Teacher Training Course at Yarina are really paying off. Most of the new Amuesha teachers are believing God's Word and teaching it, and the people seem so anxious to hear it. Pedro invites me to lead in prayer. I am happy to be praying in the Amuesha language even though it is as new to me as the Word is to them! We want to start studying new Scripture with Pedro soon so he will have more to teach from. We have to remember that Pedro himself is just learning to read in Amuesha.

At the end of the service, which goes on all morning, the women start dishing up food for everyone. The men are all seated apart from us women, but when all are served, I notice that Pedro is motioning for us to come and eat with him, and Guillermo, and the men. I hesitate, since I know it is the custom for the men and women to eat separately. But Pedro insists and we decide it must be all right; he just wants to honor us upon our arrival. What a joyful time! I even forget that the bowls which we are eating from are the same ones from which I have previously seen them feeding the pet monkey. However, we can see that it means so much to the Amueshas for Mary Ruth and I to be one with them.

Before Guillermo and his students head for home, I help him make a schedule to follow for his daily classes. He also wants to sing the songs again before leaving so he can teach them to the people there.

"Teach these great truths to trustworthy people who are able to pass them on to others."
— the Apostle Paul, (II Timothy 2:2 NLB)

(Thank you, Lord, that both Pedro and Guillermo want to pass on to their people the great truths that they have heard from your Word.)

# 32
# Making Merry to "Our Father" (the Sun)

"Why are the horns blowing this morning?" we ask some of the people who are around.

"That is to invite the people who live far away to come late this afternoon for the start of the fiesta."

We realize that the chief is going ahead with plans for the fiesta *(coshamñats)* for us. We still do not know that they are calling us "the daughters of 'our father,' the sun" among themselves. The Amueshas like to start their merrymaking in the late afternoon when the sun is the most prominent in the sky. We too join the people as they gather together. We notice the carved-out tree trunk containers full of the *co'nes* drink. The chief assures us that the drink is newly made, not fermented. Some of the women are still grinding corn for another drink.

We wear our tunics, and the women want to paint our faces as all of them do for fiestas. The men are already starting their dances. They are now doing a kind of dance where they cross hands with their fellow dancers on each side and move along together very rapidly. With the late afternoon sun shining directly in their faces, they are quite picturesque, wearing their crowns with feathers and their long tunics as they "make merry to our father, the sun." When they make a sudden turn it is something like "Crack the Whip." Different kinds of dances go on all night, each with its own name, and accompanied with drums, panpipes, and reed flutes. The women come along after the men, each holding the hand of

the one behind as they intone chants called *she'rareñets*. At the end of each dance, both men and women line up facing the sun and offer prayers of thanksgiving to " 'our father,' the sun" for making their manioc and corn grow.

During the night as the dances go on, much of the *co'nes* drink is consumed. The smell of the drink, along with the scent of the various wood fires, fills the air as darkness approaches. The party lasts as long as the drink lasts, until about ten o'clock the next morning.

We rush home and head for the small river down the mountain to wash our clothes and hair and bathe. When we get back, Pedro is there waiting. He wants us to help him improve his reading skills. He wants to be able to read the translated Scripture more easily. So I take the time to teach him the sounds of the complex letter symbols he has not yet taught in his school. Amuesha has many more complex sounds than the Spanish language, such as *čh, rr, sh, ts*, and other palatalized sounds like *b̃, c̃, m̃, ñ, p̃*, and *t̃*. It is not easy to learn to read Amuesha, especially for an adult. The children learn much more quickly. Pedro's students, especially the fourteen- and fifteen-year-old youths who are also starting in the new school along with six-year-old beginners, will probably be reading sooner and better than Pedro.

I'm thinking especially about Julio. When we first arrive at this place, Julio, a young fifteen-year-old apprentice, is away living with the "diviner," a kind of shaman, hoping to learn how to help his people by divining what is making them sick. When Julio hears that a school is opening in his home village, he returns to verify that it is true since he is very interested in studying in a school. Julio enrolls in Pedro's school. In no time, it seems, he is reading fluently and writing legends in his own language, far exceeding the ability of his teacher. As he begins to hear and read God's Word, he never goes back to the shaman apprenticeship.

Julio's eighteen-year-old sister, Kosepa, is beginning to hear our translated Scriptures read and wonders if what she hears is really true. If so, it is different from that which she and her family believe and practice in their native culture. How will she know which is true? Kosepa decides on her own that she must learn to read so she can determine for herself whether these translated Scriptures are really true. She too as an adult, enrolls in Pedro's school along with her brother Julio. She tells Pedro that she does not want to learn arithmetic, she only wants to learn to read so she will be able to read the newly translated "our Father's Word" for herself. She learns to read in a short time and becomes one of the first, eager readers of the newly-translated Word of God in Amuesha.

The people are giving us a lot of food — manioc, bananas, squash, and sugar cane. There are no fish here in the small streams, but they have been giving us a large rabbitlike rodent they call *yap* (agouti). It is good and tastes something like pork and chicken combined. We have so much, we often share it with the many people who come to visit us everyday.

I help Pedro again after school with reading Scripture. I have to realize he is just learning to read his language well, even as he teaches the children. The children also stay after school and play the syllable game. How we enjoy teaching them the fun games we taught downriver — "Cat and Rat," "Flying Dutchman." They love it; I don't think they have ever played games before.

Today Pedro comes to tell us his wife, Petita, "babied" at two in the morning and that she is having some problems. We go to visit her and see the cutest little baby. She is still having some pain so we give her some pain medicine. While there, we try working on our ailing motor again. It hasn't started since we let it run out of gas. We've tried everything — cleaned the spark plug, reset the point, took off the gas line and blew it out, drained the gas out of the tank and cleaned it, cleaned the fuel bowl — all to no effect. It plainly refuses to start. What will we do?

Upon arriving back home, who should we meet but Pedro's sister arriving from Cacaso (Fish River), the village across the big mountain from us. Pedro is just getting acquainted with his long-lost sisters who live there. While he was still a very small child, his parents died, leaving Pedro an orphan. Taken in and cared for by a compassionate Amuesha man and carried far downriver to live with this foster father, Pedro grew up not knowing any of his true relatives.

When Pedro was consulted about leaving his downriver area and coming here upriver to teach, he was a little hesitant to leave the only family he had ever known. He says, "If God wants me to do this, I am willing." Now upriver, Pedro has found his true sisters. Not only has he found them, but he has shared his new faith with them and they believe also. Pedro is experiencing the reality of God's Word, that when we leave our houses and lands, God gives us much more in return. Pedro's older sisters are so happy that they have at long last found their little brother whom they lovingly call Ca'. One sister will be helping Pedro and Petita with the care of their new baby.

Pedro walks out to the nearest civil authority today to register the new baby. I tell him that I will teach school for him. The kids are all so sweet and eager to learn. What fun! Little Poso'mer (the "Tail End," barely six years old) is twisting and turning on his table, under the table, and putting his writing book in and out of his *poshac* (bag). When I ask to see if he has written the last addition problem, he has, with the right answer. He's really sharp!

The next day, after Pedro's return, we eat as many biscuits as we can to hold us over on a walking trip to Guillermo's school. I need to start visiting each of the Amuesha schools to observe how each teacher is doing and help him where he is weak. Pedro decides to come along with his school kids to repay Guillermo's visit. It takes us a little over four hours to walk there. The last part is up a very steep and high mountain. Of course, we arrive tired and hungry, but the people there have very little food. New colonists coming into that area from the outside are taking more and more of the lowlands, leaving the Amueshas only the mountaintops.

Guillermo and Pedro share in the evening meeting, singing and reading God's Word. Guillermo also does a good job in sharing the Word.

True to his promise, Guillermo has fixed up a nice little room for us, but the altitude is so high here that it's very windy. It is cold at night even with our blankets. The mountaintop is barren — even manioc doesn't grow here.

There really isn't enough food to feed all the children. We are wondering what we will feed them when suddenly they start bringing out bowls of rice, a food they have brought in from the outside. When we realize the great need for food here, we offer them money to replenish their supply.

Sunday morning the people all gather to sing and hear God's Word. Guillermo has done a fine job of teaching the people all the Christian songs he copied from our books over at Singing Water. We teach them our new song, "I Have Decided to Follow Jesus." How they do enjoy singing. Then Pedro preaches again from the Word. All of them talk along with him and at times one even takes over the preaching. How great it is to see their interest. They call on me to pray in Amuesha. I'm sure I make mistakes, but they like to hear us speak their language.

Pedro and his school children leave about noontime to get back home before dark. Mary Ruth and I stay on another week to help Guillermo improve his teaching skills. He is working hard at it but can use some assistance. I make a provisional writing book for him to follow. He has not been keeping a daily class record, so it is hard to know what to do with his monthly register.

We are outside during recess when two boys from Pedro's school come bringing us a note. It says that one of our colleagues (Ray Liedtke) has arrived with a new generator for us. *Praise God for answered prayers.* There are several things we need to attend to while Ray is at Singing Water. If we work hard, we can finish up with Guillermo tomorrow, so we send a letter back to Ray telling him we will return soon and that he should wait for us.

It's good to get back to Singing Water village and to see Ray and read all the letters from home he brought for us. We try to write some quick responses that he can take back for mailing. Ray has gone with the chief to look at a possible location for an airstrip, but in the end they decide it is not feasible because it is too mountainous here.

When we return to the village, we find that the chief has finished our new house. We don't lose any time in moving in right away. The school kids help us carry our things. Ray gets the new motor and radio set up right in our house, which will be much more convenient than outside. He also makes us some shelves upstairs. What a delight to be in our new house after the cramped "loft apartment."

After we finish our evening devotions, Mary Ruth, Ray, and I sing our songs in English. The people like knowing we have the same songs in our language.

It has been so rainy it is hard for Ray to be on his way, and the trail will be in bad shape. Then the rain stops, and he decides to leave. We give him a good, hearty breakfast for walking the trail.

We are told over the radio that the Old Testament storybooks of David and Joseph are finished in the print shop. I must try to get some out here for Pedro's advanced students.

Pedro has to go in the woods early in the evening to hunt for meat. Petita leads our evening devotional singing. She also leads the evening prayer, praying very simply and sincerely "I want to follow you; I want you to take out of my heart all bad things. I want all Amueshas to be my sisters and brothers."

The next evening, Pedro chooses to try reading from the translated Gospel of Mark during our evening devotions. He reads a little hesitantly and keeps asking us if the comments he makes are all right. We are happy to see him making this start. He and Petita both pray that all the Amuesha teachers will also be teaching God's Word.

Late the following evening, Mary Ruth and I head out for a bath in the river. The sun is shining, but there is also a light sprinkle of rain falling. Our neighbor lady sees us and yells asking where we are going. When we tell her, she says that the rainbow will be appearing. The Amueshas believe that when the rainbow appears, the evil spirits are out, so it is a very dangerous time and people should not go outside. While we have heard of this danger, we decide to go ahead to the river anyways. We return from the river just fine and she is very surprised that nothing bad happened to us.

A lot of our inside news regarding the village comes from Petita. She tells us that the shaman's wife is very sick and that he, the shaman, says it is caused by the bones of someone already dead. The people are now gathering wood and digging up the bones to burn them. We realize that although the people want God's Word, they still cling to many of their old beliefs.

Someone tells us a woman way up on the mountain is very sick. I go with this person, taking along some medicines. The trail is quite good but very steep in places. It takes us over an hour to get there. Thinking the woman must have some infection, I give her sulfa pills.

While I am there, the boys come in, having found a lot of large, edible larvae which are like ice cream to these people. They are anxious to get them on sticks and over the fire to roast lightly. They don't like them too roasted for they pop and the good, juicy inside comes out.

Somehow I know they are going to give me some larvae. I don't know how to politely refuse in Amuesha. When I see the mother rescue a nice, large one, I know it is destined for me.

She brings it to me barely warm, greatly anticipating my joy in tasting my first *ompa*. I know I can't refuse. These dear people are giving me their "ice cream." I can't disappoint them.[1]

I see the larva between her thumb and two forefingers as she holds it out to me saying, "Now you just try this." Even all the little boys stop their own anxious preparations just then to see me take my first delicious bite. Lord, help me do this! I take my first bite with all looking on. Evidently, I look pleased and they quickly go back to their own *ompas*. The larvae are really not too bad. They taste something like bacon that's not cooked crisp. Thank you, Lord. Since they are busy preparing their own *ompas*, I slip the rest into my skirt pocket. It is good to always wear a skirt with a pocket!

Later that day in Singing Water village, we hear the people talking about how babies and small children can lose their spirits. They are saying that one of the pregnant women has gone off into the jungle to have her baby alone so the many children who are around will not be able to carry off the new baby's spirit. Even Pedro is joining in the talk as if he believes it. The Amueshas are always concerned about getting the baby's spirit back. We are learning more and more regarding their fears.

As we end our evening devotions, Pedro asks Mary Ruth and me to lead the evening devotions from now on. He says that the people want to know so many things about the true God, and he doesn't always know how to answer them. We don't give him an immediate answer. Instead, we talk and pray about it after we get home.

"I just don't think we should take the leadership role" I say. "If we do, Pedro will get the message that we feel he cannot handle it well. The people will get the same message and lose confidence in Pedro, their own indigenous leader. We want to build him up in the eyes of his people. His personal testimony means so much to them. Besides, we don't know the language well enough."

We both are convinced that Pedro should remain in charge. Then Mary Ruth wisely says, "Why don't we tell Pedro that he, the man, should be the leader, but if he wants to come and talk to us about anything, even study the Scripture for the evening with us first, away from the people, we will be glad to do that."

Pedro agrees with our decision. We later realize that this was one of the most important decisions we ever made. We fear to think what the outcome would have been  had we taken the leadership from Pedro rather than encouraging him, allowing God to develop him into the great preacher and evangelist he would become among his people. Later, Pedro even becomes our co-translator, learning much new Scripture as he works with us in translating God's Word and then sharing it immediately with his own people. Thus, the Amuesha work continues with its own indigenous leadership, which we nurture every step of the way, keeping ourselves in the background only to encourage and instruct.[2]

"And the things you have heard . . . entrust to reliable men who will also be qualified to teach others."
– the Apostle Paul to Timothy, (II Timothy 2:2 NIV)

(Thank you, Lord, for the good work Pedro has begun here among his own people, which is soon to become the first indigenous church among the Amuesha people.)

# 33
# Opposition from the Shaman

The chief and several of the men come with their axes to tell us that Kosepa, one of the older women, is very sick, and that they are going to *chemnaterra*, or "get revenge on the thing that is making her sick." This time the shaman has told them the *tasoll* ants are causing it. To get revenge, they must cut down the trees where there are nests of *tasoll* ants and burn them. This is a very common practice. The Amuesha people believe a number of things can "aim at a person and make them sick" — ants, bees, termites, certain rocks, water. The shaman or "diviner" tells them which it is, and they must get revenge so the sick person will become well.

Some people tell us the shaman has been telling them not to believe what we are reading to them and calling "the true our Father's Word."[1]

While their beliefs make us feel sad, we try to help the sick ones with our medicines. No one attempts to stop us. When we visit old Kosepa, she tells us a certain rock has made "a hole in her heart."

A "diviner" from another village comes and tells us he has heard that we have a machine that will "grab words." He says he wants the machine to "grab his words." We have no idea what he wants to say, but we figure the more text we have recorded, the more we will have for our study of the grammatical structures. We set up the "grabber of words" and hand him the mike. He is chewing a coca leaf as he speaks into the mike. With Amuesha being the expressive, aspirating language that it is, we have to take some time to clean the coca juice from the mike at the end. We don't understand enough of the language at the time to realize that the message to his people is that they should not leave their old ways, like divining from the coca leaf. When we become sad and discouraged at all we see and hear, we have to remember God's words to Joshua: "Be strong and of good courage for God is with you." (Joshua 1:9) We do not know it at the time, but this same "diviner" and all of the others will also come to believe God's Word and leave their old ways.

When Pedro is reading the Word in evening devotions today, he mentions that Jesus did not get drunk when he was here on earth. The chief immediately remarks, "We don't get real drunk when we dance — just a little, so we won't be inhibited and we'll do our dances well to " 'our father,' the sun."

Pedro makes a trip out to the airport at San Ramon to pick up his teacher's pay from the Ministry of Education and to pick up the David and Joseph storybooks. Jack Henderson, head of our print shop, tells me on the radio the books are now printed and being sent there. I can hardly wait to see my first printed Scripture books in Amuesha and share them with the older students in school, like fifteen-year-old Julio, who is already reading quite well.

While Pedro is gone, I also get to share with all the children my little lamb story using the flannelgraph pictures. I can tell by the expressions on their faces they are understanding and following all the adventures of the little lost lamb. (This is great encouragement to a translator.) I tell them we will make this story into a book which they will have soon. They are so pleased.

When Pedro returns with the first storybooks written in Amuesha, the young people are delighted to have their very own copies. They start reading immediately — surprising their teacher and parents that they can read this book! What fun it is to work with the young people, knowing that they will soon be the indigenous leaders among their people.

Because we will soon be leaving to start our school visits downriver, I again work with Pedro, teaching him how to fill out his school register. There are so many things for the new teachers to learn. I also make up a provisional writing guide for him until I can get that book composed and printed. After working in the school here, I realize we need reading books that place more emphasis on the syllables. Sometimes I am tempted to begrudge the time the schoolwork takes from translation time, but then, why bother with the translation if there are no good readers?

We must now pack up to leave for downriver. Visiting all the schools in that area, we will observe how the teachers are doing and give help where needed. We will need to go back over the mule trail to the frontier town of Villa Rica. There we will have to rent mules to carry out the things we will need on our school travels.

With our packing done, the time comes to say good-bye to Pedro, the schoolchildren, and all the people. We feel like the Apostle Paul as we have to leave the people we have come to love and move on to other places. We cry and Pedro cries. We won't be coming back here until next year.

The mule trail going out is just as bad as when we came in. We return to the saloon to ask about mules we can rent to bring our things out. The saloon-keeper always tries to help us out. He knows the mule owners who are reliable. We appreciate his help in getting our possessions out to the San Ramon air-port where our plane will pick us up to carry us downriver. Our plan is to visit the downriver schools over a month or so before heading back to Stingray village for a couple of months. Then it will be time to return to Yarina Center for vacation and to prepare for another Teacher Training Course starting the first of January.

There has been much rain lately, and the mule owners are hesitant to send their mules over such muddy trails. We are being delayed. In the mean-time, we meet up with a young Amuesha woman who would like to have a school in her community. We go with her to her community, about an hour and a half walking distance, to see what the possibilities are for a school there. As we count up the potential students, they are short of the number required for starting a bilingual school. We head back to the saloon, and although we have already arranged to have the mules bring our things, they have not come yet. We realize we are going to be late in getting to the airport in San Ramon to meet our plane on the date we have requested.

Taking advantage of the time, I write eighteen letters to send back with the plane. We have the same little room off the bar where the men drink and get pretty rough at times. Since we have no lock on the swinging door, we push our beds against it to keep some drunk from falling into our room.

Finally, the mules arrive with our baggage and we find a truck going to San Ramon. We wind up sitting in the back of the truck on sacks of coffee.

As we are descending the mountain and rounding a curve, I see a jeep coming toward us. I am about to say to Mary Ruth that the driver looks like an American when we both recognize Merrill Piper, one of our pilots. He notices us up on the coffee sacks and we wave to each other. Mary Ruth and I pound on the cab of the truck to let the driver know we want to get off, but he yells back that it is not a regular stopping place. Merrill turns around to follow us.

Eventually the driver comes to a stopping place and lets us off. After we tell Merrill about our problem with the mules and trucks, he relays his story. He says that while he was waiting for us at the airport, he met a nice, German man. They started talking and Merrill told him of having to wait for us to get there. The German invites Merrill to stay at his house for the night. He is one who has made a fortune growing coffee. He tells Merrill to take any of his several vehicles to go to look for us.

As the three of us arrive in San Ramon, we meet this same man again. He invites us all to his house for the night, which turns out to be a mansion. Mary Ruth and I are given a private room with snowy white sheets and a real bathroom — from rags to riches in one day! We never know what pleasant surprises God has in store for us from day to day.

We meet the German man's friendly wife and young child, and hear how the couple came to Peru out of great sadness after World War II, when their families had been taken to Russia. Our host and Merrill hit it off well. They talk about airplanes, as the German is planning to buy a plane and figures out the cost by the number of sacks of coffee it will take. Mary Ruth and I tell them what we are doing out with the Amuesha people and they seem very interested.

The next day we go out to the airport where Merrill has parked JAARS' new Cessna 180. It's a pretty, little thing, all white and green. As Merrill says, "It still smells like a new car." We are hesitant to load it up with our muddy bags from the mule trip, but that's what it is intended for. Soon we are loaded up, bidding our good Samaritan farewell with many thanks, and taking off again to do our school visits downriver.

Soon we are looking down on Stingray village, but we go on further downriver to start our school visits in that area. There are a few, small landing strips on the Palcaso River, and we come down on one which is nearest to Santiago's school. From there we are able to get a motorboat to take us on to the school.


"... Be strong and of a good courage; be not afraid; ... for the Lord your God is with you wherever you go."
   - (Joshua 1:9 KJV, NIV)


(Thank you, Lord, for the pleasant surprises you give us along with the difficult things.)

# 34

# Visiting the Amuesha Bilingual Schools

What is a bilingual school like?

As we arrive at Santiago's school just before dark, all the people come to meet and talk with us. They are happily surprised to hear us talking in their language. When darkness begins to fall, they leave to do their chores before the light is gone. After they leave, we take our things into the school building, where we plan to stay until we finish the work with Santiago, the Amuesha bilingual teacher.

Jannie and Al Townsend have sent us little boxes of ready-to-eat cereals on the plane with Merrill. It is so nice to have these extra things to eat while we are here. *Thanks, Jannie.*

Santiago begins his school day at seven in the morning, so we have to get up early to finish breakfast before school starts. We spend most of the morning washing our dirty clothes from all the traveling. The water is much warmer here than at the higher altitude of Singing Water. We're enjoying the warmer weather also.

The children are overjoyed when we give them the volleyball and soccer ball the Ministry of Education is sending out for all the bilingual schools.

They can't wait to get the net up and learn how to play. We play with them late in the afternoon, teaching them the rules. What great fun this is for them and us too. Santiago and his brother come after supper to talk with us for a while.

I spend the next morning observing Santiago's teaching, checking on how much the children know, and working out reports. Some of the older students who are reading quite well are delighted to receive their own copies of the David and Joseph storybooks.

The bilingual school curriculum[1] consists of five hours of classes each day, which includes reading, writing, arithmetic, natural science, and oral Spanish. Reading is first taught in the native language of the children — the only language they know well and the language in which they learn easily and quickly. Reading in Spanish is not started until the second or third year, depending on the degree of bilingualism of the students. However, oral Spanish is started in the first year to acquaint the students with Spanish which is the national language of Peru, and they do need to learn it also.

As many as five grade levels may be taught in the same room, by the same teacher, early on when there are few students. As the number of students increases over time, a second teacher is sought and often additional rooms are added. Bilingual teachers are often teaching more than one grade level in the same room. Although it is quite a lot to expect from a novice teacher, many of them learn to do this well.

This is Santiago's third year of teaching, and I am happy to see how well he handles three grade levels during one hour of class. He has already given the higher level students their work to do while he teaches the lower grades. He too is just learning to read in Amuesha. After school I go over some Scriptures with him in Amuesha since he plans to lead church services tomorrow, Sunday, at seven a.m. Santiago is a believer, and we are happy to see him starting this indigenous work of teaching his people God's Word.

After finishing our visit at Santiago's village, we walk the four-hour trail to Graciela's school. Graciela is the only woman teacher-trainee so far among the Amueshas. Observing her classes, I realize she is not teaching the oral Spanish class at all. When I mention it, she says she does not know how. I spend some time helping her learn to teach this class also.

Many of the children come back after school wanting to sing the Amuesha Christian songs and learn new ones. Since Graciela is just learning to read in Amuesha, I spend some extra time with her, helping her read the new David and Joseph storybooks. She is doing much better with her reading now.

I am reading the little lamb story (with flannelgraph) in Amuesha here as well as at the other schools. Even the women ask to hear it. All of them enjoy the story and are learning how much Jesus, our Good Shepherd, loves us.

Since we usually stay a week or so at each school, the people often give us a place to live. While I am working in the school, Mary Ruth chats with the many women who come to visit. When no visitors are around, she also tries to make some progress in the study of the morphology of the language. She prepares our food at noontime as I am still in school. The people also share food with us, which we welcome to supplement the meager supplies we carry on the trail.

Graciela has not been keeping her school register because she doesn't know how. Teaching her how to do so is one of the last things I do before we head back over the trail to Santiago's village. There we will contract a motorboat from the colonists in that area to take us to the next school — teacher Valerio's.

We get to Puerto Victoria before dark and spend the night there. Valerio hears that we are on the way and comes the next morning to pick us up. In fact, he comes so early that we haven't found any breakfast yet. We go with him anyway. He gets us set up in his house and asks if we eat *yañell* (howler monkey). We have never had monkey yet but we tell him yes. A little tough monkey is not too bad for breakfast.

Then everyone heads for school, including Valerio's fat, little wife, who trudges over to the school with baby in hand after she finishes her household duties. She wants to learn to read along with some other adults who are studying in Valerio's school. Her baby plays on the floor as she studies.

I am immensely pleased to see how successfully Valerio is teaching his students to read. He even breaks up the sight words and teaches them by sounding out the syllables. This reinforces my idea that we need to emphasize the syllables more in our learning-to-read books. His students are progressing nicely. Some are already reading well in both Amuesha and Spanish. Of course, when one learns to read in Amuesha first, he can also read in Spanish, except for the sounds of letters "d" and "f," which do not occur in Amuesha but do in Spanish.

To test the older students and determine how competent they really are, I dictate some very difficult words in Amuesha that contain complex consonant clusters. All of them write these consonants perfectly.

I decide to conduct some research on writing long vowels, aspirated vowels, and glottalized vowels, which we are finding to be difficult for readers to recognize. After various tests and talking this over with Mary Ruth, we agree that we will change our method of spelling (orthography) to omit writing such modifications since the relative functional value is very low (except for the glottalized vowels). Even in the midst of our school visits, we continue to make decisions on how best to write the Amuesha language to encourage easy reading and writing for the people. Reducing a language to writing requires some tested reactions from its readers and writers.

Seeing that Valerio's most advanced students are reading and writing so well, I suggest that he encourage them to start creative writing, allowing them to write about anything they choose. So far, they have just been writing the words from their books. So as we enter his classroom today, Valerio has written on the board for his advanced students: *"Puetare' cheshanesha* (Good morning, children). Today we are going to write our own stories, whatever we want to write about, in our language." Thus begins creative writing among the students in all Amuesha schools and in other language group schools too.

The students do not realize that having learned all the sounds of their alphabet in Amuesha, they can now write any words they want to without the spelling problems that arise in English, since all their words are spelled just as they sound. Given special notebooks for their creative writing, the students begin with great enthusiasm. They write about their favorite subjects — the many jungle birds and animals they know so well, cultural legends that have never been written before, river trips they have taken, living with their families, building a thatched roof house, planting manioc, how much they appreciate their school and teacher, and on and on. I am most interested in seeing how they wrote the modified vowels. The great majority wrote them as simple vowels, with no indication of modification which further validates our decision to not write them.

I am planning to use some of the students' own stories in our intermediate reading books that I will be composing shortly. They will be good for intermediate reading because the stories are easy and highly predictable, containing well-known cultural subjects and "simple" vocabulary. Valerio tells the students that some of their stories might be published in books, so, each student finishes his or her stories with "which wrote the student So and So" in hopes of seeing their writings published in a book sometime.

Among the stories that I publish is the one written by a student of Valerio's, about how liquid rubber is gathered from the rubber trees. Upriver where Pedro's school is, they don't gather rubber since rubber trees don't grow at that high altitude. Therefore, Pedro's students read with great interest about their fellow Amueshas downriver since they have never visited there.

We are happy to see that Valerio, the oldest of the Amuesha believers, has regular services sharing God's Word with his people. However, we are sad to see that he most often holds the services in Spanish. He has had a year of Bible School in Spanish with the help of Pete Fast, yet Valerio does not seem able to pass these truths along easily to his people in their own Amuesha language.[2] It is true that the people here are much more bilingual than the Amueshas upriver where we have been working. But it is also true that the people here want to hear God's Word in Amuesha, the language that touches their hearts. We trust that as Valerio learns to read better in Amuesha, he will share more of God's Word in the language of his own people.

"Pray that I may proclaim it (God's Word) clearly as I should."
 – the Apostle Paul, (Colossians 4:4 NIV)

(Lord, our prayer is that Valerio will learn to preach and pray in his own language, so that he will be more of a help to his own people.)

# 35
# More Jungle Jewels
# for Jesus

What will Stingray village be like after a year's absence?

After finishing a month of school visits and travel, we request a JAARS floatplane pick us up and return us to Stingray village, from which we have been gone for about a year now. Our pilot this time is Don Weber. We send our thanks back with him to Annabelle, his wife, for the freshly baked loaf of bread she sent us.

Our little house looks good after all of our travels and no place to call our own. Grandma Santos is one of the first to meet us. She is so happy she can hardly hold back the tears. Sabella says, "I saw the plane coming and I said 'Marrta is coming! Marrta is coming!'" It's good to see them all again, just like seeing long lost friends. Some of the kids have grown so much in a year that we scarcely recognize them. I ask about Shañe'. They tell me she is living downriver with her husband as his second wife. I feel for her and miss her terribly.

Before even starting to clean and set up our house, we sit down and talk with the people on our front porch. Our dear friend, Catalina, has died — the first jungle jewel for Jesus. We are shocked to hear that Llollo also has died, drowned when her canoe turned over and her arms became entangled in her straw shoulder braids. The villagers have already torn down her house here beside us, leaving only one corner pole standing in tribute to Llollo and her kindness. We are quite certain that Llollo believed in Jesus too — another jungle jewel. Sabella says they are both buried across the river. How we will miss them. I just wish that Catalina could have lived to see her little lamb story made into a book and learn how much the children in all the schools love it. It has not only shown them what sheep are (in preparation for future Bible translation), but what we people are like and how our Good Shepherd, Jesus, watches over us.

The villagers voluntarily start helping us clean up our house. We are so happy and we look forward to two whole months of living here with our friends before returning to Yarina Center.

The people return in the evening to talk with us. They like to hear about their *pamo'ts* (fellow Amueshas) in Singing Water village and our life with them. We describe our new house there and the welcome we received. We tell them of our school travels, visiting their people in all those places, how their people wanted to learn the new songs about Jesus and hear His Word, and how many are believing.

In fact, I had a very blessed time this morning in my own private devotions, thinking back on the trip. I praise the Lord for all His blessings, His provision, safety, seeing the teachers as not only teachers, but as real spiritual leaders among their own people, and the response on the part of the people desiring God's Word in their language. Thank you, Lord.

Having gotten our house cleaned up and then a little extra rest, we are now getting back to our main language work. I start right away on composing new primer reading books, for which I feel there is a pressing need. I line up the words to be used in the first book. The words are chosen carefully to not only be of interest to the children, but to contain the most common sounds and syllables in the language that will be taught later on. I make up my own charts to be able to control the needed repetitions of words and syllables. Llollo (grandmother) and Ema' (baby) — the two most lovable characters in the Amuesha family — will be the main characters. With a careful choice of words, I am able to construct simple-sentence stories surrounding the daily activities of these two fascinating characters, remembering that in the future, mostly six year olds will be using this book. As we study, at times, Mary Ruth jokingly asks me, "What is Llollo doing today?"

Mary Ruth is starting to work again with her language helper, Kosepa, on the Mark translation. She has already given a provisional copy of the Amuesha Mark to Cruz, who helped her translate it from Spanish. He does not know how to read, but is happy to see translation starting in his language.

The people come again this evening and want to sing. We teach them the new songs we have written while we were away. They like them as well as the old ones we continue to sing. Many of the older men are now joining in also. They like to see the songs in written form in our songbook.

I finish the composition of the three basic sight word primers. I realize I will need drawings for many of the words in the books. But how do I get accurate drawings of the *paña* fish, the *tome* bird, the *omo* frog, and many other things? There are many different species of frogs, fish, and birds in Amuesha. The details of the *omo* frog, for example, must be accurate enough to distinguish it from all the others — at least ten species. In Amuesha, each one has its own specific name. The same is true of the names of animals and insects I will need drawings for in the book. Suddenly, a great idea comes to me: have a "treasure hunt."

When the people come to visit, I start to tell them of the many things I'd like to have for my reading book. My idea is, if I can see a real *paña* fish, a real *tome* bird, a real *omo* frog, etc., I can make a close-up photograph of it with a white background, from which a drawing with exact details can be made in our print shop in Yarina. I list all the things I'd like to collect and promise some rewards to those who find and bring them to me. The people start discussing among themselves where they can find these things and scatter out immediately to search. Some little boys come asking for their own list as if they can read too. I wonder, will they really do it?

I don't have to wonder long. Here comes old Grandma Santos with the *omo* frog. She carries him alive, covered with a cloth so he won't try to jump. He's a very large frog, about a foot in length. How can I ever get a close-up picture of this live frog without him jumping into my camera? I see a large pineapple with its long stem nearby. Why not tie a leg of the frog to the pineapple while he is still covered with the cloth so he can't jump? Grandma thinks it is a good idea and helps me do it. I creep up close with my camera. As she uncovers the frog slowly, I snap a good picture of Mr. Omo before he tries to jump. (Later on, the artist at our print shop, Dottie Jackson, will draw the picture with such accurate detail that no one will ever fail to recognize Mr. Omo.)

One of the young boys brings the *paña* fish, which turns out to be a pirana (caribe or piranha), the much-feared, blood-sucking fish with sharp, pointed teeth. Fortunately, it is already dead, so we easily open its mouth for a close-up picture of its sharp teeth. Someone else brings the big *pona* ant that has a terrible sting.

Why do I want these particular items? Because their written forms contain the letters and syllable sounds that I want to use as key words in upcoming books to teach those particular sounds: the *"o"* in *omo* for the *"o"* sound; the syllable *"pa-"* in *paña* for that syllable sound, which is most common in Amuesha; and the *"po-"* in *pona* for that syllable sound. After learning all the syllable sounds, they will then be able to independently read words they have never seen before. Who would ever think a "treasure hunt" would help to enable many hundreds of Amueshas learn to read God's Word in the future!

*Thank you, Lord, for the good idea and for the many people who will learn to read.*

I also make a close-up picture of Grandma Santos so she can be the Grandmother Llollo of the book. (Later, Dottie Jackson, draws the picture with so much likeness, wrinkles and all, that all the people upon first seeing it say, "That's Grandma Santos!")

Cruz is helping me get all the Amuesha words in the primers translated into Spanish since we make our books in diglot form. The format of all the pages is laid out in first draft, including the supplemental primers with

more syllable practice. Then comes some final checking of the book with Cruz's wife, Shoncare! A good thing! In one place I have a sentence about the "*tome* bird's nest." Shoncare' quickly informs me that the *tome* bird does not make a nest. Another sentence reads "*caca'm* bird walks." I am told that the *caca'm* bird does not walk, it hops. Wow, another bad mistake averted! Amueshas love birds and are true ornithologists.

I type the formats for all the primers, complete with introductory pages and instructions for teachers, and instructions for the artist. We will soon be leaving for Yarina Center. I want to have the primers ready for checks and printing shortly after we arrive there, so the printed copies will be completed in time for the next school year.

Among our many visitors, someone new comes from downriver and is looking at a book with a picture of the Crucifixion of Jesus. I hear Cruz tell him, "This is when Jesus died for us, for our sins. Jesus loves us very much." It's good to hear Cruz testifying. His help in translating Mark has given him much knowledge of the Word.

We turn our radio on several times this morning to give the weather conditions from our location. Chief pilot Larry Montgomery is flying JAARS' new Helio Courier plane fresh from the States out to the jungle. We tell our radio operator to request Larry to fly low over our area on his way to Yarina so we can see the new plane. (This new type of plane will become extremely useful to us in the future because it can use a much shorter landing strip than other planes.) Sure enough, about two o'clock we hear the plane and look up to see Larry circling low over us. What fun for us and all the people, who wave to Larry in the new Helio.

The people know it will not be long before we return to Yarina. They want to learn all the new Christian songs well before we leave, so our long porch is always full of people wanting to sing.

We start our packing early so when the people come we will have time to stop and talk with them. Toward late afternoon we have progressed enough so we can take off for the river for a bath and our last swim. The women and children want to go with us on this last swim, so we all have fun together. Some ask if we can sing again after supper since we leave tomorrow. Many adults also are coming and taking part in the singing.

The plane arrives after lunch. We start saying good-bye to everyone.

"We may be dead before you come again," some are saying. They know their lives are very uncertain, as were Catalina's and Llollo's. This makes us feel bad, but it may be true.

Again, we leave our village location and head for Yarina. On the way, we circle over Valerio's school downriver to let him know he should come down to the river a short distance to meet us. We have teacher's pay from the Ministry of Education for him and other teachers in the area. We have a good, short visit with Valerio when he arrives to meet the plane.

We thank the Lord for another successful six months out with the Amuesha people.

"Look in the scroll (book) of the Lord and read . . ."
    (Isaiah 34:16 NIV)

"Sing to the Lord, all the earth; proclaim his salvation . . ."
    (I Chronicles 16:23 NIV)

". . . I will sing of you among the peoples."
    (Psalm 108:3 NIV)

(Thank you, Lord, for the enthusiastic cooperation of the people in helping to make good, culturally relevant books to teach reading.)

# 36

# Books for
# Bilingual Schools

Of the making of books there is no end!

Soon after as we arrive in Yarina, I get my primer books processed and into the print shop, hoping they can be printed and ready for the bilingual teacher-trainees (who will soon be coming in for another Teacher Training Course) to take back with them for the upcoming school year. I take the photographs I have made of Mr. Frog, the various birds, animals, etc. for the artist, Dottie Jackson, from which she will draw the pictures. What fun it is working with Dottie; she enjoys her work so much.

For the bilingual schools, we also need to translate some arithmetic and natural science books from the official Peruvian school system. As soon as Pedro Lopez arrives for the Teacher Training Course again this year, I ask him to help me translate the natural science books.

We soon find ourselves trying to say things that have never been said or even known before in Amuesha. For example: "The earth revolves around the sun." With an orange and a grapefruit and enough hands to show the movements, the concept can be demonstrated. Pedro had to think long and hard before coming out with the form of a verb that expresses the movement:

*potesme'tampenana (potes-* to turn around, *-me't-* intermittently, *-amp-* a thing included, *-en-* continuing action, *-an-* an object to follow, *-a* reflexive. So we have *Potesme'tampenana pats atsne'*. (revolves the earth around the sun). Even the word for sun is a problem since the Amueshas have called the sun *Yompor*, (our father). Pedro, as a believer, does not want to use that word here. He originates a noun form of the verb "to shine" — "the shining thing" — *atsne'*. What a challenge it is working with Pedro. He is sure nothing can be said in another language that cannot be said in Amuesha. Hopefully, these books too will be printed in time for the next school year.

Arithmetic books must also be translated. Again, Pedro, as well as some of the most advanced Amuesha students — Julio Gaspar, Raul Sinacay, and Andres Huancho — help me translate these books. Describing the processes of addition, subtraction, and division must be explained well enough in the language and within the culture for the students to understand what they are trying to do. Yes, it can be done. We use such things as "arrows," "canoe paddles," "fish," "birds," and "bananas" instead of apples for counting and performing the mathematical processes. Our thanks go to Dr. Olive Shell, Dr. Beverly Holcomb, and Viola Galenzoski (Escobar). These are our fellow SIL members who, as sub-directors in the Bilingual Schools, have changed the Western examples in the math and science books to reflect a more culturally relevant indigenous way of life. From these modified texts in Spanish, each of us linguist-translators can then translate the books into the various languages of the Peruvian Amazonia.

I also compose new writing books to accompany the reading books, starting with the printed forms of the letters and progressing on into cursive writing. Little do I know while making these writing books what prolific creative writers the Amueshas will become, writing everything from their simple thoughts to multi-page legends.

Literacy is so important that I willingly put aside my study of the Amuesha grammar and even translation of the Scriptures for a time to concentrate on literacy. The young people and children already in the schools now need to have a good system of learning to read so they will become fluent readers in their language to be able to read the Scriptures for themselves and others. This is one of the most crucial principles for the development and continuance of an indigenous church among the people — where they, as good readers, become their own preachers and teachers of God's translated Word.[1]

I appreciate "Corny" (Cornelia) Hibbard's special help in the print shop, trying to get each run of Amuesha books ready on time for the scheduled flight to Amueshaland. It means so much to the progress of the work to have the books right when they are needed. Thanks, "Corny."

Each of us linguists — with his or her particular language group — works with our own teacher-trainees, not only helping them learn the basic academics but how to teach these same concepts to their young students.

All the language groups of teacher-trainees continue to come in to Yarina each year from January to March (their vacation time) for another Teacher Training Course to advance their own academic studies. Many of them are in the process of finishing their own primary education. In the early years, the Bilingual Education Program of Peru only required that the indigenous teacher-trainee be at least one grade ahead of the highest grade being taught in his school. Therefore, the trainees often find themselves teaching their young students the same academic facts they have so recently learned themselves.

After each busy TTC is finished, we linguists visit the new schools within our language group and give further on-the-spot training for the bilingual teachers wherever they need it. I remember my own practice teaching days at college and sympathize with these teacher-trainees. It is truly amazing how much the children learn from teachers who speak their own language and have such a great desire to see their people learn.

"... and (Jesus) stood up to read ... and opened the book (of Isaiah)."

(Luke 4:16-17, KJV)

(Thank you, Lord, for books that will help Amueshas learn to read your Word.)

# 37
# Back to
# Stingray Village Again

We are a little late this year in leaving for the Amuesha area, taking more time at Yarina to move as many school books through the printing process as possible in order to take them with us for this year's school needs. But now we are finally off again, loaded with many of the newly printed books. Despite this being our fifth time out to live with the Amueshas for extended periods, I still get some butterflies in my stomach as we begin our journey again.

After an hour and a half of flying over the beautiful, green jungle, we are already descending for a landing near Valerio's school. I plan to make this downriver village my first school visit on the way to Stingray village. I stay here while Mary Ruth and the pilot, Don Smith, go on upriver to Stingray to shuttle additional supplies we had left here before. Then the pilot will come back for me and take more of our supplies.

Although we have arrived unexpectedly, Valerio is busy teaching in his school. He and all his school children come running down to meet us, along with many adults. The kids are always anxious to see what new books we have brought. Valerio's little, old mother is so cute and sweet. She is very proud of her son teaching school.

After we greet the people, Valerio returns to his classroom. I begin to observe how the children are learning and help Valerio with several questions he has. I am very pleased to see what a good teacher he is becoming, plus he is able to follow the charts and guides I've been making to help the teachers. Imagine learning to teach in your language, which has only been written a short time.

It is encouraging to see Valerio's most advanced students stand up and read the Amuesha side of their newly diglotted science studies book and then discuss what they have read. The lesson for this day is "Plants and How They Serve Us." Even little, old grandmother (Valerio's mother) who is listening in has to join the interesting discussion in their own Amuesha.

I am pleased to see how much the new series of reading books is profiting the students. Some of them are already using the syllable books. As I look closer, they know their syllables well and are reading independently. What a pleasure it is to know that readers for the translated Scriptures are already being prepared!

The morning flies by. Someone brings me a lunch of two boiled eggs and boiled manioc root. Just as I'm beginning to eat, we hear the plane land down on the river. I run with the second egg in hand to get more things ready for the plane trip upriver.

I am not able to visit Santiago's school (the next one upriver) since the water landing strip is very short and we have a full load. However, Don stopped there earlier today, leaving books and letters for him.

Soon we are landing at Stingray again. Sabella and all the kids are there to greet us. I hug them all as they giggle. They don't usually show emotion like we do. Mary Ruth meets me with good and bad news: "Our old house is *puetsohua* (worn out), not good enough for us to spend a night in. Ahuash has a little house he has built for himself for later on, which he says he will loan us for the three months we will be here."

"Thank you, Ahuash, and thank you, Lord." The Lord does wonderfully provide.

Ahuash's little house is well built and right out near the edge of the cliff, where we have a fantastic view of the river below and the mountains beyond (foothills of the Andes on the rainforest side).

We manage to get in and out over boxes and bags to prepare our supper. Since it is now so late in the day, Don decides he better spend the night here in the plane. Boy, does the old sleeping bag feel good tonight!

In the midst of arranging our new house, the villagers visit us often. Soon I have new shelves for keeping our paperwork in order. Since this house is quite high off the ground, Mary Ruth makes nice doorsteps out of sawed-off logs of wood placed into the ground. The view from our eating table — out across the river and mountains beyond — would be called a million-dollar view in the U.S.

Before starting a new project, I decide I need to review all our vocabulary files to bring to mind words I have forgotten. Mary Ruth and I frequently work at night after the people have gone to bed, reviewing the words we might be able to use in our conversation with them the next day.

In the afternoon, many people return to join us on our porch. It is fun to show them all the newly printed reading books. They get to see the drawings of the items they collected for me — fish, birds, etc. — and had so much enjoyment in doing. Old Grandma Santos thinks we did a good job on her *omo* frog. Everyone, upon seeing the drawing of a grandmother says, "That's Grandma Santos!" Thanks, Dottie, for doing such a good job.

They tell us on the radio this morning that Dr. and Mrs. Hatch, one of our Bible professors from Bible college and his wife, are at Yarina and would like to visit us. What a pleasant surprise! We spend the morning preparing for them. I bake a chocolate cake that doesn't turn out too well. They arrive late in the afternoon. Landing in the middle of the jungle, Mrs. Hatch must have been greatly impressed by the isolation; her first words on stepping down from the plane were, "How long have you been here?"

The villagers come in the evening to see our new friends and also to sing. The Hatches follow the words in the songbook as the people sing. Seeing the Amuesha words, Mr. Hatch confesses, "I'm glad the Lord didn't call me to be a linguist."

We manage to find space on our floor for their air mattresses. The next morning it is raining. The Hatches enjoy our biscuits for breakfast and the four of us have devotions together. Mr. Hatch leads us in a study of the Word from Philippians. What a delight to listen to our beloved professor bringing new truths from the Word just like he used to do in Bible college. They are amazed as we show them stories written by the school children — words written in their language the children have never seen written before, and indeed are now being written for the first time.

As their short visit ends, we send greetings to all our CBC (now CIU) friends and professors, and bid them farewell. Now it is time to read the mail that came with them. Soon we are back to our studies study again after all the excitement.

I finish my review of all the words we have on file so far and begin the preparation for writing a paper during my furlough next year as part of my advanced studies at the University of Oklahoma. Hopefully, I can get all my source materials together in our two months here in Stingray village.

Little Benjamin comes this morning and wants me to read to him the *Besllom̃* story (the little, lost lamb story). Benjamin is still too young for school, but he sits very quietly listening to every word I read. He is hearing for the first time that Jesus is our Good Shepherd who saves us just like *Besllom̃'s* shepherd saved him from death. How would we ever know at the time that little Benjamin will grow up to become one of the best Amuesha schoolteachers, teaching other children the same *Besllom̃* story.

Many people look to us for medical help today — "Little Spider" with a bad cut on her leg, Pachari with sore fungus feet, Martin for medicine for his child, and Cesar with malaria. It's ten o'clock before we finish with giving medical care and realize it is the 4th of July. However, there will be no celebrations here and we are happy to get back to our studies. I continue to work on my syntax materials of Amuesha sentence types and Mary Ruth on her study of morphology, how the parts of words (morphemes) fit together.

About midmorning "City Woman's" daughter, Elena, comes to tell us that Shañe' has "babied." Shañe' had returned to living here in Stingray village, but we are surprised nonetheless about the birth because she didn't look that big. As soon as we can get free, we rush over to see her. We find her sitting on the ground with banana leaves under her and the tiny, new baby boy wrapped in a piece of old tunic in her arms. We give her some clean, white flour-sack cloths that folks at home had given me for just such purposes. She is very appreciative and quickly wraps up little Tontelleso'n (the "porcupine rat" — her name for her newborn with stiff hair). Births are very simple here, but love is not lacking. As she looks down at her firstborn, she whispers in loving rhythm, *"Tontelleso'netall,"* (my sweet, little porcupine rat). Shañe' seems to be happy, despite being a second wife to the man who took her. We rejoice with her in her first-born baby. They eventually go back downriver, so I rarely get to see her.

Brrr! We are having a "frio." This is cold weather that blows up from the South Atlantic, coming by way of Brazil, which sometimes kills the coffee plants there. Living out in the open, it feels very cold to us. We eat under our mosquito net to block some of the wind and cold.

All the villagers who are taking worm pills come for them this morning. Adults are now joining the children, including grandpa **T̃o'**. We are all shivering as I administer the pills and Mary Ruth prepares us a hot breakfast. Despite the cold, several people come in the afternoon to sing and review some Scripture verses they are learning. They listen attentively as Mary Ruth reads the story of the Prodigal Son to them.

Rosa visits us often to make use of the new reading books. She is reading quite well. I have given her a copy of the little lamb storybook to read at home.

I have been working on my syntax file, classifying all the sentence types from the animal stories. "City Woman" did not spare any grammatical means in describing the habits of the animals. I think she used every sentence type possible, with direct objects in every possible position. It is my job to find out why the object can change its ordinary position in the sentence.

This morning we have "scheds" (scheduled time) on the radio with some of our friends at Yarina. In my talk with Pat McKerihan (Davis), my prayer partner, she says she has written to my mother for me. Thanks, Pat. In another "sched" with friend Jan Bergman, she tells us our new house at Yarina is about finished. Great news! Now we will have a proper place for the Amuesha teacher-trainees to study and have devotions with us during the Teacher Training Course.

Later in the day, many of the villagers come to learn and sing the new

Christian songs. We are happy that the men are joining too and singing with the others.[1] They like to see the songs written in our new hymnbooks. The singing has certainly been a wonderful means of bringing more and more people together to hear about the true God.

"May all the peoples praise you, O God; may all the peoples praise you."
— the Psalmist David, (Psalm 67:2 NIV)

"Sing to the Lord a new song, his praise from the ends of the earth . . ."
(Isaiah 42:10 NIV)

"May the nations (people groups) be glad and sing for joy"
(Psalm 67:4 NIV)

(Thank you, Lord, that many of the men are now coming to hear about the true God, and that they like to sing praises to you. May you speak to their hearts and help them to truly receive you.)

# 38

# Committing Our Ways to the Lord

"Commit your way to the Lord . . ." (Psalm 37:5)
"and he will direct your paths." (Proverbs 3:6 NIV)

"All of us want to come and sing tonight since you will be leaving soon," Shañe' comes to tell us as we finish supper. Come they do — young fellows, old people, and children; our little house is not only full but running over. We have a great time singing with them.

We have been packing up because tomorrow we plan to start our school travels again downriver. Since next year is our furlough year, we will not be back here for a long time. We spend more time in prayer this morning because we will not be using our plane, but will need to depend on the people to take us from place to place in their canoes. In a very literal way, we are "committing our way to the Lord and trusting in Him" that "He will direct our paths."

Encarna and the "Old Maid," both of them older women, come today and request that I read them the lost sheep story. As I get to the application, they become very quiet. I trust they are understanding more of their need for salvation. *Lord, do they understand that yet? Do they understand yet* how Jesus, our Good Shepherd, died for them? Due to our limitations yet in the Amuesha language, we are never sure just how much the people are understanding. Lord, help them to understand.

Midmorning, we finish all our packing despite the many people sitting in our little house. Babies are crying and roosters are crowing amidst all the excitement of us leaving for over a year. Finally, we are all packed and ready to go, but the one man who has said he would take us in his canoe now comes to tell us that his wife is sick and he cannot go. We are happy that Santoma' (one of "Playboy's" older brothers) said he would take us if our first volunteer could not. Thank you, Lord, for starting to "direct our paths."

We say good-bye (allaso'tach) to everyone. Grandma Santos seems so sad, thinking no doubt she might be dead by the time we return. I give her an extra hug as we step into the canoe and shove off. Kids plunge into the water and swim along beside the canoe. How we have grown to love these dear people and they us in the few years we have been with them.

The young men, Santoma' and his brother, Meshe'll, along with their younger brother, "Playboy," handle the canoe well. They even put out their lines to catch fish as we go gliding down through the beautiful, clear water. What lovely mountain views and colorful birds there are all along the sides of the river. We enjoy the extra thrill of hitting the rapids just right — in that center spot — so you don't flip over. It's a vacation! Mary Ruth and I relax and enjoy the trip, thanking God for "directing our paths."

Along our route we visit those who have come upriver to visit us. At each stop, we tell the people again that we are going to our home country, but we will be back again in a year. After one of our visits, we return to the canoe to find a fish has taken off with the entire fishing line. We chase the line and catch the biggest fish we have ever seen. We share the fish with those where we stop; there is enough food for them and us too.

After supper at the place where we stop for the night, our hosts ask us to sing. We sing a lot with Meshe'll explaining the words of the songs and the teachings of Christ. Then we spread our blankets out with our traveling companions and sleep on the floor. It's a little strange to be sleeping so closely to the others, but they think nothing of it; that's just the way they live.

On this journey, we are finding out how the people feel about having a school for this downriver area. They tell us they do want schools. The next day we arrive at a little settlement called Sheringamaso (Rubber village). The people are all out working, however, we finally get in contact with the man who has been asking for a school to be established here. He tells us that all the parents want the school. They say: "We don't want to study ourselves we have too much work to do, but we want our children to learn." We count up the number of children in the village and find it to be twenty, yet the number always increases once a school is started. This is the village where teacher Guillermo is from, so he will surely want to teach here once a school is up and running. We make plans with the parents to ask the Ministry of Education to allow a school to be started here soon.

We are on our way by noon, and are just passing another Amuesha house, when we hear someone call out to us and ask us to stop and visit. These people too have visited us up at Stingray village. They fix us fresh pineapple and ask us to sing while they cook fish. We oblige and then eat with them.

Once again we on our way with "Playboy" guiding the boat, when all of a sudden we find ourselves going through a bad rapid spot with rocks and rough water. Just as I am expecting a turnover, we get into backwater that turns us around and pushes us over to the riverbank. Thank you, Lord. And to think we could have turned over and lost our cargo.

By 4:30 p.m., we are far downriver where the German homesteaders live. Although they invite us in, we do not feel comfortable with them. They do not speak the Amuesha language; we communicate with them in Spanish. They do give us a small room and some food, for which we are grateful.

In the morning we set out on the waterway, and we reach the mouth of the Chuchuras River. Here we contact a German colonist who has befriended us before. He agrees to take us by motorboat to Santiago's school for a certain price. We say our good-byes and thank-yous, and pay our Amuesha friends for delivering us safely this far.

The motorboat speedily takes us to Santiago's school, where we will sleep and set up operations. After a bath in the river, we are feeling refreshed and thankful to have gotten this far. We thank God for "directing our paths" as we "committed our way to Him." We set up our hand crank generator to call in to

Yarina, but they cannot hear us this late in the day. We will call again early in the morning, informing them by radio that we are safe and on schedule.

The people soon realize we have arrived and come in the evening asking us to sing with them. In the morning, teacher Santiago and the children are at their school by seven to start classes. I spend the morning observing Santiago's classes and am happy to find the new books are helping the children to learn much more easily.

After classes, Mary Ruth and I are back on the road, this time accompanied by Santiago and his buddy, Juan, who walks with us over the trail to Chispa, where Graciela's school is located. It takes us just under four hours to reach Chispa this year. We are becoming pros at walking the trails. We set up in the school again, eat some of our rations, and rest a bit before the people realize we have arrived. When they hear that we are in the village, they come bringing us wild tapir meat *(ato')*. There's nothing like wild pig steaks to renew your strength. Thank you, Lord.

Shortly after reaching Chispa, Cesar, another of the new bilingual teachers in this area, comes and tells us that his school is three hours from here. We will, however, need to ford the river seven times to get there. He says the water is low now, so perhaps we should leave right away with him before it rains again. We agree, and pack up quickly to go there first and then come back here later.

The people start coming to see us as soon as they hear we have arrived. A crowd quickly gathers. We are happy to see Cesar, who is also a new believer, take over and volunteer to lead the people in singing. He and another young believer stand up together before the people. It's their own idea to have more than one lead a service to support one another. What a smart, indigenous concept we wouldn't have thought of. Thank you, Lord.

Cesar reads several of the salvation verses in Amuesha and asks us to comment on them, which we do in a very informal way. We are happy to see several of the older men showing great interest. They tell us, "We believe and we want someone to teach us all the time more of God's Word." Several of the younger men are telling us, "We want to study God's Word so that we can teach others." Maybe this is part of the movement of Amuesha teachers and preachers reaching their own people — just what we have been praying for. Thank you, Lord.

Today I work with Cesar, checking his school register and observing how he teaches his classes. He is very sharp and has his register in good order. His teaching methods need improvement, so I suggest that I teach a demonstration class in reading and have him observe. He is so young he realizes he needs help and readily agrees. It's cool teaching the kids; they are so responsive and learn quickly. Cesar appreciates the help and asks me to go on and teach the arithmetic and writing classes also. What fun for me, despite my sore throat and sore feet from walking.

After school, more people come again to sing. Cesar and Mary Ruth meet with them. Cesar also reads to the people some stories from the translation of Mark. He is good in reading Amuesha, for which we are thankful as it helps the people understand God's Word more easily.

The next morning before school, the children and many older people come early before school. They want to hear the story of the little, lost lamb and see the flannelgraph pictures. They seem to get the point of the story, and I trust it will be a step in helping them come to Christ, the true Shepherd. We're a little hesitant to ask for their decisions until we know they are sure of what they are doing. We have learned that the people often put up their hands to please someone, not necessarily because they understand what they are doing.

In classes today, Cesar teaches and I am so pleased to see he is incorporating much of what he saw yesterday. It's gratifying that he's interested in improving his teaching methods

It has been raining a lot since we arrived here. We decide we better head back to Graciela's school before the river rises too high for us to cross the seven times. Some of the villagers decide they want to go with us, including Cesar's little mother.

The young fellows wanting to study God's Word decide to help us carry our things. By noontime we are packed up and ready to go. The trail's condition is nothing compared to the muddy mule route we took to Singing Water village. Even the seven river crossings are not bad since the water is not above our thighs. As we wade through the wide, shallow, and clear, rocky bottoms, we have the added bonus of the mountains in view — beautiful scenery all untouched by "civilization." After our arrival, the people give us bird soup and fish roasted in a leaf in the fire. After supper, the people here too want to sing. The word about our singing has gotten around. We are a little tired, but enjoy singing with them and seeing another group becoming interested in hearing about the "true our Father." We are more than ready for bed when they leave.

I spend the next morning in Graciela's school observing her classes. I decide demonstration classes might benefit her too. She needs quite a bit of help on how to teach reading so the children don't just memorize the words by their order on the page.

By noontime, the people from the area outside Chispa hear that we have returned and they come to see us. They request that we sing right away since they need to return to their distant homes before dark. In the evening, another group gathers and wants to sing again. Luis, one of the young men wishing to study God's Word, reads some of the Scripture verses and Mary Ruth reads the Prodigal Son story. The older people are anxious to have someone teaching them God's Word regularly.

As I work with Graciela again in the school, Mary Ruth meets with the three young men who want to study God's Word in order to teach here regularly. She talks to them to make sure they understand how to receive Christ. One of them isn't sure he has asked for forgiveness and received Christ. Mary Ruth helps him to do that — more jewels for Jesus. Thank you, Lord.

As we get ready to leave, we are happy to hear that the fellows have made a raft for us to return downriver to Santiago's school. I am especially glad since my feet are very sore. Thank you, Lord, for making a way for us in the wilderness.

This is the same stretch of river on which our raft overturned before. The water is much higher now from all the rain, and we make it through okay. The two fellows bringing us downriver want to go back to Chispa right away, so we hurry to get song books, Bible storybooks, copies of Mark, and other Amuesha reading materials ready for them to take back to those new believers who want to continue teaching the Word there.

At Santiago's school, where we had left the hand crank generator, we try to call Yarina Center to let them know we are fine, but they have trouble hearing us. They finally read us well enough to get our order and tell us the plane will come for us tomorrow. We get our clothes washed and packed again ready to leave for the airstrip at the German place on the Chuchuras River.

The oldest Amuesha we know, who is about eighty, comes bringing the bow and arrows he promised to sell me. He still prays to the sun as god. We talk to him again about believing in the true God and his Son, Jesus Christ. He is not yet ready to believe and leave his old culture. *Will he believe before he dies, Lord?* I am happy that this elder's son, Juan, is believing already and trust he will urge his father to believe.

The old German lady at the airstrip takes us in and fixes a lunch for us. Just as we finish eating, we hear the plane. We look out expecting to see the wheel plane that will take us to the San Ramon landing strip to start our trip back to Singing Water, but we see a floatplane landing on the water instead. The pilot, Leo Lance, explains that the wheel plane was not prepared and it was thought best that we return to Yarina Center and then head out when the wheel plane is in order.

In just a short time we arrive back at Yarina, to everyone's surprise as well as our own. The two weeks and a day that we are at the Center come in handy. I am able to prepare the "dummy" copies for three new reading primers.

This time we depart in the new Helio Courier plane. We are off the ground in no time, despite our full load. In only an hour and a half we are landing on the little airstrip in the midst of the mountains at San Ramon. Happily, it is a good day for flying, and all the mountaintops are clear. With our baggage unloaded, Leo is on his way back home to Yarina.

We wait around a while for a ride into the pioneer town of La Merced. Finally, the same little man with the hand crank truck picks us up and takes us into town. We ask around about a truck going to Villa Rica but are unable to find one. Since it is late to leave anyway, we check into the same little "jail room" hotel and again "commit our way" unto the Lord. What a blessing it has been in all our travels to do this. Although it is early, we both fall asleep immediately.

The next morning, we go to this little eating place next door, with a nice open veranda, and enjoy a delicious breakfast of ham and eggs. As we are eating, the waitress there tells us of a truck going all the way to Villa Rica. *Thank you, again, Lord, for "directing our paths."* After the truck driver picks up people and baggage all over town, it's our turn. We continue our travels sitting on baggage in the back of the truck. The view is wonderful as we start climbing the road into the mountains, following the rapidly flowing, rocky rivers.

When we reach Villa Rica about three in the afternoon, we get another truck to take us out to the German lady Veronica's place and are able to rent her mules to carry us on to Singing Water village the next day. We find the muddy mule trail a little bit better than last year, but still it takes us six hours to get to Singing Water. Arriving back at the village, we are greeted by Pedro, his school kids, the chief, and his wife. The kids can't wait to see the new books we have brought. They peek at them in the boxes, reading the little they can see. Sure enough, as soon as the children get the books in their hands, they are able to read them right away. The children have certainly learned a lot while we have been away. Pedro says they have already finished the books he brought back with him after the Teacher Training Course. He takes great pride in what his students can do, and of course, that encourages them to do even better. Even little Poso'mer (the "Tail End") and little "Hard-head" have read all their books. Pedro adds that people from areas further away are planning to come next year so they too can learn how to read. Lots of adults want to study because they see how quickly the children have learned. He has certainly done a good job of teaching.

Pedro comes to us wanting help with some portions of the Mark translation. While Pedro still has some trouble with reading, he has greatly improved. We are pleased to see he has been studying Mark and has a real interest in it. He says he wants to learn it all. He marks the parts he likes — some with arrows and some with circles. The portion Pedro has chosen for tomorrow, Sunday, is about the rich man coming to Jesus. What a joy it is to see him understanding the truth of forsaking home, parents, and numerous other things to follow Jesus, for he has done that himself.

People from more remote areas start coming early on Sunday; we scarcely have finished our breakfast yet. It is good to see them again. All of us proceed up to Pedro's house, where many more have gathered — the men in their best crowns and tunics. We let Pedro hand out the new songbooks we have brought. The school kids help their elders find the numbers. Even though the elders don't read, following the words helps them to learn.

Domingo, Pedro's oldest and best student, stands right behind Pedro as he reads the Scripture, helping Pedro out where he has trouble since he reads better than his teacher. Pedro talks about how the Lord gives back to us so much when we leave everything to follow him, as Pedro himself has experienced.

The people have built a new school in a new area a little distance away, which they intend to make the center of the village eventually. In the afternoon, I help Pedro with his register. He finds adding up all the days students are present and taking an average almost impossible. But his good teaching skills, combined with his great enthusiasm, compensate for his lack of ability in taking an average.

One day, little Huancho's father comes to tell us that his son's ear is sore and hurting and asks for medicine for him.

"We have already started him on sulfa medicine to clear up his ear infection," I tell him.

"That medicine went to his stomach and it's his ear that is hurting," the father replies.

We often don't realize how much the Amueshas don't understand that we take for granted, so we try to explain that the medicine going to the stomach will eventually help the ear. Come to think about it, it is a strange concept.

I go over to school today to give the Bible storybooks to the kids who have learned to read. It's so rewarding to see even Poso'mer reading the stories of David and Joseph. (We do not realize now that in the distant future, when the Amuesha New Testament is finished, Poso'mer will be the chief proof-reader of the text.) The kids are happy they can read. They can't get enough of it. I work with Pedro in the afternoon translating another Spanish school-book which is part of the Peruvian school curriculum.

The Amueshas here in this mountainous area grow coffee to sell commercially. They often give us some of their sun-dried beans, which we roast and have one of the women grind on her stone. (We eventually buy a small coffee grinder.) The coffee is good and strong. The people have never drunk coffee before, but we add a little sugar to the coffee we serve them when they come to visit and they like it. They have learned to grow the coffee from the early German settlers in this general area. It is really their only means of making any money.

We start hearing the people talk about the *achyo'tañ*. Apparently, he is a diviner who lives in Coshapampa (Oxapampa), a town that used to be the center of Amuesha culture. They say he can divine what is making a person sick. Although this is Amuesha culture and belief, the fact that this "diviner" is charging a lot of money makes us wonder if this is not just a money-making scheme for Miguel, the "diviner." He claims to cast the evil spirit *(pocoy)* out of the water, which is often what makes the people sick.

It grieves us see the people believing what this man says. Yet we realize contaminated water does make the people sick. Since I am composing a health book for the upper grades of the school, I see this as an opportunity to build on their belief about the water. The health book states, "The water does make us sick at times, but the way to get revenge is not by laying burning logs over it, as we do, but by boiling it before we drink it."

Pedro likes the new health books, and at times I hear him in the school preaching on the need for bathing every day just like he preaches the Gospel. However, because of the cold climate and cold water here in the mountains, the Amueshas in Singing Water do not bathe, as Pedro has been accustomed to in his warmer climate downriver.

Today Pedro comes to show us the new Christian song he has just composed — the first Amuesha starting to write songs — just the beginning of many songs Pedro will write. Pedro's song becomes No. 14 in our hymnbook. What a delight it must be to God, hearing praises coming to Him for the first time in the Amuesha language, written by one of them. We encourage Pedro and others to continue. Who would think that our hymnbook in time will grow to over two hundred songs as more and more of the believers begin writing them — some with their own native tunes, and others with tunes they have heard.

Pedro himself comes up with a word for "praise" *(ya'ye'choĉhtatoñepach)*. When I first hear this word, I think Pedro has surely just made up a word for "praise." So I ask him, "Have you ever said this word before?"

"Yes."

"When?"

"When I find a most delicious, sweet fruit in the jungle and then tell everybody how very good it is, that is what I am doing."

The word literally means "by our words let us cause (him, her, or it) to be desired." What better word do we need for "praising God," than telling how good He is. Thanks, Pedro. One of our new songs to come will use this word for praise in every other line.[1]


"I will sing of you among the peoples ..."
    – the Psalmist David, (Psalm 108:3 NIV)


"... Peoples from remotest lands will worship him."
    – the Psalmist David, (Psalm 67:7 LB)


"He put a new song in my mouth, a hymn of praise ..."
    – the Psalmist David, (Psalm 40:3 NIV)


"And this gospel of the kingdom will be preached ... as a testimony to all nations (peoples), and then the end will come."
    – Jesus, (Matt. 24:14 NIV)


(Thank you, Lord, that many people in all the areas are wanting to know more about you, the true God. Thank you that indigenous, local leaders are coming forth to teach their own people, many of them being the bilingual schoolteachers. May we soon have more of your Word translated for them).

# 39

# Finishing Our Fifth Year with the Amueshas

Is it time for home leave already? It seems like we are just getting started. Yet since this is our fifth year of working with the Amueshas, next year we will be taking a break and going home. We want to accomplish much before our leaving.

Pedro really wants to help us translate God's Word into his language, but he has been so busy learning the duties of his new teaching job that he has very little spare time. We have been working with him in translating some key verses in the evenings. We get together in the big house of Ambrocio. It is the same place we meet for evening devotions.

During our evening devotions, Pedro reads the story of Nicodemus coming to Jesus. He does surprisingly well. Yes, we help him along with it, but he seems to grasp the spiritual meanings. He talks about "being born again," and the chief and some of the other men listen.

Today Mary Ruth and I both go over to the school. She wants to give the more advanced students copies of Mark. I want to finish up some odd jobs and then be free to start packing for one more school visit on our way out to the airstrip at San Ramon before we head back to Yarina and our year's leave in the U.S.

Pedro comes in the afternoon for help with his monthly reports. He works on them all afternoon so they will be ready for us to take back to Yarina with us tomorrow.

The next day, all our packing is done, and it looks like fine weather for traveling on the trail to Guillermo's school once again. By this time, the villagers have come to say good-bye. The chief's wife is very sad and kisses me, which is unusual for the Amueshas. We tell them we will be back in another year.

We find that the trail is so slippery from the recent rain we can hardly keep up with the mules. We are a little afraid we won't make it to Guillermo's school before dark. However, we again commit our way to the Lord and arrive just at dusk. Teacher Guillermo is expecting us and has a little room ready for our guest quarters.

The next morning I go to the school to observe Guillermo and see how his school is progressing. I am pleasantly surprised to find that the kids can already read. The new reading books have helped, but Guillermo's teaching methods have also improved. He is very trainable, putting into practice all I had taught him. The people here have built a funny, little school, but it serves its purpose. The tables are even steady this year.

The villagers gather in the late afternoon to visit with us, sing, and hear the Word. How pleased we are to have people in every area of the region wanting to hear about the true "our Father." This place on the top of a mountain is so cold that we have to get into our sleeping bags to warm up.

I spend another day in the school helping Guillermo where he is weak, assisting him with his register, and just talking with him in general. He wants to follow the Lord but has many temptations. Yet he is young, only twenty years old. I also speak to Guillermo about the possibility of him going to teach in his home area at Sheringamaso where the Ministry of Education will now start a school. He says he would really like that.

Mary Ruth and I ask for a schedule on the radio to talk with the Flight Coordinator at Yarina, who happens to be our old classmate, Cecil Hawkins. Since Guillermo's school is going so well, we won't need to stay here as long as we had planned. So many people come to see us all day that it's difficult to find time to eat. Several of the men gather to talk with us about a teacher for their school here next year if Guillermo returns to his home area. We assure them there will be another teacher to take his place.

All the villagers gather in the late afternoon again to sing. One woman staying in the village has come quite a distance just to hear the songs and the true "our Father's" Word. Mary Ruth has been talking to her, helping her to understand. The people all agree that they want a teacher who will also be able to teach them the songs and God's Word, which of course, we are delighted to hear. They repeatedly ask us to sing with them.

We awaken early to pack our things and have another time on the radio to confirm when we can expect the plane to arrive at San Ramon to pick us up. Although we are a bit sad to hear that the plane will not come until after Thanksgiving, we decide to leave for San Ramon anyway.

Guillermo heads off to find the mule driver down in the new settler's village. He returns with the mules and the driver. Once the driver loads all our belongings, he leaves in such a hurry we hardly have time to say good-bye to everyone. We have to rush to keep up with him since we don't know the new route he is taking. I rub the skin off both little toes coming down the steep mountain so quickly. We finally reach the bottom and cross a rushing stream. Then we start up the other side — a mountain as high as the one we have just come down. It's a Boy Scout paradise!

After about two hours of fast walking, we come to Purus, a kind of road construction headquarters on the main road going to La Merced. In a little, makeshift restaurant, we have some coffee and inquire about a truck going to La Merced. We will have to wait until late afternoon they say. We ask for some eggs. When the lady says they have none, we pull the fresh eggs from our pockets that the people gave us as we were leaving. The lady willingly fries them for us.

Spanish-speaking men are sitting all around talking about the new road construction through the jungle — just like old Western days. A clamorous woman who runs the joint is telling them all just how it should be done.

As there is no place to spend the night here, we are happy to see a truck coming just as it is getting dark. *Thank you again, Lord, for giving us a path through the wilderness.* Since the seats are already occupied, we climb into the back and plop down on coffee sacks, the only women among several men. An empty beer barrel and a number of empty beer bottles roll around in the vacant space as the truck lurches forward. We are happy that the men do not inquire what we are doing.

In about two and a half hours, we arrive in La Merced and check into the same little backwoods hotel we had stayed in before. We have three days before the plane will come for us, so we decide to travel up into the Andes Mountains to Tarma where there is a beautiful, new Turista Hotel. There we can rest and clean up before going back to Yarina. We buy two small, straw bags to carry what we will need and leave the rest of our things here until we return.

On the trip up we keep climbing into the Andes higher. Along the way, we leave the jungle-covered mountains and begin to see only bare mountains with no vegetation. Landslides are common along the road, leaving very little room to pass any big trucks coming down the mountain. We go through several long, solid rock tunnels and reach Tarma two-and-a-half hours later.

This is where the mountain Quechua live. Their way of life is quite different from that of the jungle people. Yet both cultures are a great contrast to the Turista Hotel.

We take a taxi to the Turista, and as it comes into view we begin to wonder if we are in the right place. As we go up to the desk with our little straw bags, our everyday village clothes (we brought no good ones), and our long, stringy hair, all the men at the desk stop their work and just stare at us. They scarcely have the words to ask if they can help. We stutter out our request for a room. By this time, about six men in their best suits, ties, and gold rings come to peer at us in awe. Finally, the register is pushed over for us to sign and they all look on to see what our names and occupations might be.

Thankfully, we are given a room. We can hardly believe our eyes. What a beautiful room it is — hot showers, air foam beds, and lovely drapes.

When we left Yarina we had no idea we would ever be coming here. We could have brought some better clothes. We decide that since we are paying for this indulgence, we will enjoy ourselves. It is already time for the noon meal. We wash up a little and go into the spacious, gorgeous dining room and have a wonderful lettuce and tomato salad (the first we have had since leaving Yarina) and a big steak. Some people look at us with curiosity and we try to ignore it.

We go back to our room and can't wait to take a hot shower and curl up on the big beds. We sleep till late afternoon. *Thank you, Lord, for all the good things you give us along with the hard ones.*

About eight o'clock we head for the dining room for our evening meal. Although several distinguished-looking people and foreigners are there, we carry on as if we were as appropriately dressed as they are. We enjoy a full meal — soup, a vegetable dish, a meat dish (lamb), and ending with a dessert.

Back in our room again, we take another hot shower. It feels so good to be bathing in hot water for a change. It's much colder at this altitude. We sleep like logs until eight o'clock the next morning which is late for us.

After a delicious breakfast, we stroll past a large chandelier-studded drawing room and find magazines in English. Although it is beautiful outside — with flowers galore, a swimming pool, tennis, and lovely sunshine — we prefer to enjoy the modern conveniences inside. Our day is spent reading and taking it easy.

Back in the lovely dining room that evening, who do we see as we first walk in? Cec (our flight coordinator) and June Hawkins, Annie, Jeannie, and Bob — all our co-workers on a vacation, driving across the Andes to Lima. They are as surprised to see us as we are to see them.

"Hey, what are you doing here? You're supposed to be in San Ramon waiting for our plane," Cec reminds us.

"Yes, but since we learned we have to wait until after Thanksgiving, we decided to have our Thanksgiving Day here," I reply. "We will be there by the time the plane comes."

What fun it is talking with them until late that evening. The next day, they rise early to be on their way. We have a leisurely breakfast and then walk down to the town to see if we can locate a vehicle that is going toward San Ramon. We find one, but the driver tells us there has been a big landslide and he doesn't know if he can get through. Becoming concerned since we need to get to San Ramon to meet the plane, we again "commit our way" to the Lord.

The driver eventually returns to tell us he will try to take us at least part of the way to San Ramon. As we approach the spot where the landslide occurred, we can see from afar that about twenty vehicles are lined up, waiting while a tractor pushes away the dirt that is blocking the road. After a while, the cars are able to go through. As we drive over the dirt on the road, more is falling from higher up on the mountain. Looking down over the side of the mountain isn't too pleasant either, but we make it through okay. Thank you, Lord, for "directing our paths" again.

We reach the little hotel in La Merced where we have stayed before. It certainly does not compare to the Turista. Both Mary Ruth and I are somewhat sick to our stomachs, with me vomiting twice. Maybe it's just the altitude change.

We look for a vehicle that will take us to the San Ramon airstrip. We get there in time to meet the plane and are happy to see it arrive just about eleven o'clock. Ralph Borthwick is the pilot.

We fly low through the mountain valleys and stop near Valerio's school to pick up a passenger. We send for Valerio to join us while we wait since there are some things I need to tell him. Dear Valerio squeezes my hand when we meet.

We're soon in the air again and landing at Yarina Center. Several of our friends are there to meet us. Thus ends our first five years with the Amueshas. Our Savior has been leading us all the way. Thank you, Lord.


"In all your ways acknowledge him and he will direct your paths."

(Proverbs 3:6 NIV)


(Thank you, Lord, for enabling us to finish well our first term with the Amuesha people. Thank you for sparking their desire to know about you and your Word. May we finish our home leave soon and return refreshed and ready to do more translation.)

# 40

# Back to Peru
# after Home Leave

Who is that man?

"I would like to pick up my ticket to Lima, Peru. My name is Martha Duff," I tell the receptionist at the travel agency in Miami. I have just finished my home leave in the U.S. and am anxious to get back to Peru and the Amueshas.

The receptionist starts to look for my ticket when a young man arrives and also asks for his ticket by the name of Robert Tripp. As the lady searches for both of the tickets, she looks puzzled and admits to us, "This is very strange. I have one ticket for Martha Tripp and another one for Robert Duff."

As this young man and I try to figure out what has happened to our tickets, we realize that we are both translators with Wycliffe Bible Translators and are both heading for Peru, he for the first time. What an unusual accident that they would switch our last names in writing out our tickets!

We get our tickets straightened out and take seats together on the plane for the twelve-hour flight to Lima, Peru. Since this is Bob's first trip to Peru and he is planning to do linguistic and translation work as I am, I feel obligated to relate to him how wonderful the work is and how responsive the people are. He is anxious to hear all my stories of raft turnovers, muddy mule trails, early believers Pedro and Valerio, some early translation, and so on. The long trip seems short, and Bob and I become good friends.

Mrs. Cudney, our Lima guest house manager who calls me one of "her girls," is there to meet me at the plane with a bouquet of red roses to welcome me back, and to welcome Bob as a new member. Bob and I keep up our friendship and find that we both like ping-pong and tennis. He occasionally asks me for a date, but realizes as I do, that I am committed to God and to the Amuesha translation. It is my first commitment to which I feel I must be faithful, now that I already have a five-year start in the language. Bob and I must remain only good friends.

Bob himself soon becomes involved with a different group of indigenous people called the Amarakaeri and starts his own journey of learning their language. He entrusts me to take care of his frisky cat while he and Ray Hart go out to his tribal location.

On my home leave in advanced studies at the Summer Institute of Linguistics at the University of Oklahoma, I was able to write a paper on Amuesha sentence types called "Amuesha (Arawak) Syntax 1: Simple Sentence Types."[1] Mary Ruth was able to finish work for her Masters degree in linguistics. The more we know about Amuesha syntax and grammar in general, the better able we are to insure that our translated Scripture texts are within the grammatical rules we find operating in native texts. More importantly, this assures us our translation will be understandable.

Home leave passed so quickly.[2] I was very busy speaking in over fifty churches, happy to be invited to share my experiences regarding the Amuesha work. We now have many more people partnering in prayer. Thank you, Lord.

It feels good to be back in Peru. I arrive just in time for the Teacher Training Course at the Yarina Center. Teacher Pedro, his wife, Petita, and their little five-year-old girl are here, as well as several other Amuesha teachers and their families. About twenty-five of us make up the Amuesha group. Teacher trainees from other indigenous language groups, along with new Amuesha candidates continue to join the student body and boost the total enrollment every year.

All of us in the Amuesha group meet in our new house for times of devotion, study, and fun. The trainees are taking turns leading our devotions together. We are using the newly translated Gospel of Mark, reading and discussing it together. A special joy for me is to hear Pedro pray so honestly as he did today: "Lord, as I go around, I don't always do what is good. I sometimes even think what is not good. I want you to 'throw' this all away from me." He is growing so much in his knowledge of the Lord.

Pedro tells me that the children in his school are reading *"huomenc"* (strongly). He gives me a whole notebook of stories written by Miguel, one of his best students. He says, "The stories are all written correctly." I take one look and decide I need to get these typed up for extra reading practice for the older students. I remember how Bernardo always looks around in our baggage as we arrive back in his village to see if we have brought any new books. Thus, Miguel's stories form a book of thirty-nine pages, called *The Jaguar's Heart and Other Stories*. And other stories written by Valerio's best students fill new intermediate reading books. The students will surely enjoy reading the new books this year.

Several government officials from Lima are planning to come out here for the closing exercises of the Teacher Training Course, including the Superintendent of all Peruvian schools. We linguists are usually asked to contribute either some linguistic papers or skits as part of a special program just for them. I have been asked to perform a skit with Pedro and Petita to illustrate a linguistic point, namely, the difference between long and aspirated vowels in the Amuesha language. When I tell the two of them what we are to do, they act like old pros and even give me suggestions.

Finally, having completed further training, the teacher-trainees are off again with all their new books and other school materials, ready for another year of teaching.

Mary Ruth has not yet arrived back from her furlough.

In the meantime, I am asked to consider taking a French Countess, who has come to see our work here at Yarina, out to Stingray village for a short visit, at her request. We have been told that she is a friend of the president of Peru. I am a little hesitant, thinking jungle life might be too much for her, but she assures me she has already traveled extensively in the Southeast Asian jungles. She also invites me to come see her exclusively designed clothes, in the room where she is staying at the Townsend house. A friend and I take her up on her offer, but when we arrive, she is not there. Since she told us to go ahead and copy any designs we desired even if she were not there, we look at all her elaborate clothes and decide the styles are not for us.

We take off with the countess for the jungle village; I with some trepidation, not knowing how this is going to turn out. When we reach the village, and I start to enter one of the houses, the countess backs away for fear of getting lice or some germ. I was planning to have Shañe' come back with me to Yarina, but when the countess hears about it, she says, "Oh, no, we can't do that. I might get lice from her being that close in the plane."

"She will sit with me in the back of the plane," I reply.

"No, we cannot do that," she insists.

I am happy that Shañe' does not understand this conversation in English, yet Shañe' is disappointed. She already has her little bag of things ready to go with me to Yarina. Tears come to her eyes. I am disappointed too, since I was planning to concentrate on learning much more Amuesha with her at Yarina before Mary Ruth arrives back.

We conclude our short trip to Stingray village and are on our way back to Yarina, when thick, black rain clouds drop upon us and the wind blows us about. We have to fly very low under the clouds and follow the big Pachitea River. We are so low it seems that we are actually gliding along on the water's surface beneath us, much like a wide highway. The countess becomes petrified. She holds onto the rod above the door of the plane — as if this could save her life — and begins saying her prayers. As we arrive safely back at Yarina, I think to myself, I'm sure the countess is convinced that she has never seen jungle like this.

With Mary Ruth's return to Peru, we know there is a great deal of work to be done in translation and with the schools, so we are anxious to get back out with the Amuesha people. New teacher-trainees are being named as permanent teachers by the Ministry of Education, and we need to help them get off to a good start.

Pilot Ted Long flies us out to Stingray village from where we will begin our downriver school visits. Getting nearer to our landing strip on the river, we can tell that the water is very high and muddy from recent rains. As we land, we see little "Spider" and her father in a canoe. Ted thinks the river is high enough that we can taxi closer to the village. He suggests bringing "Spider" (about ten years old now) aboard the plane to guide us away from the more shallow, rocky spots. She agrees, and sitting on my lap like a big shot, tells us to head right or left as we taxi up to the village.

We can hardly recognize the children that have grown so much in the two years we have been away and are anxious to hear all the village news. Shane's little Tontelleso'n died from pneumonia at about six months old, but she already has another darling, little baby — a girl with long eyelashes and shiny hair. However, her husband has left her again. Old Grandpa Santos has died. "He would not have died if you had been here," Grandma Santos informs us. They tell us about many other deaths and mate changes. Some man took little Sabella, and she already has a baby. With the great number of mate changes, we realize there are few binding marriage relationships in this culture, which creates many problems among them.

We are hardly back "home" when we begin getting many requests for help from the sick ones. This keeps both Mary Ruth and me busy. "City Woman's" young daughter, Amo, is very sick with fever. Her mother has not been able to give the sulfa tablets consistently, so I decide she really needs a penicillin shot, which I am not looking forward to doing. I learned how to give shots at our clinic at Yarina, hoping I would never have to give one. Now that the moment of truth has arrived, I go with fear and trembling to give Amo a shot. When I tell her mother what I am planning to do, she is as scared as she knows I am, but pretends not to be. Humming a little tune from her nervousness, she starts getting Amo ready for the shot. I make the plunge quickly so I won't lose my nerve, but in so doing forget to clean the skin with alcohol. The next time, I remember the alcohol. Amo's fever has already gone down and she is feeling better. *Thank you, Lord, for making the penicillin available and giving me the courage to use it; it works much better than the sulfa.*

We choose not to get involved in our language studies now, since we plan to go downriver soon to visit all the schools, as we did the year before furlough. Teacher Guillermo is now instructing students at the new school in his home area. He is happy to be back home at Sheringamaso (Rubber village) and is doing well, having two years of practice behind him.

We visit the schools up the Chuchuras River and higher up on the Omaiz River where the people have asked for a school. One of the recent, young believers named Luis wants to study to be the teacher there. He is one of the young people who became a believer the last time we visited. How good it is to have another believing teacher.

We head back downriver, ending up at Santiago's school, and then still further down to Valerio's school. It takes a lot of our time, but we know the more schools there are, the more readers and preachers there are for God's Word. It's a joy to see the bilingual teachers at the schools also teaching God's Word of their own desire, and in accordance with the curriculum from the Ministry of Education, which designates the first fifteen minutes of the daily schedule to "religion."

As we talk with Valerio at our last stop, we learn that this has been a tough year for him. Valerio has had health problems, land problems (outside people wanting to take his land), outsiders coming in and telling him he doesn't know anything, he should not be teaching, and that we are deceiving him. Even his oldest son Vicente, his pride and joy, is not following the Lord, which is a great disappointment to Valerio. We listen and sympathize with him, sharing verses from God's Word that have helped us with our problems. Yet as Valerio talks, there is every evidence that he intends to follow God's Word, no matter what. Thank you, Lord.

The plane picks us up at Valerio's school to take us back far upriver to San Ramon to start our trek back into Singing Water village. We have problems contracting mules for the last part of our journey and have to spend some nights in Villa Rica along the way as we wait for them. Are we ever happy to arrive back at our little house here in Singing Water village after many weeks of travel on school visits.

The fellows help me get the radio set up so we can call in to Yarina right away to let them know we are okay. The people offer to build us a new house since ours is old and leaking quite a bit. We decide, however, that we would rather just stay in it, with a roof repair, and not have to move again. We are anxious to get back to more language and translation work.

Pedro's school is progressing nicely. Some of the students are in their fourth year, and many are reading very well. He often has some of his older students like Julio, Domingo V., or Bernardo read the Mark scriptures for the morning religion class the first fifteen minutes of the school day. What a delight to hear of all these good readers of God's Word and to realize the impact the Word is making in their young lives.

Observing the great abilities of Pedro's students, I realize we need to be challenging them in more ways. They already know all the sounds of the letters in their alphabet but don't realize that with this knowledge they can not only read, they can also write any new word they want that they have never seen written in their books. To get the students into creative writing, I suggest to Pedro that we have a contest to see who can write the most bird names. Amuesha people love birds and have legends about them. We give the students each a special notebook, telling them to write all the bird names they know and to even ask their parents and grandparents for more. Just writing a name on each line, they will not need to use punctuation or capitalization. That will make for an easier start in creative writing. We can't wait to see who wins!

A week after the start of this extracurricular contest, we take up the notebooks. To our amazement, we see that even the younger students have written over one hundred bird names each. An older boy, Andres, has written 336! We finish the compilation of all the individual lists and are astonished to find a total of 470 different bird names written by the whole student body — the first time the majority of these bird names have ever been written.

Teacher Pedro decides, as do I, that some special recognition should be given to the students. We plan a little school program that Pedro directs. The three students with the longest lists read some of their bird names and are awarded prizes. I sit in the back of the school, along with the parents who have been invited. Although the parents take great pride in what their children are accomplishing, being the typical parents that they are, I hear one of them remarking, "The children nowadays, they don't know any bird names."

"That was so much fun. Can we have another contest like this?" the children ask.

"What names would you like to write for another contest?" I inquire.

"Tree and plant names," they answer.

I know when I hear "trees" that the number of names in this contest will climb into the hundreds since we are in the Amazon Rainforest. Yet since the kids ask for it, we hand out notebooks again. The compilation of tree and plant names adds up to about seven hundred — names written in Amuesha for the very first time in history! We realize what a wealth of education the native culture provides its people. You have to know quite a bit to be considered "educated" in the Amuesha culture. They think I am uneducated in some respects because I can only name about ten birds and even fewer trees in my language.

Although we are not thinking about it at the moment, all these names are destined to find their way into the Amuesha dictionary. Despite the impressive collection, these are only the names of birds and trees found at this 4,500 foot altitude. At a lower altitude, many more large birds will be found, and other species of trees.

To further reward the students, I make a book of all the bird names, listing them in alphabetical order with pictures of many of the birds drawn by one of the older students. The children are happy to have their own book — a bird dictionary — in the classroom. They continue to think of more birds and often they ask me, "Is the bird *tsetse* in our dictionary?"

"I don't know," I answer. "Look it up in your bird dictionary, in the order of the alphabet."

Near the end of the school year, a little delegation of children arrives at my door with a sheet of paper containing the names of thirty more birds. "We have come to tell you that these birds are not included in our dictionary," the delegation states.

Their request is evident. "Will you please see that they get added in our bird dictionary?" they ask. This brings our total count to an even five hundred bird names!

The original purpose of the contest has been accomplished; the students have learned alphabetical order. Better yet, they now realize they can write any word in their language, whether they have ever seen it written or not. With a little encouragement in creative writing, the students begin authoring all kinds of stories from their own experiences. They write about the habits and descriptions of birds, other animals, and fish (with pictures drawn); their families; how they live and grow their food; hunting trips; raft turnovers; and even long legends. One of the older boys writes a long, well-known legend of how the sun and moon came to be. Others write about their thoughts and feelings. One little boy writes how he felt on his first day of school: "I felt that all the other children knew everything, and I didn't know anything" (just the way we all felt on our first day of school.) They are giving me scores of notebooks filled with their stories, each one hoping that his or her writings, ending with their name, will be printed in future books. What fun it is to be working with these kids and teachers!

We have not been here at Singing Water village for very long when we hear that some Amueshas have measles. We know immediately that this can be very dangerous for the indigenous people. Entire populations of them have been known to die off. The problem is that they already have weak lungs caused by intestinal parasites. Thus, when a native person gets measles, it most often turns into pneumonia, from which they die easily without treatment. A high fever at the end of a bout with measles indicates pneumonia.

We start checking whether the people with measles have a fever. It turns out to be an almost full-time job as more and more people become ill. I am kept busy giving penicillin shots to those with high fevers.

We hear that the people a thousand feet higher up on the mountain are very sick. Petita accompanies me to show me the way. When we reach them, we find many people just lying on the ground, unconscious with high fevers. One girl with a fever of 105°. Even the shaman is among the sick. I give him a shot, along with the others, without him knowing it. There is one lone "diviner" who has not yet come down with measles who is trying to burn all the termite nests around to get revenge on the termites so the people will get well. The situation is heartbreaking. How would I ever know that one of the unconscious men I give a shot by the name of Gasparepe'n, will later become my chief co-translator — saved from physical death to give spiritual life to many of his people as he helps me translate God's Word. Eventually, the measles epidemic is over.

Today as I walk through the newly cleared and burned-off jungle ground for the new center of the village, I suddenly get the urge to plant some of my lettuce seeds here. It would be good to have some lettuce out here. I meet the chief coming along the path and I ask him, "Would you give me just a little piece of this burned-off ground to plant my lettuce seeds?"

I show him the picture of lettuce on the package of seeds since he has never heard of lettuce. He takes one look at the leafy thing and replies, "You don't want those leaves, that's for grasshoppers."

I insist that lettuce is one of my favorite foods, and he says, "I'll give you all the land you want, but you should not be eating that grasshopper food." (Amueshas do not eat any green, leafy thing.)

With his permission, I quickly get my lettuce seeds planted. They sprout up in no time and grow quickly in this fertile ground. When they get to be about two inches high, and I am passing the spot with the chief again, I notice they have all been chewed off by grasshoppers. The jovial chief's only remark is, "See there, I told you that was grasshopper food."

But I can taste the lettuce. I am not to be outdone. I plant the rest of the seeds in a wooden box filled with the good soil and place them under the open window of our house. There they grow lushly and we pick off enough leaves for each meal — lettuce in the jungle! I give the children the seeds of other vegetables they are just learning about so they can plant them in their school gardens. They bring us all the vegetables they grow. They wouldn't think of eating that green, grasshopper food. Of course we pay them, and they like that.

We hear that the Amueshas across the mountain from us, at a place called Cacaso (Fish River), want a bilingual school. We decide to go visit and make plans to start a school there. Pedro volunteers to go with us since we have never been to Cacaso. He is especially interested in going because Cacaso is where he found his true blood sisters and their families living when he came to live in this area. He has already shared with them his knowledge about the true "our Father" and His Son, Jesus. His sisters quickly and happily believed since they knew these were true words coming from their long lost little brother. Now Pedro wants them to have schools and learn to read God's Word we are translating.

We are told it is a hard, eight-hour trip to Cacaso over this large mountain that appears so close — four hours up one side and four hours down the other. While it's not a muddy mule trail, for which we are thankful, it's just a glimpse of a trail covered with foliage and vines.

We start off with a bang, but as we immediately begin the steep incline, we realize this is the worst trail we have hiked yet. Some parts are so steep and slippery that we have to pull ourselves up by saplings along the way. After about four hours, we reach the very top of the mountain where we can see all around. Pedro points out Stingray village way downriver.

A family of Amueshas live right on this mountain top. They take us in and offer us food and their fermented drink, *co'nes*. Some of them are sick with the flu, so we treat them with the medicines we always carry. We hasten on since we must get to our destination before dark.

We thought the "up side" of our journey would be the hardest, but we find the "down side" of the mountain to be equally difficult. We can't keep from slipping down the steep declines. We laugh as I slide on my bottom much of the way down. Happily, we arrive just before dark. Pedro's dear, sweet sisters, who are now believers, take us in with joy, sharing all kinds of food with us. Despite them talking all night, we sleep soundly from sheer exhaustion.

Pedro shares the Word with all the people who gather the next day to talk about the school. Many of them are also believers, including Pedro's nephew, Juan Francisco, who is already a leader of the people here. They want God's Word along with the school, they tell us. We advise them on arrangements for a school in Cacaso next year, and then leave for Singing Water village right away, hoping to return there before dark. We stop only to check on the sick people on the mountain top. After sixteen hours of walking in two days, we are happy to snuggle into our sleeping bags.

Today we receive a request by radio from Pete Fast, who is now working in our office in Lima, to ask if the chief and his wife would be willing to come to Lima to be a part of an Indian exhibit in an International Fair there. He also asks for two Amuesha schoolboys who would be willing to demonstrate their skills by reading in Amuesha and also in Spanish for the people who will visit their booth. At first we are a little hesitant, thinking that the Amueshas will be stared at or laughed at, but Pete feels that will not be the case.

Jovial person that the chief is, he thinks it might be fun, and says he would like to go to Lima to see the sights for the first time. He travels in full native dress, with crown and feathers, seed and bead ornaments, and bow and arrows, happy and proud to show off the Amuesha culture. Pedro has chosen two of his best readers from the young boys who want to go, Marin and Raul. They take their Natural Science diglot books which have an Amuesha side and a Spanish side, so folks will hear them read in both languages.

In their booth at the fair, the Amueshas are seated by a wood fire in a typical, thatched roof house. Hardly anyone in Lima has ever seen the natural habitat of the jungle people, thus, many of the fair goers approach out of curiosity. When a group gathers, the boys stand up to read. Even the President of Peru and his wife are there. The chief is delighted to be introduced to the president and have his picture taken with him. The president compliments the two boys on them reading equally well in both languages.

Upon his arrival back home, the chief tells everyone of his experiences in the big city of Lima. He gazed upon the "big lake" (Pacific Ocean) for the first time. He marveled at the motorcycles that go "sput, sput." And he was amused by his wife Ascencia hobbling along as she tried to walk in the first pair of shoes she ever had on (given to her by a shoe store).

The two boys write about their experiences. Their greatest problem was trying to keep the cars from "stepping" on them. All of them decide the city is not for them, and they are happy to be back in the safety of their jungle.

Teacher Pedro now has a large new, house built over near the new school and village center. He invites the people to come regularly to his house to sing and hear more of God's Word. More people keep coming. We join the people sitting on the floor — men on one side and women on the other according to Amuesha culture — as we listen to Pedro read and share new Scriptures from Mark.

Pedro has now written another song that reflects all the new concepts he is learning and believing from God's Word:

Look to Jesus, the Savior,
He is the loving Lord.
On the cross there He died for me,
Because I am a sinner.

Chorus:
I want to prove your Word,
The Savior who died for me,
For me, for me,
For me He died.
I also see the cross,
Wherein we are saved.
My whole heart I give to Jesus,
I very much want His joy.


Pedro's second song is his personal testimony and becomes No. 15 in our hymnbook, and of course everyone wants to learn it. His testimony is having great influence among his people — in their own language and culture.[3] A live, personal testimony from one's own people has more credibility for others than a recorded message from a stranger. Despite Pedro's shortcomings, he surely has a heart to follow the Lord, which is the only thing that really matters. We praise the Lord to have him as a leader of the people here.

By this time, the Ministry of Education of Peru has published its Program of Moral and Religious Education containing selected Scriptures to be used in public schools, including the Bilingual Schools. The passages include Genesis 1-3 and also a large number of passages from the New Testament on the chronological life of Christ. These are to be taught in the first fifteen minutes of the school day.

Pedro agrees to help me translate these passages in the afternoons after he has finished his school day. We realize this may overload him, but he wants to do it, and there is no one else available. We start on the Genesis passages. I am happy to be translating the creation story early on to make known how the true "our Father" created the sun, since Amuesha culture considers the sun itself to be god. Now translating Scripture for his own people, Pedro is the same young boy who once prayed to know who the true "our Father" is. His search has ended, for today Pedro knows the true "our Father" is the one who created the sun!

As we start each translation session, Pedro's prayers are a joy to me, "We want to translate well your Word for our people, even for all the little

Amueshas who are not even born yet," he prays. "Help us there where it is hard. Your Word is very good. I'm so happy, receiving your Word. I want to follow you well. We thank you that the children are learning well to read your Word."

Thus, it is translated there in Gen. 1:16: *"Yečhcatan Parets epa ate-sha' ñeñĩcha' čhoyo'tatsa."* (The Deity One created two large lights to light the day and the night.) As we arrive at the point where the Garden of Eden is spoken of, and the Tigris and Euphrates Rivers are mentioned, Pedro asks, "Is this a real place in the world? Where is it?" I show him on a map where this location is.

As we get to the end of Chapter 3, where the "flaming sword" is placed at the entrance of the Garden of Eden, Pedro asks again, "Is that flaming sword still there?" What would you answer? "I don't know," I can only answer.

Mary Ruth is working on a revision of her translation of the Gospel of Mark. We both realize we have much to learn yet in order to translate God's Word meaningfully and accurately. There are so many new concepts the Amueshas have never heard of. We trust you, Lord, to enable us.


"The entrance of thy words giveth light . . ."
    (Psalm 119:130 KJV)


"People who never before inquired about me are now seeking me out. Nations who never before searched for me are finding me."
    (Isaiah 65:1 LB)


(Thank you, Lord, for your enabling us to carry out all you have called upon us to do.)

# 41

# "All Thy Children Shall Be Taught of the Lord"

A library for indigenous people!

"These books will make the children so happy," Valerio says as he sees all the different new booklets we have typed up to create an Amuesha library. The library series is composed of twenty-six booklets which will provide children and adults extra reading practice and information. Improving the fluency of the new readers will help them to more easily read the Amuesha New Testament when it is published.

Within this series of booklets, we have several selected stories of Jesus from the Gospel of Mark (with colored pictures); descriptions of African animals with pictures; my little *Tempo* fish story; a chicken story of a mother hen who died in saving her chicks in a fire; the two schoolboys' written accounts of their trip to Lima to read for the president; teacher Cesar's account of the ten-day raft trip down to the Teacher Training Course at Yarina; and many other stories. Teacher Pedro also wrote up his account of getting lost in the jungle. He said, "I want my students to know how they almost lost their teacher."

We have also included various stories written by students themselves, like "How Our Raft Turned Over on the Meshtaso River." With all these stories typed up in individual booklets, plus the previous storybooks of David and Joseph, Valerio realizes that a number of students can be reading different books at the same time. We make a sign-out sheet to keep track of the books. Even some former students like Domingo V. come to the school to sign out books for himself and his new wife to read at home. For people who have never had a book, newspaper, magazine or even a letter, reading can be most fascinating.

Valerio is delighted with all the new reading material in Amuesha, and is happy to see the new *Life of Christ*, a book composed of passages from all the Gospels containing the chronological life of Christ. These passages were translated with Pedro's help the last time we were in Singing Water village. They have now been printed up along with the Genesis portions — conforming to the program of Moral and Religious Education designed by the Ministry of Education for all schools in Peru — and will be used in the Amuesha schools this year.

From Valerio's school, we fly on upriver toward Stingray village, stopping en route to leave books at Sheringamaso (Rubber village) for Guillermo's new school.

How good it is to see all the people at Stingray village again after all our travels to other parts of Amueshaland. This still seems like our "home" despite the fact that our former house has now fallen down. We have been given another house where we can live during  our short visits here. The villagers want us to stay in Stingray village and say they will build us another house, but we plan to go back upriver to Singing Water after we finish our school travels downriver. We want to get into more Scripture translation with Pedro there.

The people in Stingray tell us all the news since we were last here. Shañe' is downriver with her husband, who has now taken another wife. I feel so sorry for her. Although she wants to believe and follow God's Word, she is trapped by her culture. Old Grandma Santos looks much older and more feeble. She comes by often and wants us to read her the Bible stories in Amuesha. As we talk to her, we feel that she really believes. She also loves the songs. Ahuash has taken a wife. Sabella's little baby died.

Several people request the newly printed portions of Genesis. Now they will be reading about the true "our Father" who made "our father (the sun)."

Soon we leave for Guillermo's new school downriver in Sheringamaso (Rubber village). After a pleasant, four-hour canoe trip with Santoma' and his buddy, the people proudly escort us to a new, little house they have built for us. This is the first time we have ever had a house built for us at one of our school stops.

The people come to our little house right away and want to sing the first night and every night that we are here. We are happy to find teacher Guillermo leading the meetings and often reading Scripture verses to the villagers. He is also having some of his students quote verses they have already read and memorized from the new Genesis Scriptures, that were translated just last year (including the passage where God made the sun). They seem to be understanding well what they read which makes a new translator quite happy.

The kids are delighted with the recently inaugurated Amuesha library booklets. They learn right away how to sign out a book — "big stuff" for them!

In talking with the older man, Luis, who is the head of Sheringamaso village, we are pleased to find out that he is glad to have God's Word taught here. Guillermo has been teaching the people God's Word and has even written a new song about Christ's second coming:

"We will see Jesus someday, the one who saves us,

When He will come back here to earth;

That's what He told us upon leaving."

This is our first song about the Second Coming of Christ. Thank you, Lord.

We leave to continue our visits to other schools, and Guillermo, on his own, prays for us right there on the riverbank, in the presence of the unbelieving Spanish speakers who are taking us in their motorboat to our next stop.

We venture on to teacher Luis' new school way upriver in the Omaiz area. He is doing well as a new teacher and in sharing God's Word with the people. While he reads from the new Genesis portions in school, I hear interesting reactions from two older men sitting near me in the back of the school, just listening in. When Luis reads where God made man from the dust of the earth, one of them comments to the other, "That's why we are such "diers" (mortals); if He had made us from rocks, we would have been more durable." As Luis reads on about Eve wanting the fruit, again they comment to each other, "That's just like women; when we take them out anywhere, they always want all the fruit they see."

Later, I have time to share my lamb story with the children and all the villagers. They seem to understand the application well.

Mary Ruth and I notice how anemic the children look here. Barely having the strength to play, they just sit lifelessly. Some are not even strong enough to attend school. Teacher Luis informs us that he can scarcely keep chalk in the school because the children are eating it. We realize right away that they are very anemic from many intestinal parasites, so we treat all who come to us with worm pills and then start them on iron and vitamin tablets. Some show such improvement that even before we leave they are already back in school.

It's a rainy day when we leave to head back downriver to Cesar's school, arriving in time for Sunday services. Cesar directs during the "church" meeting. He reads from Mark about the things that defile us and presents good examples. When Cesar is through, I share my chicken story with its application of how Jesus died for our sins. While I meant for the invitation at the close to attract new believers, it winds up being a testimony meeting. Those who already believe state how they know Christ died for their sins and that they want to follow Him.

One young fellow by the name of Domingo S., a student of Cesar's, speaks openly and says, "From this time on forever, I want to follow Christ." He shares with me later that this is the first time he realized why Christ had to die to save us. He and another young fellow, José, tell us that they want to go to Bible School to learn more of God's Word. We trust they will come to preach the Word because there is so much drinking and fighting in this area. This is just what God will lead them to do. God's Word is producing such wonderful results!

We open up a medical clinic after church. Many of the people seem sickly.

Abel, a student of Cesar's, is thinking of studying to be a health promoter here, which we encourage.

Cesar is doing a good job in teaching his classes. On Monday during his Peruvian history class, I hear Cesar instructing his advanced students: "San Martin, (the liberator of Peru) freed us and gave us our own land." One boy, realizing how the villagers are trying, with little success, to get titles for their land from the government exclaims, "But teacher, we don't have our land yet."

We have made arrangements for our plane to pick us up at the Iscozacin airstrip. While we are still en route down the Chuchuras River, we hear the plane fly over us. Ted Long, the pilot, is waiting for us when we reach our destination. Flying back over the mountains to San Ramon, we look for a possible place for an airstrip in the mountains near Singing Water, but the clouds are so thick we are unable to see anything.

At San Ramon, Mary Ruth and I get the idea of trying to hire only one vehicle that will take us as far as we can go before we have to travel on foot. In the past, we would take different vehicles just as far as they would happen to be going, leaving us to have to look for another vehicle. We do find one that costs us more, but we think it is worth it not to have to stop and find other vehicles along the way.

When we get to the end of the road, we contract for mules to take us to Singing Water and then on to the school at Palomar where Guillermo has taught before. Vicente, Valerio's son, is assigned to teach here now. This is his first school assignment and a very difficult place for him, with the cold, windy climate on top of this mountain. He has been used to the much warmer climate downriver. And with the shortage of food here, his wife has already gone back downriver. Vicente and his wife are both so young and have a new baby. We trust they can make the situation work. We admire him for sticking with it. Despite Vicente's good training from his dedicated father, Valerio, Vicente is not a committed believer. Still he is holding services for the people here and has even written some new children's songs.

The mules we contracted for come on time and we continue our trek on into Singing Water village. We are disappointed to find the villagers have been unable to build our new house yet, but we are happy that they are giving us another makeshift house to live in for the time being.

We get here just three days after Petita has given birth to a baby girl. They proudly tell me they have named her Marrta (Martha), so I now have a cute, little namesake. It's always good to see Pedro and Petita after being away from them for as long as we typically are.

How soon something sad thing happens. Just after we have gone to bed one night, Pedro comes and calls for us explaining that his foster mother's little baby isn't breathing. (Pedro's foster parents from downriver are visiting him.)

We know the child has whooping cough, and we rush over. The baby is already limp. Pedro is working on the baby, trying to get him breathing again. The mother and sisters are wailing and crying. We try everything the health book says, but nothing works. Pedro blows and blows into the baby's mouth. Finally, we all give up, and they get a board and lay the little child out in the middle of the floor, as is their custom.

We sit and talk with the family to comfort them and take the opportunity to tell them about living for Christ so that they understand they can be with the baby when they die. While Pedro's foster parents love all their children very much, they have heard little of God's Word.

Since the baby died with whooping cough, Mary Ruth and I think we should try to get vaccine for all the children, especially the babies. We talk to our doctor by radio, and he tells us we can get the vaccine from Lima. He instructs us in how it should be administered, and says it requires refrigeration, or a very cool temperature. We decide our cool weather and cold water will be sufficient.

At issue is the fact that someone will have to make the long trip into Lima to get the vaccine. We talk to the chief and people to see if any of them want to make the journey. Following the death of the baby, the people are scared and desire the vaccine. The chief agrees to go to Lima since he has already been there. We make arrangements with our Lima buyer to secure the vaccines for us.

We set up a regular procedure. For the babies, Doc advises us to give a preliminary shot in addition to the three regular vaccines. That means four shots for each baby. In all, we give shots to forty-two children.

Since Pedro has learned to give shots at our Center, he does the actual injections, which is a great help. I take on the role of nurse, preparing the syringe with the proper dose and needle, and handing it to Pedro all ready to go. Mary Ruth records the names of all the patients so we can keep track of whom we have given shots, when they need the next one, etc. The mothers find all this difficult to understand, especially needing the three shots.

One night in our makeshift house, when I am unable to fall asleep, I keep thinking of the future of the Amuesha work, and of the potential leaders the Lord is bringing forth in various areas of the work. In the back of my mind the verse Isaiah 54:2, which arose in my devotions recently, keeps coming up: "Enlarge the place of . . . your habitation . . ." All of a sudden it is like the Lord himself is speaking to me. "Why not have a Bible School for those wanting to study this year, with Valerio doing the teaching in Amuesha!" The revelation is so startling, so direct, and so forceful that I can only believe it is the voice of the Lord.

Being unaccustomed to such divine instructions, I tell Mary Ruth in the morning of this unusual happening. Since we always like to agree on our decisions, I ask her, "What do you think of this; what should we do?"

"Since you feel strongly that it is of the Lord, you go ahead with what you think the Lord is leading you to do."

For further confirmation, I ask Pedro what he thinks about it. As soon as I mention it to him, he is all for it. Right away, he says, "I can walk with the students down through the mountains all the way to Valerio's place."

Pedro is volunteering to make the four- to five-day trip downriver on foot with the students, which is something I failed to consider. I take this as further evidence of God's leading.

The fact that Pedro is pleased Valerio is being selected as the teacher of the Bible School instead of himself is also encouraging. I realize, however, there are problems with Valerio teaching in Amuesha. Having lived far down-river near Spanish-speaking people coming into Amuesha areas, Valerio is more bilingual in his speech than other Amueshas. He has already studied one year in a Bible School taught all in Spanish, as our predecessor, Pete Fast, encouraged him to do. The sad thing is, when Valerio came back from the Spanish-speaking Bible School, he was unable to pass on many of the spiritual concepts he had learned in Spanish to his own people in their Amuesha language. He continued to preach mostly in Spanish, even praying in Spanish as he had learned.

Because Valerio was designated as teacher in the first concept of this Amuesha Bible School, I feel we should continue with the plan. To have Pedro agree is further assurance. In addition, Valerio is older and the first believer — more affirmation. It is very much in keeping with Amuesha culture that younger men work as apprentices to older men, just as young Julio was doing with the older shaman when we first arrived in Singing Water village.

Convinced we are heading in the right direction, I start to consider what we have already translated to use as study materials in the Bible School. We have the newest book on the whole life of Christ, arranged in chronological order and taken from all the Gospels. We also have the book of Mark, which Mary Ruth has been revising. In addition to these, the Lord indicates that we need to translate a set of selected verses that show clearly the way of salvation, plus another set of verses that illustrate the Christian life of the believer — the heart of the Gospel.[1]

With some 130 verses selected, Pedro is happy to start the translation. He realizes the verses are also helping him to understand more clearly the way of salvation and the Christian life. He thinks they will be very useful for young Amueshas who want to believe and share the Word with their own people.

Yet we face a few challenges. Can we get that many verses translated and printed before the end of this school year, ready for vacation time when Valerio will be available? How can we contact Valerio within this short period to see if he is willing to teach and go over all the translated verses for his approval? How can we contact all the potential students and assure them there will be a Bible School when we don't even have Valerio's approval?

Although these issues all seem like impossibilities, yet the Lord gives me such faith and peace about setting up the Bible School that I am convinced it is not only possible, but certain. *Thank you, Lord, for such faith that I have never known before.*

Mary Ruth and I still have another school to visit this year before the summer break. It's the new school at Cacaso which is over this big mountain. The villagers chose Enrique, a young fellow who lives there, as their teacher. Although he has already attended one Teacher Training Course, we realize he needs much help. It only takes us six-and-a-half hours to cross the big mountain to Cacaso this time since the trail is much drier.

We visit some Amueshas who live on the mountain top. The lines on one old woman's face seem to show all the years she has weathered the exposure, hardships, and sicknesses of that cold mountaintop in a house with no floor or walls. Since we have to hurry to get down the other side of the mountain by dark, I wonder when we leave her, *How will this dear woman ever hear enough of your Word, Lord, to ever believe in you?* How could I ever have imagined that in the not-to-distant future this same woman would be hearing God's Word read to her by her own son, Casper Mountain, and that she would later be saying to me, "The more he read to me the verses on how we are saved, the more I believed this really is the true our Father's Word to us, and I believed it. Then I asked my son to take me down to live at Singing Water with the others who believe there." *Thank you, Lord.*

While working with Enrique on school matters, I have a good opportunity to help him assure his commitment to the Lord. He prays very simply, "I know I have done many bad things, but I know that you died to pay for my sins. I want to follow you."

Back in Singing Water, Pedro wants to work every afternoon after school to help me finish all the selected verses on *Salvation* and the *Christian Life* booklets for the Bible School coming up soon. Assisting with the translation is a great blessing for Pedro. We hear every new thing he learns because he shares it with his people. His prayers are a blessing to me too as he often prays, "Your Word says . . ." (quoting something we have just translated). Such prayers make all our efforts worthwhile.

Mary Ruth is still revising Mark. She wants to include the opinions of women as well as men, but finds it difficult to hold their attention since the women usually have babies that distract them. Mary Ruth has chosen Tomas, one of the older schoolboys who is reading well, as her translation assistant. He has a strong interest in the Word and wants to attend Bible School.

One Sunday after "church" we give all the kids their second whooping cough vaccine. In short order we vaccinate forty-two children with our new system. Poor kids, they are becoming afraid to come to our house now. Pedro's little boy, Juanacho, just stands at a distance and looks at our house giving up his frequent visits.

Pedro makes the trip back over to Cacaso to administer the second round of vaccines. He wants to see his relatives there anyway. Upon his return, he tells us that a little boy not wanting to get another shot took the vaccine from the cool water in which Pedro had been keeping it and hid it out in the jungle. Luckily, the villagers finally found it.

We continue to conduct church services in Pedro's house, where the people gather and he shares the Word. However, we still have not seen a real moving of the Holy Spirit among the people. Pedro is having some of his best students read the Word during the service. They read well and seem anxious to take part. The older folks like to watch their youngsters recite like this and are learning to really listen to the words and what they mean. To see the school children standing up in the middle of the group, reading Bible stories without any difficulty, and the adults paying attention, is a thrill and reward for both Mary Ruth and me.

Although sometimes we think the Amueshas are letting go of their old beliefs, something like the words of old Selano's wife bring back to reality the fact that they are still enslaved by them. She explains to us the reason the villagers were having so many drinking parties at the time we returned to Singing Water.

"They were having them," she says, "so that this man visiting from Chispa could shoot the demons. He killed three during that time."

"How did he kill them?" we ask.

"He shot them with a shotgun he had."

It strikes us as ironic to think a demon can be shot with a gun, but at the same time we realize they still don't trust the Lord to deliver them from their fears.

Pedro's life is a good example to his students. Already several of his older students have heard about the possibility of a Bible School and tell us they want to study there, including Tomas, young Selano, and his younger brother, Miguel. Tomas replies, "I want to go if it is in our language and not in Spanish." Selano adds, "I would like to go to Cacaso to teach the people there after I have studied God's Word." Later, Ernesto, another of Pedro's students, comes and says he and his younger brother Raul want to go too. Such comments confirm our Bible School idea. And Pedro continues with his plan to walk with the students on the long, jungle trip.

With these inquiries, Pedro and I begin to move forward with our Bible School concept, but then we both start to have second thoughts. *What if Valerio does not want to teach the school when we see him? It will be impossible to tell Pedro and the boys not to come once we leave here.* Nevertheless, I express to Pedro, "This is faith. We believe God is leading us this way." Seeing faith in action encourages us both. I have never been so assured of something in my life; this is the "stretching forth." Has the Lord not said, "And all thy children shall be taught of the Lord . . ."? (Isaiah 54:13)

I have been creating a sample of the booklets for the Bible School courses on *Salvation* and the *Christian Life* to show Valerio when we stop at his place on our way back to Yarina. We plan to spend a week there going over the selected verses with him and getting his answer to our question about leading the Bible School.

Now as we finish translating all the selected verses, Pedro breaks into spontaneous prayer, "I pray to you in all my happiness, to thank you for all your Word you are giving us." He goes on to thank the Lord for heaven, "where there won't be any more suffering or snake bites."

At last, we have finished our work at Singing Water for this year and are on our way out, flying downriver to spend a week or so at Valerio's place before returning to Yarina Center. Valerio is willing to work with me on checking the selected sets of verses to see if he thinks we have translated them well. It's important that he approves of the way we have translated the verses if he will be teaching them. However, I say nothing of a Bible School yet, thinking I need to wait for the most opportune time.

Valerio is delighted to hear the same verses he has studied in Spanish become so much more real and understandable in his own language. *"Atarr cohuen yeñoño"* (It is so good in our language), he says over and over. At times he says, "Oh, is that what that verse means; I always thought it meant such and such," or, "Is that what this verse means; I never understood what this verse meant when I studied it in Spanish."

As we get into such passages as the "fruit of the Spirit," "joy in suffering," "complete surrender," and "trust," Valerio is thrilled. "This is very good," "these are new thoughts," and "these are strong words," he comments time and again. A passage that opens up to Valerio for the first time is John 15:4-7, "abiding in Christ" (we remain united together with Christ). As Valerio grasps the wonderful truths these verses contain, he realizes that this is what he needs in his own Christian life.

The opportune time has come, so I ask, "Valerio, have you ever considered teaching God's Word to your own people in your own language?"

"Oh, no, I couldn't do that."

"Well, I know you can," I respond "You know a lot more of God's Word than many of your people upriver. Many of the young ones up there want to be taught more of God's Word."

I refrain from saying any more. I do make suggestions, but I never want to make anyone feel obligated for my sake. We continue on with checking verses. I am not even disturbed. Somehow I know that God will take care of it.

About a day later, as the Word itself again grips Valerio deeply in his own language, he confesses, "I've been thinking about what you asked me. I've decided that if God wants me to teach my people, He will help me. You tell those who want to study to come on."[2] Thank you, Lord. I lack the nerve to tell Valerio that we had already told them to come when we left and that we won't be seeing them again.

The next Sunday in Valerio's morning service, he announces to the people of his own village that during his vacation months he will be teaching God's Word to those who want to study. He never even mentions us in connection with it. This is just what we want because we have prayed that if this is really of the Lord, Valerio will take it as coming from the Lord, and through his own conviction.

Before we leave, he is already telling us his plans. One day he says, "See that house over there? I think I'll fix that up for the students to sleep in. The house where you are staying, I think I'll put flooring all the way across and walls around, and that will be where we will study the Word." With hearts full of praise, we leave Valerio's village, knowing that God has accomplished this important step toward the Amuesha Bible School. *Thank you, Lord.*

Arriving back at Yarina Center, we work hard to get the Scriptures all ready and printed in a form that will be suitable for study. Soon the books are finished and sent out to Valerio in time for him to start his Bible School the first of January.

However, at Pedro's village, Satan begins his work. Pedro has planned to gather the students from the various areas and get them down to Valerio's place in time for the Bible School. In the meantime, Pedro, it seems, might have to go to Lima for an eye operation and not be able to make the trip to Valerio's. We pray and wait for the outcome. What a happy day it is when Pedro lets us know he has delivered the students to Valerio's and that Valerio is starting his school the next day, January 2.

We later ask Pedro why he didn't go into Lima for the eye operation. He says, "I just thought, and I said, 'If I go into Lima, these young fellows who have never seen Valerio's place will never get there.'" We rejoice again to see the Lord working through Pedro and Valerio to accomplish His plans.

Satan's next attack is upon Valerio himself. Valerio will later tell us about it upon his arrival at Yarina after completing his first summer of teaching Bible School. He relates to us how just a week or so before it was time for the students to arrive, Valerio's only little girl was bitten by a snake and died the same day. He could not understand why this sad thing had come upon him. He and his wife were so sad. He said, "We just wanted to go away someplace where we could bear our sadness. We planned to come to Yarina."

"Just at that time," he proceeds, "the new Scripture books arrive. I open the first book. The first verse I see is Romans 8:28: 'All things that come upon us, we know our Father makes them fitting for us, for those who love him, for those who are chosen to fulfill what he plans.'"

"Then," Valerio continues, "I knew that I was chosen of God to fulfill what

He wanted. I knew that God loved me, that it was even because of His love for me that this came upon me. Then I read there I Peter 4:12-13 (another of the selected verses), 'Do not, my loved one, be startled or afraid if severe testings come upon you, because they come upon you to test you . . . always be happy.'"

"Then just at that time," Valerio adds, "Brother Pedro arrived with the students. Then I knew God wanted me to stay right there and teach the young men and not go anywhere. Even in my sadness, I was extremely happy."

What a victory! Not only is Satan defeated in this final attack to stop the school, but we feel that through this, Valerio is further prepared for the work ahead of him. The very verses he is teaching have experientially become reality to him.

I have the joy of visiting Valerio's Bible School once while it is in session. As I sit in and hear Valerio teaching so beautifully the Amuesha Scriptures, and see the young fellows sitting on the edge of their seats drinking it all in, I can hardly believe it is happening. There are the two sons of the shaman from Pedro's area. There is Tomas, who said he really wanted to study if it was in his language, just beaming as he listens and takes part in the discussions. After the class he keeps telling me over and over, "Our Father's Word is so good, so very good in our language. We are so happy." "Delight yourself in the Lord" is already real to them. There is no doubt from their enthusiasm, questions, answers, and discussions that they are assimilating what they are studying. Valerio continually reminds his students as he teaches, "We must tell these words to our people as we go back." For practical experience, he has his students share the new Word with the people right there in his own village and nearby areas.

All those who have studied leave with the promise that they will not only return next year, but bring others with them. I receive a letter from one of the students after his arrival back home. He writes, ". . . Now I am very happy that I know God. Already I have been preaching the Word, as our Father tells us. If we know Him, we will preach His Word, thus will we cause to serve Him the good words which we have heard. My people are very happy that I preach to them. Very well they listen. My mother also, she is very happy. I always pray for you."

The students go back to their various home areas and carry with them the verse booklets on *Salvation* and the *Christian Life*. They read and share these verses first with their parents and family, then with the people of their villages. How many parents, especially mothers, have told me, "When my son came back and started reading to me all those verses from our Father's Word, the more he read, the more I believed that these were really our Father's Words to all of us and I believed too." These stories are repeated in all the villages to where the students return and start preaching the Word, and the number of believers grows. What a great advantage it is to have the students studying in their own territory, language, and cultural setting. A "people movement" has already begun.[3] Thank you, Lord.

In subsequent years as Valerio continues to teach during each vacation period, his desire to have the bilingual schoolteachers also study at the Bible School is accomplished as almost all the Amuesha teachers take time off to study God's Word. And they too return to their various villages where they teach, often becoming the Christian leaders of their villages and starting regular services for their people.

Our seventh year with the Amuesha people has certainly been a jubilee year. Thank you, Lord.

". . . You will be my witnesses . . . to the ends of the earth."
— Jesus, (Acts 1:8 NIV)

"I myself am convinced, my brothers, that you yourselves are . . . complete in knowledge and competent to instruct one another."
— the Apostle Paul, (Romans 15:14 NIV)

(Thank you, Lord, for "enlarging our habitation" by bringing to pass the Amuesha Bible School through which your Word is spreading out into all the areas where Amuesha people live. Thank you, for the many who are already believing.)

# 42

## Go Tell It
## on the Mountain

What will the first Bible School students be doing this year as we go out?

"What shall I tell those who want to study in the Bible School this year?" I ask Valerio as we make our first stop at his village while traveling out to Amueshaland to visit all the schools again.

"Tell them all to come. I will teach them." Valerio is overjoyed with his new service to the Lord, teaching young believers God's Word in their own language. He even has written personal letters to every student who attended the first Bible School, which he gives to us to deliver on our school travels. We leave Valerio extra copies of the newly printed *Life of Christ* books for his distribution.

Omer Bondurant is our pilot this time out. As we fly on upriver to begin our school travels, we decide to eat the lunch that Cal and "Corny" Hibbard (our prayer partners) have made for us before we land. Later, we'll be too busy talking to eat.

After a short visit at Stingray village we go on downriver to Guillermo's school in Sheringamaso (Rubber village). At an evening meeting there, Guillermo has one of his older students, Jorge, along with other students, repeat from memory, what they have learned from the *Salvation* verses. Jorge is one of those who studied at the Amuesha Bible School. What a joy for us to see these verses being shared with all the people of the village. Guillermo tells us that another one of the Bible School students, Lorquin, has been helping him with preaching, and also holds a children's class for teaching them God's Word. *Thank you, Lord.* Both Jorge and Lorquin are happy to receive their personal letters from their beloved Bible teacher, Valerio.

We don't know it at the time, but many people in Sheringamaso will come to believe. Guillermo will start a Saturday class for thirty-five adults who want to learn to read so that they may be able to read God's Word in their language.

We proceed to Cesar's school on the Omaiz River. As the kids are helping us carry our bag up the riverbank, one of them says to us: "The pastor's house burned." I'm thinking, who is she calling "the pastor"? We haven't been in the village long when we realize Domingo S., the young fellow who went to the Bible School, is considered to be the pastor here. The people tell us he has already been hosting meetings every night until midnight — with the villagers holding their little, flickering kerosene lights — teaching them God's Word he learned at Bible School. *Thank you Lord.*

This very night there is a meeting, and we are amazed and thrilled beyond words as Domingo starts preaching. We have never heard anything like it — such a complete understanding of all the verses and passages he has studied and the ability to get it across. He speaks on John 14:1-7, one of the passages in the *Christian Life* series, explaining, enhancing, bringing in other verses and passages where they are pertinent with their references, and quoting parts by memory. How much he has learned in such a short time with Valerio in the Bible School. *Thank you, Lord.*

In addition to Valerio's excellent teaching, we must accredit much of Domingo's skill to the Holy Spirit's power in enabling him to teach even beyond his abilities. Domingo says that ever since he started preaching, people have come from all around to hear him. It reminds us of John the Baptist's preaching. Domingo not only preaches remission of sins, but the true repentance that goes with it.

Those who are believing can't seem to get enough of Domingo's preaching. Almost any story from the *Life of Christ* book we mention, they respond, "Yes, we know about that." It is so different from past years. Now they want to talk solely about the things of the Lord and following him. Thank you, Lord for fulfilling your promise, "All thy children shall be taught of the Lord."

Domingo's mother is one of the firm believers. She is always sitting nearby, listening to everything her son says and rejoicing. Another of Domingo's converts is his old grandfather, who used to tell us he believed in "our father, the sun." He is the oldest person we know among the Amueshas, and he has become a believer! Thank you, Lord.

At the Sunday meeting Domingo uses the new *Life of Christ* book, reading the passage about Jesus feeding the five thousand. The villagers who bought the book bring their copies and follow along as Domingo reads, using it as their first Bible.

On Monday night, Domingo uses Galatians 5:16-24 from the selected passages of the *Christian Life* series — the works of the flesh and the works of the Spirit — as the basis for his talk. He speaks from seven to nine on just that passage. The night meetings are good because all the babies and small children are asleep and there is no crying, so even the mothers can concentrate. Several of the villagers want to be baptized to acknowledge their new faith, and Domingo discusses their request with us.

Our next stop is upriver at Luis' new school. We are pleased to see that a larger school has been built. Luis has taken a fourteen-year-old girl as his wife. Their house and the school are the only buildings in the recently cleared area of jungle. Luis' students are progressing nicely. "Have you 'grabbed' your lesson well?" we hear him ask in the classroom.

Every other Sunday, Luis travels to hear Domingo preach and to learn more of the Word. He has been studying the verses from the *Salvation* and *Christian Life* booklets all on his own. Luis must be using his books a lot as they look so worn. Several of the villagers here buy the *Life of Christ* books. One young fellow is also interested in attending the next session of Valerio's Bible School.

One of the older schoolgirls has her "coming out" (puberty) party while we are in Luis' village. Before we leave, a big discussion arises over whether the "grown-up" girl should continue to go to school. Her mother is quite concerned since she has heard that some people don't want her daughter in school because she might "mess up" the bench with her blood. They all finally decide that it is all right. In many of the villages they are now saying that the grown-up girls should not remain so long in seclusion and miss so much time from school. Tradition is giving way to "civilization."

Luis' village is the first Amuesha village to have a health promoter. His name is Pablo. Last year, this young man asked if he could travel to our Yarina Center so he could learn to give shots and provide other medical assistance. Since these people are so far away from any trained, medical personnel, it's good to see Pablo going around with his little bag of medicines which we are helping finance.

Getting back downriver to the airstrip at Iscozacin is not easy after so much rain has fallen, but Domingo, Cesar, and Pablo help us find canoes headed in that direction. When the big, two-motor Faucett plane arrives, the pilot gives us a note from Bernie May, our pilot at San Ramon who is waiting with supplies. Bernie wants us to hop on the Faucett plane to meet him there. In no time, we are over the mountains and landing in San Ramon greeting Bernie.

We are both surprised and pleased to learn there is now a lovely, new Turista Hotel right near the airfield. Even Bernie, wanting to check out the new Turista, decides it is too late for him to head back to Yarina before the 6:00 p.m. deadline. We get our supplies and mail from Bernie's plane, and all of us go over to the Turista for a delicious meal — from "rags to riches" again in less than an hour. Thank you, Lord.

Mary Ruth and I have a beautiful room. The color scheme of beige walls and lovely matching curtains delight our eyes. We even have a private bathroom with hot water! The lounges and dining room are so inviting. We rest up for another day and buy additional supplies before looking for a vehicle that will take us to the end of the driveable road going to Singing Water village.

We find the man with his little, old truck who agrees to take us to the end of the road. That point is now past Villa Rica, as the road for vehicles is gradually penetrating further into the interior. After about five hours we reach the end of the driveable road and stop at a little makeshift café. We have learned that you don't ask for a menu in places like this. Instead, you ask for *"lo que hay"* (whatever there is) to eat. Even a bowl of soup is a luxury.

Since we don't know if we can reach Singing Water from here before dark, we ask the owner if there is someone who could accompany us on foot to our destination. Mary Ruth and I, along with our guide, leave after arranging for mules to bring our cargo later. We arrive in Singing Water before dark and can hardly believe it — we traveled all the way from San Ramon to Singing Water in one day!

What a delight to see Pedro, Petita, my little namesake Marrta, and their young son Juanacho. My little *"shall"* (namesake) is a doll. Juanacho, now a three-year-old boy, is already speaking in the Amuesha language better then we are. They haven't cut his hair yet, but were waiting for us to share with them this special tradition of the first haircut for their first son.

Since Pedro's house is close to our new dwelling that still isn't finished, we get blankets from the things we have stored in Pedro's house and head for our little makeshift house from last year.

We are camping out with an open fire when the mules arrive with more of our supplies. The people come by to greet us, including the chief. The chief tells us he too has named his new baby girl Marrta. I seem to be acquiring more namesakes.

We would like to get moved into our new house but the flooring is not down. In fact, the one who was contracted to build the house has not even cut the palm-bark flooring. Dear Pedro always comes to the rescue when it regards helping people. He says that we can use the boards his stepfather sawed for him by hand while he was here. Sawed boards are precious since there are no sawmills in the area.

All of us gather for "church" at Pedro's house. He now has benches made that he moves from school to church and back as needed. We introduce the new *Life of Christ* books while the people gather. All of them sell quickly. We are happy to see the readers buying books. Pedro plans to go through the entire life of Christ in the meetings. He begins teaching from the first of the book about the announcement to Mary (Luke 1:26). The villagers follow along with him in their own books.

Although there seems to be evidences of increased interest in the Gospel on the whole, the people just have not been turning to the Lord here as at other places. As Pedro is preaching, and several times is almost in tears, I am overcome by thoughts of his faithful preaching, teaching, and living, and yet not a real turning to the Lord resulting from it. Overwhelmed with sadness for him and his people, I can't hold back my tears either. Oh, that there would be a real work of the Spirit of the Lord, turning the people in repentance to Himself like we are beginning to see in Cesar's village.

On Monday morning, many of the villagers appear to finish the work on our house. The chief lays out all the work that needs to be done and then everyone takes off to the jungle to get the materials. By nightfall we have palm-bark walls around the kitchen and a new end roof. Since I like to drive nails, I build a counter across one side of the kitchen along with shelves and a cupboard for our dishes with some of Pedro's prize boards. Mary Ruth arranges all the kitchen utensils.

Each successive morning another fellow shows up, telling us the chief is sending him for whatever needs to be done. One builds us a little cookhouse so we can have an outside fire for boiling water and roasting coffee. We think it is cool the way the chief organizes the work. And we are happy that we can really get down to work on translation again.

Mary Ruth continues with her rechecks of Mark since we now have received the *Handbook of Mark* from the American Bible Society to refer to. Having finished all the exegetical studies for the Gospel and Epistles of John at Yarina, where we have a library for assistance, I am now starting to write a preliminary rough draft translation of these books. This will serve as a starter when I later work with Pedro. We will then talk about it in detail and Pedro will provide the final rendering. Also, I am studying the transcription from the tape of the diviner's speech, which is a discourse style that should help with this translation.

On the two Sundays Pedro has to be away, the two sons of the shaman who went to Valerio's Bible School take over the Sunday meeting. The older one they are now calling Bernardo. Although he is young and a bit shy, he reads the stories from the *Life of Christ*. After he reads through a story a little hesitatingly at times, his younger brother, Miguel, immediately reads it through again in a voice that is loud and clear and filled with expression. The people are amazed at how much better they understand the stories with the good reader. However, Bernardo is a changed person since he went to Bible School. Before, he was a heavy drinker. Now I've not seen him drunk. Both he and his brother are so happy to receive the letters from their Bible teacher, Valerio. They want to attend again this year and take another younger brother, Mariano, with them. Maybe they will win over their father too — old Selano, the shaman.

The chief, Pedro, and Pedro's stepfather all decide to go in to the Ministry of Justice in Lima to try to get an order for removing outside squatters off their land. While the Amueshas have titles to the land, squatters from another language group coming down from the higher Andes Mountains have just taken over some of the areas where the Amueshas have planted coffee. Although they have shown the squatters their title documents, these invaders ignore them. So a delegation of villagers journeys to Lima, stays in our Guest House there, and presents itself in tunics and crowns to the Minister of Justice.

Pedro calls us on our Lima House radio to talk to us in his village. All the people come to hear their *"pamo'ts"* (relatives) talk from Lima. Pedro tells us they prayed before they went in to meet the Minister. He says, "When we got to see the Minister, I said to him, *'Señor Ministro* (Mr. Minister), those people who are taking over our land say these title documents we have from your office are not worth anything.'"

The Minister, wanting to defend his office replies, "We will see about that." I'm sure the Lord guided Pedro to state the problem in the way he did to cause the Minister to feel obligated to defend his office.

While Pedro is gone to Lima, we decide to go over the mountain to Cacaso to make our last school visit there. Teacher Enrique needs a lot of help. He is the least qualified of all the teachers, but he is following the Lord. From selected passages, Enrique shares the Ten Commandments with his people during our visit.

On the way back over the mountain, I grab some pretty jungle plants along the way. I find a short, hollow log, plant my jungle treasures in it and place it at our kitchen window. I say to Mary Ruth, "The people will laugh at this." To them, these beautiful vining plants are like weeds. Sure enough, when the chief sees it, he laughs and laughs, but with pleasure, I think. Pedro admires them as I do and educates me about the names of the plants. Later, I notice over in the school they have started a planter in their classroom.

We have just returned from our trip over the mountain when Pedro arrives back from his trip to Lima with mail for us. Coming along with Pedro is Tomas, the Bible School student. Pedro is anxious to inform us about his Lima trip and Tomas is just bursting to relay his experiences since he has been home.

After Pedro and the others leave, Tomas remains to talk with us privately. He can't hold back all his joy he has in learning more about the true God and in knowing and serving the Lord Jesus since then. As with Domingo, we are amazed by what he has learned, but most of all, we marvel at the reality of it in his own life. Tomas goes on and on about the wonderful ways of Christ. He's the same beaming, young fellow who kept saying to me, "Our Father's Word is so good" on my short visit to the Bible School. It is still possessing him.

Tomas informs us he has been preaching the Word in his own little village and has also been visiting teacher Vicente's area to share the Word there. He has just returned from another mountain where he has been preaching. He explains how he wants to go around to all the little villages, even to individual homes scattered throughout these mountains, and share the Word. I can hardly believe what I am hearing! We have prayed much for Amueshas to carry the Word to these remote places. Because the people are so scattered, they could never all come together, even just on weekends, to hear the Word. Here young Tomas, beaming with joy in the Lord, is telling us that's what he wants to do.[1]

He says, "The only thing I need is for someone to go with me." Amueshas never travel alone on long trips. But who else would ever want to do this?

We assure Tomas we will surely pray about it. I can still hear him saying, "I love my people. I want them to be saved. We need to tell them God's Word.

We are strengthened by his Spirit to do this."

The next day Tomas comes back to say good-bye. He has another young fellow with him. "He believes," Tomas says, and with that short introduction the other fellow launches into his story:

"When Tomas came from the Bible School and started sharing with us all the Word of God, it arrived on me in my heart that these were true words and I believed. From that time on, I have believed and I want to live anew, good for the Lord. I want to study in the Bible School also, and I want to go with brother Tomas to tell the good words to all our people."

Am I hearing this correctly? What just yesterday seemed like an impossibility is already being taken care of by the Lord, who is supplying a partner for Tomas. Both of the young men are not yet married and free to travel.

Before Tomas and his friend leave, Enrique and several others from Cacaso arrive. Tomas suggests we have an evening meeting. He takes over, and without any timidity, boldly speaks the Word from heartfelt joy. Taking a selected verse from Isaiah 53:5, he preaches about Christ suffering, bearing our sins. He, like Domingo, does not let up on repentance and forsaking sin, yet makes it clear it was only through Christ's payment for our sins that we are saved. Tomas and Pedro are both so full of the Spirit they can hardly contain themselves.

"And all thy children shall be taught of the Lord."
(Isaiah 54:13 KJV)

"... I will pour out my Spirit ... and your sons and your daughters shall prophesy ..."
– the Prophet Joel, (Acts 2:17 KJV)

(Thank you, Lord for fulfilling your promises to the Amueshas.)

# 43

# The Entrance of Your Word Gives Light

"God is light." What does that mean?

I start working with Pedro in the afternoons on translating I John. He wants to help translate, but it is hard for him, teaching all morning and then translating until six in the evening. We hardly get started on chapter one when in verse five we run into "God is light; in him there is no darkness at all . . ." What does light really mean in this instance?

I have already completed my preparation in exegetical studies on I John at Yarina. The commentaries agree that "light" in this sense is a symbol of all the ethically good qualities of God: goodness, holiness, purity, righteousness, love. Some commentators also speak of light as a metaphor and say that the ground of comparison is that light and God both illuminate.

Very few metaphors and similes are used in the Amuesha language. The ones that are used most often do not correspond to the ones in Scripture. Thus, if "light" is translated literally in this case, it would be misrepresenting the true or intended meaning of the ethically good qualities of God. Also if translated literally, it could be interpreted by the Amueshas to mean that the sun truly is God, which they have always believed.

As Pedro and I discuss the meaning of the metaphor, we come up with the following: "Everything that God is or does is all good. Thus, He is like light, which we consider to be very good." In this way, the intended meaning is made explicit[1] and the figure of speech, "light," is maintained. "Darkness" is then treated as the opposite of "light."

We, as translators, are greatly aided in our translation efforts by specially prepared books covering each book of the New Testament, created by the Greek scholars of the Translation Department of the Summer Institute of Linguistics. The verse by verse *Exegetical Summaries* give us the meaning of the original Greek words and also a compilation of the interpretations made by various commentaries. This saves us a lot of time that each one of us would have to spend looking up all this exegetical information on our own.

We continue working on the translation of I John. Verse 1:7 becomes, "If we show forth all good things in our living like our Father God does, it is like we are walking in the light with him . . ." Verse 2:2 becomes "He is given in order to pay for us our sins . . ." Verse 2:6 becomes "If someone says, 'I am united together with God,' then that one should show forth all good things in his living like God's Son used to do." Pedro drinks in all he is learning from the translation.

One particular Sunday, I notice a stranger at the Sunday morning meeting in Singing Water who is taking a great interest in hearing God's Word. The people call him **"Gasparepe'n."** They put the "mountain" suffix *–epe'n* onto his name Gaspar because he is "tall like a mountain." Thus, "Casper Mountain" (as we freely translate his name for English speaking friends) comes into the picture. I slowly realize that he was one of the people unconscious with a very high fever following the measles outbreak. I gave him a shot of penicillin up on the mountain some time ago. We are later to find out that after we had returned to Yarina, Casper Mountain's

wife and two of his children came down with measles and died at that time. Just he and one of his three girls survived.

One day, Casper Mountain shares with us about a hernia he has that keeps him from being able to work. He asks if we can take him to Yarina for an operation. Mary Ruth and I decide we should help him. "While you can't work, why don't you go to school with your little girl and learn to read," Mary Ruth suggests. He thinks this is a good idea and enrolls in the bilingual school, studying right along with his daughter. He learns much more quickly than she does. In two weeks, he has already learned all the sounds of the Amuesha syllables. He is then allowed to take the next higher level reading books home with him to practice reading for greater fluency. *Could Casper Mountain possibly be the full-time translation helper we are looking for?*

Pedro and I finish the translation of I John. It is a real pleasure to hear Pedro adding new points in his preaching that he has learned from the recent translation. He has been beautifully bringing out the idea that we love other people and want them to be saved because of our love for God. I'm sure the greatest delight for a Bible translator is to see the newly translated Word being accepted and applied in the hearts of those early believers. Translation is a great challenge, but at the same time it is fascinating, fulfilling, and rewarding. It is something I truly love doing.

Mary Ruth is now working with Pedro on I Thessalonians. Since Casper Mountain is taking such an interest in the Word of God, which he is now hearing, I ask him if he would like to help me in checking the recent translation of I John. He readily agrees. As we read it together, I ask him questions about what we have read to see if he is grasping the correct interpretation. Casper has never done any paperwork like this before but does a fine job. He adds in little words and suffixes here and there that enhance specific meanings. On the whole, he is understanding the message quite easily. Where he doesn't understand, we talk about the intended meaning and revise the translation accordingly. I'm happy for him to be hearing this much more of God's Word because he is definitely interested. He is already starting to read the Genesis passages I translated with Pedro earlier.

Pedro shares with me the concern of some of his students and others who are asking him, "If we want to believe, how do we receive Christ?" He shows me a prayer he wrote up all on his own for helping them accept Jesus Christ as their Savior: "I know that I have done bad things and I want you to forgive me. I know that you died to pay for my sins. I want to receive you into my heart and follow your Word."

Our policy of just staying in the background and allowing the believers to develop as teachers and preachers in their own way is really paying off. Whatever tips we give Pedro for his preaching is done privately so that whenever he preaches, the people will think he has always known these things. It also instills greater confidence in their own indigenous leaders, and that's the way it should be.[2]

There aren't many native songs still known by the Amueshas. However, we continue to search for them and find one that is appealing. I'm thinking I would like to use actual words from Scripture as lyrics to this one. I look through our selected verses translated some time ago for the Bible School. Isaiah 41:10 seems to fit, "Do not fear, for I am with you. Do not be dismayed, for I am your God. I will strengthen you and help you."

Then I realize that in Amuesha culture, this is a tune just for women to sing. Even so, the words from Isaiah are very fitting for the women who experience many difficult things in their lives. Why not have a special song of encouragement for the female believers? I sing the new song for some of them, and they are delighted. When we women sing it at one of our meetings, Pedro hears it for the first time and thinks it is wonderful.

"We men should be allowed to sing this song also," he says, and asks me what I think.

"Well, that's for you men to decide," I reply.

"Yes, we men want to sing this good song of God's care for us."

That settles the question. It becomes No. 31 in our Amuesha songbook. Pedro also keeps writing new songs and our songbook continues to grow.

We still haven't seen the real turning to the Lord here that we want to see, but it seems the Lord is preparing people's hearts. One Sunday after the meeting, Pedro tells us that Kosepa (the village harlot) and Losaria both came after we had left and said they wanted to receive Christ. He prayed with them. When Kosepa first learned that we had come to write God's Word in their Amuesha language, she decided she needed to attend school so she could learn to read. Later, she could read for herself what we wrote and make her own decision as to whether it is "the true our Father's Word." As a young adult, Kosepa enrolled in the school and has already learned to read well. She has been coming regularly to the Sunday meetings and is reading her own copy of the *Life of Christ* book. Since Pedro is using this book in his Sunday meetings, Kosepa comes prepared, having already studied the new lesson. She likes to enlighten us with all she has read before the service starts.

Late one afternoon, Pedro comes to see us and is very distressed. "They have 'grabbed' Tomas." Our hearts sink as we think somebody has killed him. Then we get it straight; military officers have taken Tomas in for the army. Tomas lives closer to the outside world. Remembering that Tomas has just been planning to reach the Amueshas in more remote areas with God's Word, we grieve with Pedro. We feel it is a real attack of Satan to keep the Word from going out. We, along with Pedro, pray Tomas will be released. Can you believe it? The following Saturday we look and see Tomas coming with his mother. They are overjoyed. They came all the way from their distant home just to let us know he was released. *Thank you, Lord.* By this time, both his father and mother have become believers. They are happy he can stay with them to teach them more of the Word.

We have heard that the people in Metraro and Huocas want to have bilingual schools. Mary Ruth and I are reluctant to stop our translation work to go and make arrangements for this, but we have already seen the great value of having readers ready for the Word. We have never been to these places before, but Pedro and some of the boys want to escort us. Following a long trek through the rainforest, we arrive in another top-of-the-mountain village, Metraro. After the people hear us speaking in Amuesha, they take us right in. They can't believe we are talking their language. No outsider has ever done that.

The head man has a very large house with a room for each one of his four wives. He gives us a room and we hope for the best.

After a meal with the villagers, Pedro gets out his songbook and Scripture books and tells them that we would like to sing for them. Around the open fire we sing, and he begins telling them about Jesus who came to earth, lived, died for our sins, rose again — the whole story. For people who have never heard anything like this, he does a good job. They seem to understand but are astounded at all they are hearing. We are pleased to see how concerned Pedro is for his own people, even though he has never seen the people of this village before. How easily he can start witnessing to them. Thank you, Lord.

With the school business taken care of in Metraro, we head for our next destination — Huocas. From Villa Rica we start out in a truck cab on a new, narrow, dirt road along the edge of a mountain. The sun sets as we continue our journey. As I look out from my cab seat next to the door, I see nothing but darkness below. We climb higher and higher into the mountains and finally come to a new house at the end of the road. It is the house of the administrator for a rich immigrant from eastern Europe, who has acquired hundreds of acres of land here and has started a coffee plantation. He is the one who has created the road in and is currently in Europe. The administrator and his wife are very friendly and give us lodging for the night.

The next morning, they show us the trail leading to where the Amueshas live. We take off on this trail going down the mountain. After an hour or so, we come to a house with some people. We greet them in Amuesha and they are surprised and pleased to hear us speaking their language. They take us right in.

We spend the day here while our hosts go out all over the mountain informing people we have arrived and inviting them to come. They also tell us there are more Amueshas further back in the mountains. By nightfall they have all gathered, and we start to talk about a school. You never heard so much talking — all of them at the same time.

"We heard you were coming; we were just waiting for you to come," the spokesman for the group informs us. One fellow keeps saying, "I told them that we'd wait for you to come, and then we'll do whatever you say to have a school."

After much loud discussion, they decide on the best spot for the school, how they will all work together to build it, and who will be the boss.

With all the school business taken care of, Pedro says to the people, "Now we want to sing for you." They all gather around to listen.

"You go ahead; we want to hear what you have to tell us," the headman invites us.

Pedro presents the best summary of the entire story of Jesus and salvation, and he does it in such a beautiful way for his people who have never heard the

Gospel. The more we see him do this so easily with love for his own people, each new group we meet, the more we realize he is a chosen one of God.

Back home in Singing Water, we are anxious to return to our translation work as soon as we can. We are barely started when a flu epidemic begins again. Casper Mountain's little girl is at first sitting around our house, then lying around, which is strange for a young child. When I take her temperature it is 104 degrees. Manual, a little boy staying over at Pedro's, also has a fever of 104. I start giving penicillin shots. Kosepa's little newborn is sick, so she leaves her house (as is common in the culture) and goes way up on the mountain to her mother's where I must go to give the shots. Several others are brought to our house with the same symptoms that day.

The next day, more and more sick people come. The floor of our house is full of mothers with their children, all with high fevers. I administer all the shots since Pedro is teaching school in the mornings. I hear the mothers saying, "I believe in it now," meaning they trust our shots more than the shaman's treatment. To have them coming to us instead of going to the shaman is a good sign, but it is taking all our time. *Is this Satan's way of keeping us from the translation?* We are thankful that none of the people die in this epidemic.

Finally we get back to Bible translation and are making progress. Mary Ruth finishes her translation of I and II Thessalonians with Pedro. She checks that translation with Casper Mountain while I start with Pedro on the first ever translation of the Gospel of John. I am choosing to start this Gospel just after the Epistle of I John since they both have some of the same expressions. Here again I am dealing with the metaphors of "light" and "darkness" common to John's writing, and also the "Word" as referring to Christ. These need to be made explicit in Amuesha for people who haven't used such metaphors and titles. Thus a "dynamic equivalent" translation is being done.

Sometimes such information — making the implicit explicit — can be put into a title of the section. For example, for the title of the first section in Amuesha we say, "The One who is called God's Word is the same one who came to earth, called Jesus Christ." John 1:29, where the section starts naming Jesus as the "Lamb of God," we give the title: "Jesus, who is symbolized as the Lamb killed for sins" (as in Old Testament times). By this time, the Amueshas have learned what a lamb looks like and its characteristics from the lamb story

I translated, along with seeing pictures of a lamb and hearing the Spanish name for it. (Amueshas do not have sheep so have no word for lamb.)

John 1:34, where Jesus is called the "Son of God" becomes a problem. The Amuesha people say, "How could God have a son when He does not have a wife?"

Then we come to John 3:16, which is expressed in Amuesha this way: "God very much loves all of us people in the world. That's why He gave us His only Son. Then whoever believes in Him will not be lost/perish. They will live completely forever." We are able to finish the first draft of five chapters of John before we must go back to Yarina. Thank you, Lord.

Pedro's little, three-year-old boy, Juanacho, likes to visit us to look at the books or play with the plastic toy animals we have. Sometimes after playing with the animals for a while, he will say to me, "Let's just kill them and eat them." He is very sharp and surprises me when, looking at the picture of the Crucifixion in the *Life of Christ* book, he says to the other children around, "This is when they killed Jesus and He died for our sins." Pedro has taught his children well.

The rainy season has begun. It has been raining almost every day for some time now. We live near the creek and hear it rushing over the rocks. Day by day it is rising and sounding louder.

Pedro wants us to go up on the mountain to see his planted fields before we head back to Yarina. He takes such pride in his plants. We take off with him and Petita up the mountain. They have lots of mature corn. Their coffee is bearing this year for the first time since being planted and is covered with little, green berries. Pedro is building a small house there from which to work his coffee. We just reach the house when it starts to pour rain and we get under the green leaves already on the roof of the house. Petita roasts us corn while we wait for the rain to stop. As we go back down the steep, slippery mountain, I start sliding. I am covered with mud by the time we reach the village, but for Pedro's sake it was worth it.

Many young men, including Julio, are asking if they can go to Valerio's Bible School this year. Those who studied last year would like to attend again, however we are asking them to instead consider becoming teachers for the new schools being started. Tomas has said he would like to go to Huocas since this is the mountainous area where he would also like to teach God's Word. Bernardo wanted to go to Azules, where we hope to open a school soon, but his shaman father who doesn't yet believe is not permitting him to do so. Domingo S. will be teaching along with Cesar at his school since the number of students is increasing and two teachers are needed. What a pleasure it is to have the recent Bible School students wanting to go to various areas in their tribal region to share God's Word in their own language. This is truly the most effective form of E-1 evangelism (when a person of certain language and culture testifies to another person of the same language and culture).

We finally get our things packed away for our next visit here and are ready to go. Tomas and his father want to walk with us on the mule trail until it meets the road. Pedro and Petita want to accompany us also. Another young fellow planning to go to the Bible School meets us along the way. Mary Ruth and I carry a change of clothing for the end of the muddy mule trail. Happily, a little bus is there, and we are on our way back to San Ramon to meet the plane. *Thank you, Lord, for another good time with the Amuesha people.*

At Yarina, we need to get our translations of 1 John, and I and II Thessalonians checked by the Translation Committee, and the page dummies typed up and turned in to the print shop. With the number of new believers growing, we want to get each newly translated book printed in provisional form and out to the people as quickly as we can. The new schools require that we also reprint editions of the reading books, writing books, arithmetic books, and the social science books for next year. Then there is always the exegetical work in preparation for future translation work. When we are at the Yarina Center, there is more than enough to keep us busy.

While we have been away, our new house at Yarina has been finished, complete with a large study room for the increasing number of Amuesha teacher-trainees. A class in pedagogy has now been added to the trainees' study schedule in the Teacher Training Course. We, the linguists, are assigned to teach this class within our particular language groups. We are fortunate to soon have a Teacher's Manual composed by one of our co-workers, Martha Jakway, designed especially for bilingual teachers, with simple steps for teaching each of the classes. I am happy to teach this new class because I see the need for more training in pedagogy in the language of the trainees before they go out to teach. Using the large blackboard in our new study room, the trainees now will also be able to practice their teaching skills with supervision. The goal is to create more competent teachers.

Casper Mountain comes to Yarina to schedule the hernia operation for which we promised to help him. We go with him to make an appointment for the operation at the small Albert Schweitzer Hospital near Yarina. While he waits for the appointment date, I ask him if he would like to help me check more of the I John verses. He is happy to work on translation again.

One day we get to I John 5:12, "He who has the Son has life; he who does not have the Son of God does not have life." Since the word "to have" in Amuesha has more of the meaning "to own something," Pedro and I have translated this verse to state, "The one who receives God's Son, also receives that which will cause him to live forever . . ." As we read this verse together, I feel strongly that I should ask Casper Mountain, "Have you received God's Son, Jesus, into your life?"

"No, but I've been thinking lately that this is what I want to do."

We talk briefly about how we receive Christ into our hearts. Casper Mountain begins spontaneous prayer, "Lord Jesus, I know I have done many bad things, but my sister here tells me that is why you died for us, to pay for our sins. I want you to forgive me and come into my heart. I want to follow you as your Word tells us." Thank you, Lord.

Casper Mountain goes for his operation without fear. As he is coming out of the anesthesia, he tells me he is hearing beautiful songs coming from our Father, God.

"I will also make you a light for the Gentiles (nations, people groups), that you may bring my salvation to the ends of the earth."

(Isaiah 49:6 NIV)

(Thank you, Lord, for Casper Mountain's decision to follow you. We feel you are giving us a great helper to translate your Word for his people.)

# 44

# From Apprentice with the Shaman to Apprentice with the Bible Teacher

*What can you do when the engine of the plane starts misfiring as you head for the mountains?*

After a busy session at Yarina, we are off again for Amueshaland. Almost all of the cargo we have on the plane this time consists of Scripture books. The new books we translated just last year (I John and I, II Thessalonians) are now printed up in provisional form and fill the plane, along with reprints of the selected Bible verses, a new, bigger edition of the hymn book, and a newly printed health book that Pedro and I worked on last year.

We stop first at Valerio's school to leave books and then Santiago's school upriver. We are anxious to see how Valerio is doing after another devastating blow to his family. Another of his children died from a scorpion sting about a month ago. He and his wife, Rosa, are in good spirits, trusting God in every way. *Thank you, Lord.*

Just after taking off from the airstrip, we head toward the mountains and the engine begins to misfire. The pilot, Don Weber, quickly turns back and lands. After talking with the mechanics at Yarina on the radio, and cleaning the spark plugs (a lot of lead contamination from bad gas), we take off once more. Don says he wanted to check with the JAARS people at Yarina first since we are heading into the mountains. The motor gives us no more trouble, and we are reminded again of God's care, in allowing this to happen before we get to the mountains and need full power. Thank you, Lord, for competent, careful JAARS pilots.

Don drops us off in San Ramon and it takes Mary Ruth and me all day to reach Vicente's school in Palomar. We arrive there at dusk. We are happy to find that Josefina is back with Vicente after leaving last year because of a shortage of food here.

What a delight it is to see Domingo C. (one of the new students who studied in Valerio's second Bible School) share a portion of Scripture with the people on the next day, Sunday.[1] He reads from the *Life of Christ* book about how people mistreated Christ long ago and caused him to suffer. Domingo C. applies the reading to us when we don't believe in Christ. We are surprised and pleased at how much he has learned and how well he is now sharing it all with the people.

After Domingo finishes speaking, Vicente announces that it is "question time." He invites those listening to stand up and summarize what Domingo has said. One after another rise and speak, giving not only a summary of what Domingo said, but adding their own ideas on the subject. Tomas' father is one of those who gives a good testimony of how he believes in Christ. He says, "When we believe in Christ, we *'parrocmat'* (are one together) with Christ." He uses the word we have been trying out for the phrase "to be in Christ." Since there are no prepositions in Amuesha, his usage helps to assure us that this is the word we want to express that concept.

Several of the older school kids and adults show real evidence of believing. We are very pleased with Domingo's and Vicente's work here. On Wednesday evening, the people gather again and Domingo shares the parable of the sower. The people listen well. Domingo always explains what it means to believe and how we believe. The people need that explanation here since they have not heard much of the Word yet. We can tell that those who are believing are doing so with a good understanding. Thank you, Lord.

During prayer time, the villagers pray out loud about the things they need. Dominga (the sister of teacher Tomas) prays to the Lord, "Take care of my brother, Tomas, way down there in the jungle teaching school and teaching your Word."

Vicente's school is also doing well. He even holds night classes for the adults, three hours in the evening. That's quite a schedule for Vicente. Josefina helps with teaching the female students. The women get their babies to sleep and study peacefully.

Leaving Vicente's school Mary Ruth and I plan to visit the two newest schools downriver, including Tomas' school. His father and mother want to travel with us to visit their son. They don't have enough money to cover their expenses, but we pay their way so they can join us.

We must first get back to Villa Rica to find a truck that will take us to the end of the road downriver. The four of us go into a restaurant in Villa Rica to have something to eat. Tomas' parents are shy. They have never been in a place like this. His father does not know how to pull out a chair from the table to sit down. People always stare at Mary Ruth and me when we are with the Amueshas and speaking their language. We don't mind.

We find a truck going only part of the way, but we pay the driver to take us on to the end of the road. Arriving at dusk, we decide to continue on foot. Tomas' father knows the route through the forest since he has visited his son here before. This is the first time we have traveled by foot at night, but we do have flashlights.

Before long we reach the place Tomas is staying. He is so surprised and happy to see us and his parents. He is also delighted to receive the new Scriptures we are bringing. He wants to sing the new songs every night with us.

The next day, Sunday, the people come together and Tomas does a good job of sharing God's Word with them.[2] He is truly fulfilling his desire to spread God's Word to his *"pamo'ts"* (fellow Amueshas). The more I see the Bible School students conducting services for their people and proclaiming the Word so clearly, the more thankful I am for the Bible School.

Tomas' school here at Huocas is doing well too. The new pedagogy classes at Yarina are helping his teaching. I assist him with some problem areas before Mary Ruth and I decide to go on downriver to the newest school at Azules and then come back this way.

We expect the trip to Azules to be difficult. They tell us it is a day and a half of hard walking. Pedro has told us we should not try it; he remembers the condition of the trail from walking it with the Bible School students. But we feel that we need to go. The new teacher, José, is there and may need our help.

Valentin and Espiritu from here at Huocas say they will accompany us as our guides. We leave with only the bare essentials. Around mountain ledges, down into creek valleys, up the other side, and across landslides we go. About one o'clock in the afternoon we arrive at a house where some Amueshas live. They tell us this is the last house before Azules. We are still a day's walk from our destination. Since we can't make it all the way before dark, we decide to spend the night here.

Two sisters live here with their one husband and sixteen children between them. All the children call both of the sisters *"ach"* (mother), according to their kinship system. Their life here is very simple. Only one other house is near this family. The occupants happen to be two other sisters of the first sisters who live there with their one husband and their children.

We are offered much of their slightly fermented drink, *co'nes*, which is the polite thing to do. We drink only enough to be appreciative since we realize the drink is made with contaminated water and other contaminants from the masticated portions it contains to start the fermentation.

We go down to the stream to bathe and find an ideal spot with clear, cold water. Looking up and down the stream, we see nothing but big, close mountains — beautiful scenery. "For you shall go forth with joy and be led forth with peace; the mountains and the hills shall break forth before you into singing, and all the trees of the field (jungle) shall clap their hands." Isaiah 55:12

We sing with the people and share God's Word. They listen well, but it is all so new to them, I doubt they really comprehend much. How will people living off by themselves like this so far away they cannot go to where the teachers and preachers are, ever hear enough of the Word to really understand? I pray that Tomas will reach this distant area.

The next day looks rainy, but we decide to go ahead. Soon the rain does come, making the rocks along the stream very slippery, but we keep walking.

We are following the stream because Pedro told us it was easier than trying to cross the high mountain ranges. This high up in the headwaters of the river, large boulders break up the swiftly rushing water. The hardest thing to do is walk along the narrow, rock ledges and not slip off into the rushing water below. "He gives me the surefootedness of a mountain goat upon the crags. He leads me safely along the tops of the cliffs." Psalm 18:33 (Living Bible)

Many times we have to cross the river to find a ledge on the other side in order to continue our journey. In crossing, all four of us hold hands so we will not be swept away with the force of the water. On the other side, we have to find roots or bushes to pull ourselves up out of the swift water and onto a ledge. We start counting the crossings, but after twenty-five we stop counting! Our two guides help us greatly. We couldn't make this trip without them.

Finally we leave the river and start through the jungle, coming unexpectedly upon an abandoned building. As we stand there looking around, a woman appears out of the jungle. She tells us this is the old school building they abandoned when a new one was built.

We go on and find the new teacher, José, who is just recovering from malaria. We surprise him with our sudden arrival. We see that the people have built a nice, new school with benches and tables hewn out of soft balsa logs. José has taken our new pedagogy class at Yarina and is doing a good job of teaching. He is also one of the early believers from teacher Cesar's area. He has been holding regular services for the people.[3] They have already learned all the Amuesha Christian songs. We give José copies of the new Scripture books, from which he reads to the people using I John the Sunday before we leave. Although we don't know it at the time, students from this village of Azules, the remotest of the Amuesha villages, will soon become teachers and leaders.

After finishing our productive visit at José's school, we head back upriver the same way we came down, with guides accompanying us. Getting a good, early start, we are able to make it all the way back to Tomas' school in one day. We are completely exhausted! We take three days to rest and finish up with Tomas. He has been reading his new copy of I John and must read parts of it aloud to me that he thinks are especially good (as if I hadn't translated it). These are the joys of a Bible translator that make the sore feet and toes more than worth it! Thank you, Lord.

On our little nine-kilo radio we talk with Luke Tanner, the radio operator at Yarina, and tell him about all our foot travels.

"How are your shoes holding out?" he asks.

"Not so good," I answer truthfully. "I've already worn out one pair on this trip."

Our next destination is the Cacaso school, which is just over another mountain on the left — luckily I brought another pair of shoes. It's another rainy morning, but we decide to press on. Three fellows decide to go with us. We are barely on the trail when we meet up with two others from Cacaso who are returning there. This is good fortune for us since our three leaders are not too sure of the trail the entire way.

Along the route on the very top ridge of the mountain, they see where a *ma'ñor* (large jaguar) has pawed the ground and left his tracks. We have never thought seriously about jaguars before, but there are some that run the mountain ridges, or so they tell us. We just hope this one is running the other way.

Cacaso is the place Pedro's sisters live. As soon as they hear we have arrived, Margarita comes with all kinds of food for us. She and her sister are true believers and want us to sing with them this very night. Their brother, Pedro, has already lead them to believe.

I start working with teacher Enrique right away. He needs more help than any of the other teachers. In fact, he is discouraging to me at times. He finds it very hard to handle a school. I hope he will learn more from our pedagogy classes. Yet he does well in sharing the Word with the people.[4] Many people come to visit us and be treated medically while we are here in Cacaso.

Now we face our last mountain — the one between here and Singing Water — with another six hours of hard walking. After living out of our duffel bag for four weeks, are we ever glad to get back to our side of this mountain to our own home, even if there are cobwebs we need to clean out.

Petita meets us with some hot food. Casper Mountain comes as soon as he hears we have returned. Rejoicing in his new-found faith in Christ, renewed in strength after the operation, and glad to see us, he can hardly contain himself. Juana, wife of Domingo V. (a marriage of the first two graduates from Pedro's school), comes with some cooked manioc root. Since the student body here has increased so much, Domingo V. is now named by the Ministry of Education as a second teacher, joining Pedro.

We spend all day cleaning and repairing our house. Petita and other women cut the grass around it. Casper Mountain, never having built or seen a table before, makes us two tables, one for dining and one for paperwork. We work with renewed energy, knowing that we are setting up to live here for four months, free now to continue with our translation. Although our school work takes time and energy, we realize its great usefulness in producing new readers for the translated Scriptures who may very well become Christian leaders among their own people.

By the time we have things arranged for work to begin, it's Independence Day in Peru (July 28) again. The schools have two weeks of vacation that usually start with celebrations. Pedro and some of the Bible School fellows suggest we start the celebrations with singing the Christian songs and reading God's Word.[5] The two sons of the shaman, Bernardo and Andres (Bible School students), take over. Bernardo leads the singing and Andres reads from the newly translated book of Thessalonians about the Second Coming of Christ. In the past, Bernardo would likely have been getting drunk for this occasion.

In the evening, Pedro and the school students present their school program. It's a typical little program of poems, songs, and speeches in the midst of colored paper chains the students have made, along with paper lanterns that have lighted candles inside.

On the second day, teacher Vicente and his school children all come marching over, from Palomar, complete with flags flying. Vicente and Pedro think up contests and games for the children. Mary Ruth and I have a good number of toys and trinkets that people at home have given us, which we provide as prizes for the winners. The "slick-pole" contest is the funniest of the contests the teachers have devised — the kids try to climb a newly debarked tree. Time and again a child gets almost to the top of the pole and then suddenly slides all the way back to the bottom. Finally, one makes it, winning the best prize. Every child wins a prize before the day is over.

Again at night, both teachers have their students perform alternately reciting poems, singing songs and giving speeches. The school is running over with visitors. Pedro ends the program with his usual patriotic address, all in Amuesha, of how Independence Day came to be, with its heroes and battles. The people of the jungle are hearing this history for the first time since their ancestors were not a part of the battles long ago in which the Inca Empire was destroyed by the invading Spaniards. Pedro ends his talk by reminding his audience about the great value of the schools, and suggests that the parents support their schools to serve the Amuesha people. Finally he pays tribute to us, their linguists.

Then it is time for the torch parade. The parade begins with all the children from both schools marching around the school field holding their torches and lighted paper lanterns, with Vicente directing. It is very impressive, indeed.

On the next day, a soccer game is held between the students of both schools. Although it rains, the games go on. You never heard such yelling and rooting for school teams. Pedro's school wins, and I am glad because Vicente's students made a better showing in the school program. We sit back and wonder what these people will be doing next. Many are learning that there are better ways to celebrate than just getting drunk. Finally the four-day celebration is over and "a good time was had by all."

This year's Bible School students are doing even better back in their villages than last year's students. Julio and Andres, two from this year's group, speak in "church" on our first Sunday back here in Singing Water.[6] Julio takes Acts 4:12 and explains very well how there is no other way to be saved.

"There is no other way," he announces, "since there is no other One except Jesus Christ who died for us that we might be saved." He continues: "We had heard something about 'Yoos' (God) dying, but we didn't know what for. Now we know that Christ died on the cross to pay for our sins that we might be saved." Julio goes on to say, "We should not make somebody or something else our god or father, for we would be just like a child who asks someone else other than his real father for something; he will not be given what he asks for." Is this the same Julio who just a few years ago was an apprentice to the shaman? Yes, from apprentice to the shaman to apprentice with the Bible teacher. Thank you, Lord.

Andres, the second son of the shaman,[7] speaks up and announces his Scripture, I John 2:3-11. He reads it through first and then goes back and comments on it verse by verse. As I listen to his comments, I can tell he is "getting" the intended meaning without having been taught this text, as we have just recently distributed I John. Yes, Andres is interpreting "walking in the light" and "walking in the darkness" correctly. And to think, just a year ago we were translating this text! Thank you, Lord.

The Bible School students and Pedro make preparations for their services such as who will lead the singing and who will speak. Even the youngest of the Bible School students, Miguel and Alberto, have been teaching the Word some.[8] We are fortunate that the older Amueshas are pleased to see their young people take the lead, since living nearer to the outside world than some groups, they realize the "know how" will come through the youth.

Pedro informs us that he has started meeting informally with the boys in his school. He says that he invites them all to come to his house on Friday evenings just to talk with him and share things. He invites us to join in, if we like. We assure him we would like to come just to listen in, and that he should continue as he has been doing.

On Friday evening, Mary Ruth and I go to Pedro's house and sit inconspicuously in the back of the group. We hear Pedro tell the young boys about his most recent experience. "I was so angry," he relates to them, "when I learned someone had stolen my sacks of dried coffee beans (representing a lot of hard work and a good sum of money when sold). When I found out who had stolen my coffee, I decided right away to go into Villa Rica (the nearest civil authority and a day's walk on the muddy mule trail) and turn in charges against this person. After another day's walk back home, I just happened to pick up our book of selected Bible verses, and the first one I read said, 'Repay no one evil for evil.'" (Romans 12:17, a verse I had later translated with Valerio at his request to include in the selected verses, hence Pedro was seeing the verse for the first time).

"As soon as I read that verse," Pedro continues, talking man-to-man with his young students, "I realized what I was trying to do, to repay another one for evil he had done to me. I knew that I could not do this if I call myself a believer following God's Word, so I decided to walk all the way back to

Villa Rica and take out the charges I had made against this person. On my way back, I came by way of the thief's house and told him what I had done. I asked him to forgive me."

Wow! What a testimony Pedro is leaving these young boys. What an impact this will make on their young lives — the power of a personal experience! Is it any wonder that in later years almost every one of these young boys will turn out to be a believer? Some will be preachers of the Word, some health promoters, some schoolteachers, and some Christian leaders of their village. Thank you, Lord.

Seeing Pedro's good example, I wonder why our own schoolteachers don't do something like this, just invite their students to come and talk with them during off-school hours. I learn so much myself from seeing these people "do their own thing." In fact, at their request, we are inviting the Bible School students and any believers to come to spend time with us, just to talk and study the Word in an informal way. They had mentioned that they would like to meet and review the new Scriptures as a group. So we set Saturday evenings aside for our get-togethers.[9]

We gather around our one table, our kerosene light glowing in the darkness. Those who are with us choose to study I John first. Some of their first questions are, "How long had Jesus been back to heaven when I John was written?" "Was this John the same as John, the disciple of Jesus?" They want to know the background of each new Scripture book.

We study the first chapter of I John and I am glad that for the most part, they understand it. It's a good check for me on the translation itself, to see how much of it they understand without further explanation. Then our students want each of us to pray. How it touches our hearts to hear Bernardo praying for *"apa"* and *"ach"* (father, the shaman, and mother). We pray with them for parents. The shaman listens very attentively and agrees in the meetings, but we feel we have not really reached him on a personal level yet.

I am happy to be starting translation work again after all our school travels. Pedro and I are beginning with the Gospel of John, Chapter 6, where we left off last year. Mary Ruth is preparing to start the book of Matthew soon.

Pedro is having to study more to be able to teach the higher grades in his school. He is also teaching from the new health book we made last year.

I hear him over in the school teaching health like the Gospel. I hear him saying, "It's our dirtiness that makes us sick; it's not ants, bees, rocks, dead people's bones that 'aim' at us and make us sick."

"You mean there is nothing that aims at us and makes us sick?" asks little Espiritu, whose mother is constantly burning rocks for revenge because she says the rock is making them sick. Following their way of thinking, we state in the health book: "The way to get revenge on the water when it makes us sick is not to burn it, but to boil it before drinking. The way to get revenge on our dirtiness that makes us sick is not to burn it, but to bathe with soap and water regularly." The people in this upriver mountainous area do not bathe because of the cold, but Pedro is preaching the need for bathing.

Pedro informs us that some time ago the villagers dug up the body of one who had recently died. The shaman had told them it was this dead person's body making someone else sick. Pedro says the flesh was still fresh on the body, but the villagers burned it to get revenge before reburying it.

After one Sunday meeting, when Pedro and the Bible School students proclaim God's Word so clearly to the people, I say to Mary Ruth, "It's remarkable how they present the essence of the Christian life and don't put undue emphasis on the nonessentials, which religious groups are apt to do. Few people at home have the essence of the Christian life presented to them as clearly as the Bible School students are presenting it here." Just to hear Julio preaching on Roman 12:1-2 with such sincerity and understanding is a great joy to us and a challenge to his people to accept.

Casper Mountain and Kosepa (Julio's sister) make public their personal faith in Christ at the Sunday meeting. Casper Mountain tells the people how he received Christ as his Savior while he was in Yarina. Kosepa tells how she now believes the true "our Father's Word." As I listen to Kosepa's statements of faith, I'm thinking: Is this the same Kosepa who was the village prostitute not only here in Singing Water, but in all the villages upriver and downriver? Is this the same Kosepa who prided herself on being able to take away the husbands of other women, the same Kosepa who took Ambrocio from his wife and child? Yes, it is, but a redeemed Kosepa. Thank you, Lord, for bringing Kosepa to know your truth through reading your Word.

Both Casper Mountain and Kosepa want to join our Saturday night study and prayer group as well as several more of Pedro's older schoolboys who are believing. They pray much on these Saturday evenings that more of their people will come to the Sunday meetings to hear God's Word. Since we have started praying together on Saturday nights, more and more people have been coming on Sundays. Kosepa remarks about this matter and sure enough on Sunday morning many people have come, "We prayed just last night that the Lord would bring many people and here they come!"

Casper and Kosepa (who are relatives) like to sit on our porch and read the new Scriptures together during their free time. I hear their comments to one another as they read, and I can tell whether or not they are interpreting the translation correctly. This is another good check on our translation work. Casper is always reading ahead in I John and sharing what he reads with anyone who may be near.

The old shaman, Selano, father of Bernardo and Andres, is now very old and the boys tell us, "He has just given himself up to die; he has quit all food." Mary Ruth prepares medicines to send up to him on the mountain. Ironically, he gets well and is so grateful that he comes down from his mountain to see us. We persuade Selano to stay nearby. Then he can come to hear God's Word, which he does. I talk to him one afternoon alone, explaining to him the way of salvation. He responds, "I do want to believe." Thank you, Lord.

"Pray for one another . . . the prayer of a righteous man is powerful and effective."

— the Apostle James, (James 5:16 NIV)

(Thank you, Lord, for answering prayers of the believers for their loved ones.)

# 45

# "This Is What We've Been Looking For"

What have the Amuesha people been looking for?

Pedro and I have been working steadily on the translation of the Gospel of John in the afternoons, continuing with Chapter 6. He finds it hard to believe that the majority of the Jewish people never did believe and accept Jesus as the Christ. He says, "It's just like the people here. We tell them many times about Christ, but many don't believe." It helps him not to become discouraged if everyone does not believe and accept Christ.

He chuckles at the wisdom of Jesus, who says to the people that bring the woman taken in adultery, "Let whichever one of you has not sinned throw the first stone." Pedro is already using new truths he is learning from the book of John in his talks to the people. One day he cites John 8:31,32, about Christ's true words setting us free from sin. Pedro's people are such a burden for him and he prays for them by name. Truly an inspiration to me, I don't know of any other Christian anywhere who has a more sincere, Christ-like attitude in everything he does than Pedro.

Recently, in the midst of our translation work, Pedro says to me out of the blue, "Why are we not doing anything for the Amuesha people at Oxapampa?"

Since Oxapampa is a place where the Amueshas are quite acculturated, I reply, "They don't speak much Amuesha there anymore. The children don't speak any Amuesha, and they don't need a bilingual school like we do here."

"The older people speak Amuesha there," Pedro counters. "I need to go there and tell them God's Word. God will fulfill his promises to us." (Pedro will later make the first missionary trip to Oxapampa, and from there he will continue on downriver sharing the good news *(cohuen ñoñets)* of the Gospel of Jesus Christ. He shares with us his joy how he felt the fullness of the Holy Spirit inspiring and directing him all the way.)[1]

As we continue with the translation of John, we get to John 14:1 ". . . trust in God, trust also in me," Jesus says. How can we translate "trust" in Amuesha since we have not found a word for trust? We have a word for "believe," but not for "trust." Sometimes the word we are looking for is just a step away.

One day I hurry over to Petita's house next door. As I enter the house, I can tell something bad has just happened. Petita is bemoaning what has just happened. My little two-year-old namesake, Marrta, is sitting near the open fire in the kitchen. I listen to Petita as she relays her story. "Pedro was so much *'yemtenana'* his new trousers for his speech in the school celebrations." She shows me Pedro's brand new pants, all folded up with a newly-burned hole going through each layer of the folds.

She informs me that my little namesake had been playing in the open fire with a stick and had flipped out an ember that burned the hole, despite the fact she had been told not to play with the fire. I have never heard this word *"yemtenana"* before, and don't know its meaning, but from the context in which she uses it, it sounds like it could mean "counting on." Can this possibly be the word for "trust"? I duly sympathize with Petita and Marrta, yet mark down in my mind to investigate this word as a possibility for "trust."

As I later check out *"yemtenana"* with others, I find that it does mean "to count on, to confide in as one's best friend, to trust." The noun form of it *(pueyem)* means "one's best friend or confidant" (one you can tell anything). What better word for "trust"? As I run it by Pedro for John 14:1 he heartily agrees. So we have ". . . As you count on our Father God, Me also you are to count on." Thank you, Lord. Just as we need a new word, God provides it by placing it in our path, albeit at Pedro's expense.

As we get down to verse 14:6, and I know that we will have difficulties translating it. "Jesus answered, I am the way, the truth and the life." The problem here is with the three nouns: way, truth, and life. The Amuesha language uses verbs or other words, rather than some nouns. Some concepts are just not expressed in nominal forms. Pedro and I discuss how to express these nominal forms. The first one, "way," is not so hard, since we do have "path, trail." We have an adjectival form of "truth," thus meaning "true." "Life," as a nominal form, is not used in this sense; the verbal forms of "to live" and "to cause to live" are the normal usages. As we work on it, Pedro and I come up with "I am like a path . . . ," and then to make explicit the ground of comparison of the simile (that leads to a certain place), "that leads to the true 'our Father.' I am the one who tells you the true words, I am the one who causes you to live forever."

I have been so concerned about making the adjustments for the translation that I have not realized the impact the truth of the revelation God's Word has been making on Pedro. As usual, I type up for Pedro what we have translated today and give it to him so he can re-read it and see if he wants to make any changes. He also knows that he is free to use it in teaching the people who come to his meetings if he likes.

It's a beautiful morning as everyone gathers at Pedro's thatched roof house for "church" the following Sunday. As usual, we women sit on the palm bark floor on the right, facing the leader, with the men on the left. After singing all the songs in the hymn book as the people like to do (sometimes twice), Pedro stands up to speak. Holding in his hand the copy of the newly typed Scripture that was translated in the past week, he announces the text: John 14:1-6. My heart takes a leap. This is the difficult passage we have just translated. *Will Pedro interpret it correctly?* I almost hold my breath.

Pedro, on the other hand, has such a happy expression on his face, as if to suggest, "I can't wait to tell you this!" He reads the first verses of this passage, where Jesus announces that he will prepare a place for us and come again to take us to be with him. The people understand this easily and voice aloud their joy upon hearing it. *But will they understand verse 6 when Pedro gets that far?*

After Pedro reads verse 6 (where Jesus proclaims, "I am the way, the truth and the life,") he stops. Then he begins to remind the people of all the ways they have tried to find the true God. He states, "You know how we have tried in our culture to get a message from the true 'our Father'. You know how we have had our shamans sit up all night chewing the powerful coca leaf in hopes that they would get some message from our father, the sun. You know how we have tried to entice the beautiful little birds to come out of the jungle up to our houses, because as we say, 'They might have a message for us from our father the sun.'"

Pedro again reads verse 6 in Amuesha, where Jesus says, "I am like the path that leads you to where the true our Father is. I am the one who tells you the completely true words, I am the one who causes you to live forever."

"This is what we have been looking for!" Pedro exclaims, releasing all his pent-up joy in declaring Jesus is the way to the true "our Father," the path that the Amueshas and their ancestors had been looking for.

Although I am sitting on the floor, I am really in my "third heaven." With this declaration of Pedro's and him relating it to the Amuesha culture of how they have really been searching for their true God, I realize this will open up the people to believing easily — and it does. Thank you, Lord. The most effective testimony is that which is given in the language and within the culture of one's own people.[2] Coming from their much-loved teacher, many of the Amueshas embrace Pedro's words. Groups of believers start springing up near and far. A "people's movement" is beginning.[3]

After finishing the translation of the Gospel of John with Pedro, I start to check the comprehension with Casper Mountain. He is anxious to help with the translation since accepting Christ as his Savior at Yarina. Casper is now reading well in Amuesha. We read the translation together as it now stands to determine how well he understands it. I do this by asking pertinent questions. Where he finds the meaning difficult, we work to make the translation clearer. Casper's insistence on doing all things well makes him a capable assistant for this work.

He is excellent at using the pragmatic features of good story telling. Prominence and cohesion are vitally important in communicating a story properly in Amuesha. Casper is very sharp at keeping in focus the features that make it easy to understand new content. Keeping the focus marker *–pa'* on the right word and *–ña*, the sequence marker, on the right word is critical in the progress of a story.

Casper Mountain insists on giving full accounts of actions in a specific event. For example, when we read how Jesus calls Lazarus forth from the tomb, he insists, "Jesus would not just say, 'Lazarus, come out.'"

"Why would Jesus not say that?" I ask in amazement.

"Because he would know that Lazarus would have to get up first before he could come out. We need to say, 'Lazarus, I say to you, get up and come out.'"

So be it! This is the way Amueshas would express it!

We sometimes have instant readers for the new Scriptures. The other day, when I was typing up the passages we had just translated from our 3" x 5" scratch copies, Huancho, Casper Mountain's nephew, came along and started reading the text over my shoulder as the typewriter printed it word by word. How amazing it is to see newly translated Scripture go right from the typewriter into the heart of the first reader! Huancho is one of the youngest of the new believers. He comes to the evening Bible study and learns from his uncle, Casper.

Since Casper Mountain has been reading the verses on salvation to his old mother, he has led her to believe and she has come down from her mountaintop home. "The more my son read to me God's Word, the more I realized this really is the true 'our Father's Word,' and I believed, too," she tells me, her old, rugged face beaming with newfound joy. *Thank you, Lord, for more precious jewels!*

"After I believed, I told my son that I want to go down from the mountain to where the other believers are. I want to be with them." She hears more and more of the Word as her son Casper proceeds to read and share with her all he is learning from the translation work. How could I have ever imagined on the mountaintop that day that this dear, old lady would have her own private teacher (her son) help her to know the true "our Father."

Even her grandson, Huancho, shares with her. He tells me, "I read to Llollo (grandmother) the verse from I John which says, 'Do not love the things we see here in the world.'" Although he is very young, this verse has special meaning to Huancho as he is beginning to know the outside world.

The translation of the Gospel of John is completed just a week before Mary Ruth and I are to leave. Casper Mountain and I finish our second check today. *Thank you, Lord.* Now we will take it into Yarina where it will go through a committee check. Then I plan to prepare it in book form for printing, hoping it will be ready in time for us to bring out here on our next trip. Since there are already believers, Mary Ruth and I are planning to make provisional printed copies of each book available as we translate so the believers will have more of the Word to grow on even before the entire translation of the New Testament is completed. We feel that a good, understandable translation of God's Word is essential to the development of the indigenous church.[4]

We move forward with Pedro and Casper Mountain as our assistants, alternating our turns with each one of them. Mary Ruth has concluded the translation of I and II Thessalonians and is now preparing for the translation of the Gospel of Matthew.

Having learned so much from working with us, Casper Mountain is speaking more in the meetings and sharing many of the things he remembers from the book of John. He carries his Scripture books in his *poshac* (man's handbag), and wherever he goes and sits down to talk, he soon takes them out and starts to read to the older folk who do not know how. Being an older man, he relates well to them. Tenesho and his wife, who are very much bound in their old beliefs, ask him many questions as he reads and shares God's Word with them in their home. *Will he be able to win them for the Lord?*

Julio is becoming quite the preacher. He is good at reading, helping people to understand and apply the Scriptures. The older men, even the chief, are listening to him expound on the Word. Julio's sister, Kosepa, the first woman believer at Singing Water, tells me with tears in her eyes, "When I hear my brother preaching, it makes me want to cry from joy. I am sad that our mother is not believing this new way."

One Sunday, as the speaker asks, "Does anyone have a special verse they would like to share with us?" Kosepa reads the passage about Jesus being taken up into heaven and then returning in like manner. She makes fitting comments on it. She and Julio both read the Word to their mother, who is very set in the beliefs of her indigenous culture. *Will she ever believe in Jesus Christ?*

"You will seek me and find me when you seek me with all your heart."

— the Prophet Jeremiah, (Jeremiah 29:13 NIV)

*(Thank you, Lord, for making yourself known through your Word to those who have been seeking you.)*

# 46

## The First Baptized Amuesha Believers

A woman with an open stomach wound? How could we have ever imagined the unusual things we would become involved in this year with the Amuesha people?

Our session at Yarina Center has gone so quickly with the Teacher Training Course and daily pedagogy classes at our house. Now that the teacher-trainees have finished and gone back to their schools, I am able to get my translation of the Gospel of John checked by a consultant, typed up ready for printing, and turned in to the print shop. I hope it will be published in time to take with us when we return to Amueshaland.

I am also doing my exegetical, preparatory work for the book of Colossians, which I plan to translate this time out. I feel this book is needed for the situations the believers face there. Mary Ruth is continuing her preparation for translating the Gospel of Matthew.

Another new publication we are getting out this year is an Amuesha newspaper. With the people living so far apart from one another, the newspaper will keep them up-to-date on events going on in the different areas. And it will give them a greater feeling of unity since there are no roads, mail, or phones to connect them. Raul Sinacay, one of the very capable graduates of Valerio's school interviewed all the teacher-trainees while they were in Yarina for the Teacher Training Course. He collected news items of interest and compiled them into a small newspaper. Raul has learned to type almost completely on his own. I loaned him a typing manual and typewriter, and showed him how to follow the book to pick up just a few letters at a time. Within a short period, he has learned all the letters by touch.

In the future, we will be making more library reading books with Raul typing up the dummy copies. Since Raul is quite bilingual, he is able to translate the Amuesha texts into Spanish, which is handy for us because our books are now required to be in diglot. He can also translate some books from Spanish into Amuesha. And Raul is a good artist too. What a great help it is to have Raul work with us in making so many books. It's a paying job for Raul, and he loves it, and he has now taken over my desk at Yarina with his bookmaking projects for his people.

A recent project of Raul's was translating one of the best known Amuesha legends, *How the Sun and Moon Came To Be*. This forty-one-page story was originally handwritten by Julio Gaspar, who was one of Pedro's advanced students and is now one of the Amuesha teachers. Raul has turned the legend into a book with drawings and put the Spanish translation in the back. This book becomes No. 6 in the Amuesha Library Series.

Valerio has been encouraging the production of this book. I hesitated in the beginning thinking a legend book might possibly confuse the people as they are just now hearing the Creation story from the Bible. After talking this over with Valerio, who is the Amuesha Bible School teacher, he suggests that his people have a written account of their legends "just like other people have legends and fairy tales that they know are not true."

The plane is loaded with 100 copies of the new Gospel of John, copies of the newspaper for each village, and copies of the legend book for each of the school libraries. Bernie May is our pilot, flying us out in the new Helio Courior plane. He flies low over the very areas we trekked into last year. We can see clearly where the Azules River flows into the **Muenaresmaⁿ** River, and the headwaters of the Palcaso River. We do want to visit the people and the teachers here again this year. If we could get out here easily and not have to trek back into this mountainous region as we did last year. Who would ever think that this remote area will in years to come be the exact spot where the marginal highway east of the Andes Mountains will pass through the jungle?

We enjoy a good dinner with Bernie at the Turista Hotel on the airfield at San Ramon and then he is off back to Yarina. The next thing we know, here comes the same little, old man with his little, old truck. We are off to the mountainous region of Amueshaland.

We get to Vicente's school at Palomar a little after dark and soon feel the cold mountain air. Our thermometer reads forty-four degrees when we arise in the morning. We find many people sick with pneumonia here, including teacher Tomas' mother. Josefina, Vicente's wife, is kept busy giving penicillin shots, which she learned to do during her last trip to Yarina. What a help she is to her people! Josefina is running out of penicillin, however, we have brought a new supply with us.

We find the adults still studying in the evenings. They are to be commended, considering the cold nights here. The day school is progressing more smoothly, thanks to the pedagogy classes the teachers are taking in the Teacher Training Course at Yarina.

Domingo C., a Bible School student, already has a copy of the new Gospel of John and is teaching it to the villagers. Many of the young fellows who didn't seem too interested in Bible study last year are now taking part. Mary Ruth and I feel that many of them are believers already. Several want to buy copies of the new, translated book of John.

Going on to Julio's new school nearby at Metrado, we find many sick people here also. Julio is doing well with his teaching, but is a little discouraged, thinking maybe the people don't want him as teacher. As I talk to them I find they are very happy with Julio and want him to stay. This greatly encourages him. Meeting in a different home each time, he teaches the Word which is what the people want to hear.

Mary Ruth and I go back by way of Villa Rica to start our school visits in the downriver area. We find our way to Tomas' school in Huocas and tell him about his sick mother at home. We say if he would like to go to visit her, we will go on downriver to José's school in Azules and stop here on our way back up.

With our reliance on guides, we begin the treacherous trek once again, following the narrow passes of the swiftly flowing **Muenaresmaĩ** stream. After about eight hours, we arrive at José's school, exhausted to say the least. José is also doing much better with his teaching. Several of the older students who started school last year are already reading independently. They are actually able to read the new translation of John and want to have their own copies. It makes the difficult hike worth it! José is also reading and teaching the villagers the book of John. He gets all the way to Chapter 13 while we are here.

As we set off to return to Tomas' school, it begins to rain. We wait a while, hoping it will stop, because it makes the rocks along the water slippery to walk on. But the rain does not let up, and to stay on schedule, we feel we must get moving. It continues to rain as we walk. Not only do we fall, but our seasoned guides fall too. We finally reach our destination thoroughly soaked. Tomas' new, little school right along the stream is a welcome sight.

Tomas and the school boys help us set up the radio to see if we can contact Yarina, to let the folks there know we are alive and well since we haven't reported in for a week. I wonder if our signal can get past these mountains. Lo and behold, we hear Yarina answer us clearly and strongly. They read me a message from our director at Yarina, Eugene Loos, saying he would like me to consider graduate studies in linguistics during my upcoming home leave. Mary Ruth has already made her decision to begin studying for her doctorate. Knowing the great need to continue on with the translation work for the Amueshas, and in light of the positive response we are receiving from them, I do not want to take time off for further study, but I will think it over.

We find that Tomas is also teaching much better this year. Many of his older students are reading independently. They all want copies of John and our books disappear in no time. Tomas too is teaching the people from the book of John. His lesson this Sunday is John 14:6. Many of them are hearing for the first time that Jesus is the way to the true God. Thank you, Lord.

After a little rest here, we are ready for the longest trek yet, back upriver and across another mountain to Enrique's school in Cacaso. Three guides go along with us, but even they are not sure of the trail at times. Two of them actually drop out along the way. Soon it becomes dark before we even reach our destination. Happily, we have now left the stream, but the terrain is still very rugged. The youngest of the guides leads us on through a dark, dense depression in the ground. With our flashlights we can see a little, but it is a scary experience. *We trust you, Lord, to take us the rest of the way safely.*

Finally, after about eleven hours on the trail, we recognize the football clearing at Enrique's school even in the dark. *Thank you, Lord.* What a disappointment it is to find Enrique's school in a mess — and Enrique too. He has only matriculated nine students. We know something must be wrong. As we feel out the situation, the people start talking and tell us the many ways in which Enrique is failing as a teacher. They have even more complaints about his wife, who they claim is *atsrremñaĩ* (an angry person). The villagers are all in favor of getting a different teacher. Enrique himself tells me that he wants to quit. He did not come to Yarina for the Teacher Training Course this past year. Although he is a believer, he just can't seem to handle his school. He, no doubt, will quit this year.

The people say they want the school to continue and will have their children attend if Enrique is replaced by another teacher. I tell the people there is a possibility of teacher Santiago from downriver taking over this school next year. They are happy to hear this. While we are here in Cacaso, we receive the news that Pedro from Singing Water was on a hunting trip when he accidentally shot his nephew, Juan (from this village), through the hand.

We finally get back to Singing Water, and Pedro tells us about the accident. He says that one night while he and Juan were hunting, he saw the reflection of Juan's flashlight and, thinking it to be the deer's eye, shot, only to find he had shot straight through the palm of Juan's hand. Pedro says he was so sad and upset that he called all the believers together to pray he would not be taken in by the authorities for shooting his nephew. Later, when he went into the city with Juan to get his wounded hand treated and had to appear before the authorities, he said, "They took one look in my eyes and said, 'You look like an honest man,' and let me go." Pedro is sure it was the result of the believers' prayers. *Thank you, Lord.*

This is the first time we have come all the way from Villa Rica to Singing Water by road in a vehicle. The road now goes all the way through. We are thrilled about the road, but unhappy with the negative things that are already coming in on that road, like trucks loaded with rattling beer bottles. We are glad that the church is already functioning well here before the onslaught of "civilization" sweeps the people up in its grasp. Thank you, Lord.

Pedro and Petita are anxious to tell us about a sick woman, Pascuala, from way up on the mountain who they have been treating while she has been staying in our house. Even they have never seen anything like this. The woman has a ruptured stomach, open all the way from her intestine to the outside of her body. Pedro himself has become quite a doctor, but for lack of knowing what else to do before we arrive, he has treated her for intestinal parasites. He says large worms about a foot long came out of the opening. Some of her food comes out as well. He has also given her penicillin shots, which have probably saved her life from the infection in the open hole.

We consult with our doctor by radio. He has never heard of such a thing, but says it must be from an amoebic abscess. He replies that an operation is necessary. In the meantime, we are to treat her for worms and amoeba, then give her vitamins and iron. Pedro says the sick woman's husband was drunk recently and almost kicked their little five-year-old boy unconscious. What can we do? An operation would require a trip to Lima. What about all the translation we want to get done? What about the future medical clinic for several Amuesha villages we have already planned with our Dr. Eichenburger?

While all the teacher-trainees at Yarina for the Teacher Training Course were together in one of our many fellowship meetings, we had talked about the meaning of baptism. Those who claimed to be believers had expressed their desire to be baptized, so the upriver teachers all agreed to meet at Pedro's during their Independence Day vacation time to be baptized. According to plan, they all arrive, including Tomas, José, Enrique, Vicente, Vicente's wife, Pedro and Pedro's wife, Petita. We meet with them one evening to make sure they understand what baptism means. We create a little form for Pedro to use when asking questions in the confirmation of faith. Pedro will baptize Tomas first, then Tomas will baptize Pedro, who will then continue to baptize the others.

We go down to the nearest stream and find a place deep enough for baptisms. We sing, and Vicente reads from Mark and Matthew about John's baptizing and Jesus' baptism. Then Pedro speaks on II Corinthians 5:17, applying the newness of life to the symbol of baptism. He makes it clear that without the newness of life, baptism has no meaning. Pedro stands on a rock jutting out into the water as he speaks from the Scripture book open in his hand. With the jungle behind him, I can't help but think how much he looks like John the Baptist in the wilderness.

It is time for Pedro and Tomas to go into the water and baptize each other. Tomas says he would like to speak first and gives a good testimony of his faith in Jesus. Pedro asks him the questions, and with Tomas' confirmation of faith, Pedro says, "All right, brother, I now baptize you that you might be in close fellowship with God, the Father, and with God's Son, Jesus, and with God's Spirit" — the first Amuesha baptized by another Amuesha! Tomas then baptizes Pedro, and Pedro in turn baptizes the others. Nine in all have asked to be baptized. Thank you, Lord, for the first baptized Amuesha believers! Thank you for helping them to speak your Word in their own language so that they may understand well what they are doing.

Since we had arranged for the baptism of the teachers to go so quickly to enable them to return to their schools, some of the believers here did not even know about it. Now that they have heard, they also want to be baptized, including Casper Mountain, and Juan, Pedro's nephew. We are already planning the next round.

Three of our friends from Yarina plan to come visit us on their way to Lima. They are Lucy Eakin, a distant "cousin" of mine who teaches our missionary children at Yarina; Lucy's fellow teacher friend; and Arlene Gusman from Wisconsin, who came down to help out and typed the Amuesha John manuscript for printing. They arrive late at night, tired and hungry after the long road trip. They make short work of the chocolate cake I have made for them. Since the Amuesha people are just delighted with their new copies of John, it is good to be able to tell them that Arlene typed the copies. Lucy knows Pedro a little from seeing him at Yarina.

With the many sick people we are treating, our friends get a good picture of what village life is like. They also see the joy of the believers in receiving God's Word in their own language. Both Pedro and Casper Mountain are already telling their people about the good things they remember from the translation of John. Never do we image at the time that Lucy will later decide to switch careers — from a schoolteacher to a linguist-translator — and eventually will translate for the Yaminahua people, along with her co-worker, Norma Faust.

Mary Ruth and I are hoping to finally be able to work on our translations. It is not to be so. The villagers bring us another very sick woman. Despite many radio consultations with the doctor at Yarina and following his instructions, the woman dies in Pedro's house, where our friends have been staying. Not long after, the baby of the woman we are treating with the open stomach wound also dies. We are sad about the deaths. Yet we question if people will even want to come to Pedro's house to hear the Word anymore with another person having died there. The Amuesha people usually abandon a house where someone dies for fear of evil spirits. Although Pedro does not continue to follow this custom, we wonder what the people will do now. It seems that just when more of the people are becoming believers and wanting to be baptized, Satan is putting up another obstacle to keep them enslaved. We pray for God's overruling.

God wins! The following Sunday more people come to hear the Word than usual, sitting right in Pedro's house where the woman died. Thank you, Lord. Andres talks on a newly translated passage from Thessalonians, and the believers are hearing Scriptures to grow on. Domingo C. and another believer, Gaspar, come from Palomar wanting to be baptized. Domingo C. preaches the Sunday they are here in Singing Water.

Finally, Pedro and I can get to work on the translation of Colossians. After some orientation for Pedro to understand that this book is a letter, written by Paul to the believers in a place called Colosse, we begin:

"To: Brothers (and sisters) you who are followers of the holy God by your faith in Christ, you who live there in the village of Colosse.

From: I, Pablo, am writing you this letter, along with our brother, Timothy. I am the one who is Christ Jesus' 'sent/commissioned one' according to God's will."

Thus begins Paul's letter to the Colossians.

We have started up our Saturday night Bible study again. We make an announcement that if believers want to be baptized, they should also attend the study group Saturday nights. Agosto is one of them. We have seen his interest in the Sunday meetings grow. When baptism is mentioned, he, along with Casper Mountain, are the first ones to state they want to be baptized. Talking with Agosto, we want to be sure he is firm in his decision to follow the Lord. He acknowledges he really does want to follow the Lord, but his main problem is controlling his anger with other people. He prays and asks for the Lord's forgiveness and help.

"When do you two want to be baptized?" I ask.

"Tomorrow, after church," Casper Mountain replies.

Sure enough, there lies his extra change of clothes that he has brought from his mountain home for the occasion. There's nothing like coming prepared. After church on Sunday we take off to the baptizing hole and several people join us. Casper Mountain is so tall we wonder if the water will be deep enough to cover him, but the river is up some and just right. Knowing his sincere desire to follow the Lord, and his faithfulness in witnessing to others, it is a joy to see him baptized.

Casper tells us he has been witnessing to Miquela by reading Scriptures to her. He thinks she is very interested. When we mention it to her, she affims, "Yes, I want to receive Christ right now." Right in the midst of everyone she makes her confession and prays for forgiveness. I see the same joy on Casper Mountain's face that you see in anyone who has just been an instrument in bringing another to faith in Christ. Casper makes known he is now reading Scripture to Ballentin's father. He maintains he likes to deal with them "one by one."

We are studying Thessalonians in our Bible study group. Several of Pedro's older students are attending and showing great interest. One of these is another young fellow called Santiago. He has all of the Scripture books translated so far and says he is reading the Scriptures to his mother. I think several of these young fellows will be going to Valerio's Bible School this year. Julio's mother has been coming early to the Sunday meetings. Is she considering becoming a believer?

Pedro and Petita's children are so cute. My little namesake, Marrta, is three years old now and talking a blue streak. Juanacho, her older brother, is five. Pedro bought a pig for them that now has little piglets. One day while I am playing with Marrta and Juanacho, the three little piglets come running and flop down right in front of us, knowing that Juanacho will pull their legs up and start looking for the fleas on their tummies, of which there are many. He shows his little sister Marrta and me (his big sister Marrta) which of the piglets are male and which are female. He also tells us the names of each one. The piglets are enjoying all this scratching of their tummies. No doubt the kids are getting their own fleas, but what fun it is to watch them play with some of their first domesticated animals.

The woman with the open stomach, whose name is Pascuala, is gaining strength from vitamins and iron treatment. We are still deciding what we should do since going to Lima for this operation will take a big chunk of our time away from our translation projects this year. Then, out of the blue, we are asked over the radio to go into Lima to help with a certain project for a short time. We feel this is our answer. Yes, we should go to Lima and take Pascuala for the operation.

We ask Casper Mountain if he would like to go along with us, so we can continue with our translation work as time allows in Lima. He happily agrees since he has never seen a big city before. He shows up decked out in his crown and new tunic he borrowed from the chief. As we sit on the side of the road waiting for some vehicle to come by to start us off on our long trip to Lima over the Andes Mountains, we know the tremendous responsibility we are taking on. However, it seems to be the only way to help this poor woman. Mary Ruth and I have devised a dressing of sorts, a pad for Pascuala to wear over the open, draining wound. This, of course, will have to be changed several times during our trip to Lima. Where will we find a place to do this since there are few handy restrooms along the road?

We find a vehicle to take us to Villa Rica. When we arrive there, we are well aware we are quite a spectacle for all the Spanish-speaking people — Casper with his colorful Amuesha attire, and we two Americans with this poor, helpless native woman. They will never figure us out. And with these two who are traveling with us and have never seen the outside world, just how will we get by?

"Where shall I urinate?" Casper asks as we get to the town of Tarma where we will begin our trip over the Andes. He doesn't see any woodlands anywhere.

"You see that place where it says *'baño'*" I reply. "That's the place to go."

Mary Ruth and I must also find a restroom for ourselves so we can change the dressing on Pascuala. Thank you, Lord, for the few restrooms we find.

As we continue, Pascuala hides her face and refuses to look around, the bare mountains appear so scary and different from the jungle that she knows. We zig-zag up the mountains, gazing down from the heights of the narrow road. When we meet another vehicle, one of us has to back up to the nearest spot in the road that's wide enough for passing. As we reach the 16,000 feet level. (the highest point on the road) we see snow out our open window. The window will not roll up, but it doesn't matter; the little, old bus is so warm from climbing up the mountain. We have also brought along blankets because we have no warmer clothing, never expecting we would be going into Lima.

"This place stinks!" Pascuala remarks after our eight-hour trip from San Ramon and arrival into the big city of Lima. We get a taxi to our Lima House and Mrs. Cudney, our housemother, takes us all in with graciousness. She shows Casper Mountain how the shower in his room works and he panics. Seeing the clean, white sheets on his bed, he comes to us right away saying, "Quick, get me some soap! I have to get all cleaned up. I can't get this white bed all dirty." In our room, Mary Ruth gets in the shower with Pascuala to help her get really clean prior to her hospitalization.

Casper has a long talk with Pascuala before she goes to the hospital to help her understand how to believe and accept Christ, reading to her from his Scripture books that he always carries with him. She does want to believe and prays to receive Christ as Casper instructs her.

Pascula soon enters the hospital, but Mary Ruth or I must see her every day to keep her content until it is time for her operation. With Pascuala speaking no Spanish, and all the queer things she has never seen before, we must keep her pacified. We take turns working with Casper on translation and going to the hospital.

"Seek those things which are above . . ." (Colossians 3:1) is a little hard sometimes when we are involved in such "earthly things." But as Casper and I talk about what that means, we come up with the translation "think or concentrate on the things that Christ (who is above) wants." This has great meaning to Casper in his new Christian life. I hear him praying to God just after we get through this translation: "You will help us to concentrate on 'above things' and not on 'earthly things.'" God is helping us as we do just that. Mary Ruth and I are both making progress with our translations even though we are able to work only half-time! Thank you, Lord.

Our people at Lima House are bothering Casper Mountain by always asking whether they may take a picture of him in his Amuesha dress. We cautiously ask him if he would like us to find some other clothes for him to wear so that he will not be bothered as much. Understanding this will stop the photo requests, Casper agrees. We speak to Mrs. Cud and she looks through the good donated suits. She finds a sharp one for Casper, complete with necktie. Casper comes to us for help, but we don't know how to tie a necktie either. We call on Mrs. Cud again.

When Casper Mountain emerges after Mrs. Cud's makeover, with his hair combed back and wearing the suit and tie, we don't recognize him. Later, Mary Ruth and I put on our good Lima suits and heels to go out and Casper doesn't recognize us either! We laugh at each other.

As the time for Pascuala's operation draws near, Patsy Adams, who is a nurse (working on the Culina translation), takes great interest in this case and persuades me to go with her to see the operation. We are in a glass observation area right above the operating room. Since this is such an unusual operation, several doctors also observe.

In the process, the doctors take out all of Pascuala's intestines, hold them up, and go through them just like a woman looking for runs in pantyhose. I, not being a nurse, can only take so much. With my eyes closed, I say to Patsy, "What are they doing now?"

"They are still going through the intestines."

"Why are they doing that when they already know where the rupture is?"

"It's probably to see if there are any other weak spots that might rupture."

We return home to Lima House, and Patsy is ecstatic with what she has been able to see. On the other hand, I am recovering from the shock that anyone could ever live through such a procedure.

That very same night, Mary Ruth and I, along with fellow members Patsy and Millie Larson, put on a program for officials of the Ministry of Education. I have to shift gears in a hurry. We each are to give a short speech in Spanish, talking about the different languages we are working in. Then Mary Ruth and I carry on a conversation with Casper Mountain in Amuesha. The Minister is duly impressed by hearing us talk with Casper in his own language and hearing how Casper learned to read in just two weeks in a bilingual school. The Ministry of Education is fully supporting the Bilingual School Program to help the indigenous people of the jungle. That's why we are happy to show off some of our results. A radio station also taped the demonstration which we are able to hear later.

Casper Mountain is also asked to speak at a Methodist high school in Lima. Although there are about three hundred students, Casper does not seem to be the least bit intimidated. He tells them in Amuesha how he has learned to read in just two weeks in the bilingual school in his area, and how he is helping with the translation of God's Word into his own language. I have to interpret for Casper and am more afraid than he is.

Yet another opportunity to promote the success of our program comes in the form of an interview with a representative of Ford Foundation. He is greatly impressed with Casper and how he has learned to read so easily through the medium of his own language.

In the meantime, Mary Ruth and I are both able to reach our translation goals. Thank you, Lord. Mary Ruth's linguistic article on Amuesha verbs (called "Six levels of structure in Amuesha (Arawak) verbs" is published in IJAL. My article on indigenous creative writers is also published in *Peru Indigena*.[1]

Pascuala recovers well from her surgery and is soon able to come back to our Lima House. Mrs. Cud, who knows the two of us need to return to Amueshaland to establish the medical clinic we have already planned, volunteers to keep Pascuala for us in her own room until her recovery is complete.

"When she is well enough to travel on the bus, I will take her back over the Andes Mountains and meet you in the town there," Mrs. Cud says.

"Thank you, Mrs. Cud." I respond. "You are always so gracious and so ready to serve."

Although they can scarcely talk to each other, Pascuala and Mrs. Cud become great friends during the time they spend together until Pascuala will be able to travel back home to Singing Water.

Mary Ruth and I get on the road back to Amueshaland as soon as we can to prepare for Dr. Eichenburger and his traveling medical clinic. He will be bringing medical care to villages throughout the area, starting at Singing Water. The doctor also wants to conduct a research project on the infant mortality rate among the Amueshas, along with examining all patients who would like the doctor to look them over.

The two of us will be his facilitators. It will be our job to get the people lined up, keep records, and interpret for the doctor as he examines each person. He wants us to ask each of the older women how many pregnancies she has had, how many miscarriages, how many stillbirths, and how many of her children have died. For women who have never much counted beyond three, all fingers and toes will come into play. They name each child and use their fingers to keep count. We find that each of the women has had about ten pregnancies. Only a few have more than five children living, and many have fewer than five. Once the research is finished in all of the villages, the doctor calculates that the infant mortality rate is about fifty percent.

The people come to see the doctor with their many ailments, and we have strange self-diagnoses to report to the doctor. One woman tells me she has a "hole in her heart." I relay to the doctor exactly what she says; he is the doctor and must determine her problem. Some do not want to describe their symptoms for the doctor or tell him what their ailments are. They think he, like the shaman, should be able to divine what is making them sick. Everyone who desires is examined and treated. Almost every patient receives amoebic parasite treatment.

We finish with all the upriver villages and then go to San Ramon to meet a plane to take us to the downriver villages. By this time, Pascuala has recovered enough to travel and we arrange by radio to meet her and Mrs. Cud in San Ramon. It's good to see Pascuala looking so well and happy as they ride in on the bus from Lima. Her husband has come with us to take her back home.

Since she has gotten this far out into the jungle, Mrs. Cud decides to go on with us to the first village downriver. That is Stingray, where we will set up the clinic and proceed downriver by boat from there. Mrs. Cud wants to help us with the cooking and meet some of the other Amueshas at the first village. From Stingray she will fly on our JAARS plane back to Yarina, and eventually back to Lima.

We buy food supplies for our expanded family and are soon transported by our plane across the mountains and downriver to Stingray village. Dr. Eichenberger's wife Beth, a lab technician, flies in from Yarina to meet us, bringing lab equipment for the clinic. What fun it is not only having our fellow Wycliffe friends with us, but all our Amuesha friends who we haven't seen for some time. How we appreciate Mrs. Cud's help with the cooking.

After our medical clinic duties are wrapped up at Stingray village, we bid Mrs. Cud good-bye as she flies to Yarina, and we take boats on downriver to the next village of Sheringamaso. We conclude clinic work here and are giving out the medicines, calling the names we have been given. We call "Losaria Roman" time and again. No one answers. Finally after several attempts, one woman speaks meekly, "That must be me." We realize that some of the villagers who seem to have no names have made up names just for registering. She has forgotten the name she gave us. We decide for the next clinic to give each patient a number tag instead.

We go up a tributary to set up another clinic that will serve all the villages in this area. A large number of people seek us out. We find the number system works better. Beth gets a workout with her lab equipment here where there is more illness caused perhaps by many more domesticated animals in this area. The bilingual teachers of these villages have been a great help in the clinic, and we trust the health of their students will improve. Thank you, Lord, for the clinic help.

We return downriver by boat to where our floatplane can pick us up to take us back to Yarina Center. And so, ends our tenth year with the Amuesha people.

JAARS pilots are an integral part of our team that spreads the Word of God to the language groups. Pilot Fred and nurse Ruth McKennon become my prayer partners for the Amueshas. They hear more about the needs of the people as I share many of the problems we encounter. Fred decides he wants to pilot all the Amuesha flights to become better acquainted with the Amueshas.

Once, when one of the Amuesha women, who is a tubercular patient, ran out of medicine in a remote mountainous village, Fred suggested that he could make a drop on the soccer field. He did. The woman and her husband (who was known to be the village thief) were so impressed by the Christian love expressed to them by Fred and the Amuesha believers, they decided they wanted to become Christians themselves. They started attending the Amuesha Christian fellowship in their village.

"He sent forth his word and healed them . . ."
(Psalm 107:20 NIV)

". . . Go and make disciples of all nations (peoples), baptizing them . . ."[2]
– Jesus, (Matthew 28:19 NIV)

(Thank you, Lord, for the first baptized believers among the Amuesha people. Thank you for good medical help for the people.)

# 47

# Indigenous Churches Develop

Is that a church building?

Going back to Singing Water after my second furlough, I am surprised and delighted to find the first church building standing right in the center of the village. The people tell us, "With so many people believing now, we needed a larger place to meet to study God's Word."

The people have built it themselves, with Julio and Ambrocio, Kosepa's husband, heading up the project. It was all their idea. I thought meeting in Pedro's house was fine enough, but it is true that they need more space. Thank you, Lord.

The new church may be a typical Amuesha building, with palm-bark walls and a dirt floor, but it is the first building dedicated by the Amueshas to the true "our Father, God!" It has benches with supports pounded into the dirt floor, with a men's side and a women's side in typical Amuesha fashion.

I am sad that Mary Ruth is not here with me to see the new church. She is still in graduate school. After finishing her doctorate, and upon her return to Peru, she will be asked by our director to consider becoming head of our Linguistic Department and chief editor. Neither of us had planned on this, thinking we would continue with the Amuesha work together. Since she will have the qualifications for the new position, and both are full-time jobs, Mary Ruth has to make a choice. Deciding she should accept the new post, I am now left without a permanent co-worker. Since there are often short-term workers visiting us in Peru, the director and I both realize it will be easy for me to get temporary help. Phyllis Ament is one of those early co-workers. She soon gets to know and love the Amueshas, and appreciates their individual personalities.

As Kosepa and I chat and exchange stories about what we've experienced while we have been apart, she tells me a precious incident about her little four-year-old girl, Elsa. "One day, Elsa comes running to me and anxiously asks me, 'Mommy, is Jesus coming? I heard his horn blowing.'" Elsa had heard a strange horn blowing in the distance and remembered what her mother had read to her (in Thessalonians) about the horn that will blow when Jesus comes again. What other four-year-old girl would know that Jesus will come

when his horn blows except one whose mother reads to her God's Word.

Another day when Kosepa comes back to visit, I notice that as she gets near, she leaves something in the grass before coming up to the house. We talk and Kosepa mentions that the field of manioc she planted is now ready to eat after months of developing, but she and her family haven't eaten any of it yet.

"Would it be good for me to give some of my first manioc roots to "our Father, God?" Kosepa asks.

"Yes, it would be good," I answer as I realize she wants to make a "first fruits" offering to God. I wonder how she proposes to do this, but I don't question.

"I thought that if I give my offering to you, it would be the best way to give it to God," she replies. I am overcome with emotion, yet I manage to say, "Thank you. Bring your manioc here and we will dedicate it to God."

As Kosepa goes to get the manioc she had left out in the grass, I call Phyllis and explain to her what Kosepa has said. "Come join us now as we pray and dedicate Kosepa's first fruits offering to God."

Kosepa brings her offering covered with a clean, white cloth. She uncovers the manioc and we see the best, long, straight roots that Kosepa has chosen. Again I am overwhelmed by her gesture. Kosepa places the roots carefully in line on the palm bark floor and the three of us gather around and pray.

"Thank you, our Father, that you have caused Kosepa's manioc plants to grow and the roots to develop so large and beautiful. We want to offer these first fruits to you for loving us so much and giving us our food each day. We make our offering in the name of Jesus, who loves us and died for us."

It is with great reverence and thankfulness that Phyllis and I eat the cooked manioc roots tonight as I share with her the story of how Kosepa's life has changed since she accepted Christ.

My mind recalls the time I first got to know Kosepa, pretty teen-age girl that she was. Actually, Kosepa was the village prostitute at that time, not only in her own village, but throughout Amueshaland. She made her rounds of all the villages, priding herself on being able to take husbands from other women. After a while, Kosepa was able to take Ambrocio from his wife in Singing Water. Then Mary Ruth and I arrived and started translating the Word. Kosepa wondered, *can these words be true?*

She decided right away that she needed to enroll in the new school Pedro was starting. She wanted to learn to read along with the children so she would be able to read what we were writing and calling "our Father's Word." Only then could she make her own decision as to whether these words were true. With her sharp mind, she learned to read in no time and immediately started reading all of "our Father's Word" that we were translating. Written in her own language, the Word spoke to her heart, and she realized she was a great sinner. She repented and made the decision to follow this Jesus she was just learning about who died for her sins. She was always the first one to get her copy of the newly-translated Scriptures. She devoured each new book as it was printed and shared what she learned, first reading to her husband Ambrocio, and then leading him and her children to believe.

Given her history, is it any wonder that Kosepa sees the need for sharing God's Word with the women and girls separate from the men? It is true that the women are not learning much at the regular church services due to caring for their children and trying to keep them quiet, chasing out the dogs and other pets, and talking to others. Now Kosepa has started a class just for the women and girls, so they can concentrate and learn better.

Santiago also sees the need for teaching the children separately. Thus the reason for the Sunday School classes which he has now started. Casper Mountain and the Bible School students are helping Pedro with the preaching. The indigenous church is developing.[1] Thank you, Lord.

Julio has had to stop teaching school in the distant village due to poor health. He is back at Singing Water, his home village, with nothing to do. I ask him if he would like to help me with translation and relieve overworked Pedro. I remember that Julio has been excellent in creative writing, in his Bible School studies, and in preaching. He says, yes, he would like to help me. I have done my exegetical studies for translating the book of Acts, thinking it would be a good book to challenge the believers to carry their new faith to every area where the Amueshas live.

The new church is just a few steps from my house. Ambrocio has even made shelves in the church on which to put our new Scripture books. Right away Julio and I find the church to be the best place for working on our translations. Soon we start translating the book of Acts.

Knowing that the Amuesha verb requires the repetitive suffix *-err* if a person ever returns to the place where he has been before, I make a large map so that we can trace the journeys of Paul and make sure we use the *-err* suffix when he returns to a place he has already visited. Julio and I keep the map before us and mark Paul's travels as he carries the Word of God to distant lands. (Julio has learned to read maps in his bilingual school.)

"When God's Holy Spirit comes upon you, He will make you to be strong ones. Then you will reveal my Word for me all around — in Jerusalem and in all of Judea, and also in Samaria, and into all parts of the world" (Acts 1:8). We locate these places on our map. The challenge is made to the Amueshas to carry "our Father's Word" to every part of their world.

Julio proves to be a great co-translator, wording his sentences with much clarity and ease for reading. How would I ever know that in the near future, Julio would be teaching this same book of Acts to all the Amuesha people of the upper mountains in a Regional Bible Conference? In fact, he will use this same map we have made to use in our translation work to teach the journeys of Paul.

Julio's sister, Kosepa, is also challenged anew as she reads Acts 2:18, where Peter is preaching and refers to the prophecy of Joel: "All who serve me, even the women, I will put my Spirit on them and they shall reveal my Word." In addition to her women's Sunday School class, Kosepa is led to start a midweek prayer and Bible study group for the women. Upon my return this time, she invites me to attend. I assure her I will come, and that she should continue teaching as she always does. I will just visit.

I could not have imagined the blessing awaiting me as I join the women. Hardly have they finished singing, praying and reading the Word when one of the young, married women falls down on her knees right in the middle of our circle. She starts weeping and confessing, "It's all my fault, it's all my fault. I have been playing around with the men. That's why Francisco (her husband) and I have been having so many problems. I want God to forgive me so that we can live well together." What a thrill it is to see all the women (including me) around her, and praying for her, and to watch her rise with great joy and peace on her face.

Her husband, Francisco (the "Tail End," now a tall grown-up), who is already a believer, has been having his own health problems. Later he will tell me, "I felt so bad, with extreme pain in my stomach and problems with my wife, that I just prayed to the Lord, 'Lord, heal my pain; if you don't, just let me die. I am so miserable.'" Then he says, "As soon as I prayed, the pain in my stomach stopped, and I thanked the Lord. He continues, "the next day the pain started anew. Again I prayed, 'Lord, do it again' and the pain stopped another time and never started again. I was profoundly touched and thanked the Lord and made a new commitment to serve Him."

How happy Francisco is to learn what his wife has just done. They now tell me they both have decided to serve the Lord together by helping other young couples in their church who are having similar marital problems.

Thus, the indigenous church continues to grow.

Church activities are now replacing some of the social drinking fiestas of the past. As more Amuesha churches are established in other areas and the Amuesha Church Association begins to function, quarterly meetings provide Christian fellowship, food, and fun, plus a three-day spiritual retreat.[2]

As Julio and I finish the translation of Acts, I realize that Julio has learned many principles of good translation. I feel he is capable of translating some basic stories from the Old Testament all on his own. Using a simplified storybook written in Spanish, he translates some fifty stories quite easily. He has learned enough Spanish from his school studies to do this. Julio asks for help only when he does not understand what the Spanish means. I review his work and find it to be a good, idiomatic translation, and suggest relatively few changes. The indigenous church is well on its way with an independent translator.

When these latest Bible stories are printed up into booklets, they become the stories Santiago chooses for teaching the children's Sunday School classes that he has started on his own. The other preachers also use these Old Testament stories for teaching the adults. They prove to be a great help for the Amueshas in learning some of the Old Testament culture and practices which they need to know in order to understand such things as sacrifices made to God for sins and its fulfillment in Christ's sacrifice in the New Testament.

I continue to have Julio work with me as my main co-translator since he has not yet decided if he wants to return to teaching. He enjoys the translation work so much and is so good at it that it is a joy for me to work with him.

Next we start translating the book of I Corinthians. This book is very difficult to translate because it concerns historical events and cultural situations that the believers at Corinth faced but which the Amuesha people have never experienced. I Corinthians Chapter 8 is one such section. When we begin, I wonder if this chapter will ever have much meaning for people who have never sacrificed meat to idols. I can only trust that the principle involved will be clear enough to apply in other instances as well. To that end, I talk with Julio about the principle Paul is teaching in this section — that we should not be a stumbling block to someone else by what we do, even if the action itself may be considered all right. As Julio grasps the profoundness of this new teaching of Paul's, he is so impressed that he just stops and asks me, "And where is Paul now? Is he with our Father?"

Caught off guard, I stammer, "Yes."

"Well, I just want to meet Paul someday and thank him for teaching us so well!" Julio replies. Once again I am struck with a great sensation of fulfillment in translating God's Word for people who have never had it available before.

Julio and I move on to the translation of James. This book also has some tough parts to translate since certain presuppositions of the culture at that time and place are different from those in Amuesha culture.

After the book of I Corinthians is in the hands of the people, one day I go to visit Kosepa's women's Sunday School class. I sit back in the midst of the women and I hear Kosepa announcing the text of God's Word she will share with them today — I Corinthians, Chapter 8! Oh dear, what will she do with that passage?

I almost hold my breath as she reads through the whole section first and then reads it again verse by verse. She reads verse 1: "Now I am going to talk to you about what you asked me, 'Is it fitting that we who are believers should eat the meat that they have killed for their handmade god (idol)?'" Immediately Kosepa reminds her listeners, "Now we here don't have this same problem that the Corinthian people had. We have never killed an animal for a handmade god, but we do have a similar problem with some people who tell us we should not be eating some meats that they say are unclean." Then she proceeds to read and tell them that we should not be a stumbling block to anyone by what we do. I breathe a sigh of relief as I hear Kosepa interpreting this Scripture correctly and applying the principle to a similar situation the Amueshas have. Kosepa has not been taught this particular Scripture by anyone else. Thank you, Lord. Your Word is powerful! The indigenous church continues to develop with the power of the translated Word.[3]

The young men who have studied in the Amuesha Bible School, as well as others, start giving me copies of Christian songs they have written. Each songwriter contributes from five to ten songs. They know I will have them record their songs on my tape recorder so others can learn the songs the way they were intended to be sung. Quickly, our songbook shoots up to two hundred songs. The Amueshas love the songs and want to sing them over and over. These songs become a great tool for evangelism.

I notice that Julio and Kosepa's little, old mother is coming early to services on Sundays. She arrives before the others and tells me she wants to listen to the Christian songs in her language (which we now have on tape). She moves close to the little tape recorder so she can hear the words well before the others come. Is she really wanting to believe now after being so resistant to Kosepa and Julio's sharing God's Word with her? I later learn from Kosepa that her mother has made her decision to believe and wants to learn as much as she can of the Word and the songs. Thank you, Lord.

"Do you have any more books of our Father's Word?" a young fourteen-year-old teenager by the name of Espiritu asks me just after arriving from his little village in the mountains, a place we have never been before. "I have already read all the ones I have to the people in my village. They want me to read more of our Father's Word to them if you have more."

"Yes, I have more and will give them to you. But tell me, how did you learn to read since there is no school in your village yet?"

"I went to the bilingual school in Cacaso (quite far away) and stayed there long enough to learn to read. Now I know how to read well, and I read to all the people in my village. They come together for me to read to them our Father's Word."

What a joy it is to hear this news from a boy who lives in a village where there is not yet a school or a Bible School student. Thank you, Lord. I give him the new books he hasn't read and he is on his way back home. The Word is spreading to all areas!

Early one Sunday morning Cuñivo, the shaman, arrives at my door and quickly tells me, "Come, pray with me in the church. I want to believe our Father's Word and receive Christ." Is this the shaman who for years has refused to believe and has advised the chief and others not to believe? I can hardly believe what I am hearing. He continues, "I now realize that all I have been doing is in vain — trying to tell the people what is making them sick. It's all *orrena* (in vain)."

I call Pedro and others and we hurry into the new church. The shaman throws himself down and starts praying immediately: "For a long time I have resisted you, but now I want you to forgive me . . ." Thank you, Lord.

After the shaman's conversion,[4] he is the first one to arrive Sunday mornings at the church. He sits in the front and is the first to learn the Scripture memory verse which the preacher has written on the blackboard for that day. He is now eager to memorize all of God's Word that he can.

In fact, all of the older adults are now saying that they want to learn much more of God's Word. "We are not able to go the long distance down-river to our Bible School where the young people are going, but we want to know God's Word, too. Can't we study more right here in our own village?" The idea of Regional Bible Conferences is born. Since the villages are spread over such a large area, they make the decision to have two Bible Conferences, one upriver and one downriver.

By this time, a good number of the villagers have already studied in the Amuesha Bible School, and they volunteer to be the teachers at the Bible Conferences. Each one chooses the book of Scripture he feels most competent to teach. Julio chooses the book of Acts since he helped translate it, using the same map that he and I made to trace Paul's journeys. He even makes a list of questions he will ask his students as they study. Casper Mountain is assigned to all the adults who don't know how to read because he is closer to them in age. He chooses to teach them all the selected verses on the way of salvation and the Christian life. He has them memorize all the 130 verses, which they can do quite easily. Even the older adults of an oral tradition society have great powers of memory. Oddly, the converted shaman is Casper's best student.

The Amueshas do all the planning and teaching for the Bible Conferences. I am not even able to visit, nor do I need to. They will only be studying Scripture that has already been published. I receive a letter from Pedro at the start of the Conference: "I am writing so that you can rejoice with us. Some forty adults are studying, having come from five upriver villages. The chief and the converted shaman meet with us for early morning prayer. We study six hours each day and will continue for two months, using all the Scripture we have translated to date. Seven of us are sharing in the teaching. New ones are believing." Thank you, Lord.

At the same time, the downriver Conference is going on with Domingo Suarez and other Bible School students teaching there. And still farther downriver the regular Amuesha Bible School is in session again. Valerio is continuing to teach, with other Christian leaders helping him. He has twenty-eight students this year. He writes of baptizing twenty-two new believers. What a joy it is to know that indigenous Christian leaders are taking full responsibility, even as it should be.

Teacher Tomas had planned to teach in the upriver Conference. But shortly before it was to start, he drowned in the swift water downriver where he had taught. Tomas, who was so loved by both upriver and downriver people, is greatly missed by everyone especially his school students. Carlos, one of his older students, announces immediately, "I must dedicate myself to take my beloved teacher's place." That he does. He studies at Yarina in the Teacher Training Course and becomes not only a schoolteacher, but a teacher of the Word in his church, just like his beloved teacher, Tomas.

Of all the Amuesha schoolteachers, Carlos becomes one of the best, using his own creative ideas to challenge his students and guide his village. During the Teacher Training Course at Yarina, he often shares his ideas with the other teacher-trainees, helping them to improve their skills and their work in the villages. Thus, it is only fitting that Carlos should become the bilingual teacher who will finally be responsibile for  maintaining all the Amuesha bilingual schoolbooks and Scripture books in the future. He and his son, Asael, volunteer to take on this challenge for their people.


". . . I will build my church and the gates of hell shall not prevail against it."
> – Jesus, (Matthew 16:18, KJV)


(Thank you, Lord, for the developing indigenous churches among the Amuesha people. Thank you for many more believers and their desire to know your Word.)

# 48

# Finishing the Translation of the New Testament

Casper Mountain becomes a missionary?

Now that Julio's health has improved, he begins teaching school again. Thankfully, Casper Mountain is very willing to become my main co-translator. As I talk to him about pay, he says, "No, I don't want to be paid. I want to do this for God."

"We will be working all day, everyday," I counter. That means you will have to pay someone else to work your coffee plants." Only then does Casper agree to accept payment for his time.

I decide to translate Romans next to include more Scripture in the way of salvation. Romans is a difficult book to translate because of the long development of Paul's themes over various chapters. I am glad Casper Mountain already knows much of the plan of salvation and expect he will be a great help to me in the translation of this book.

As we get into Chapter 3, where Paul elaborates on the sinfulness of the natural person, I am suddenly reminded of the Amuesha people of Sancachari. Mary Ruth and I visited them several years ago, but they told us they did not want God's Word there. They didn't even want a bilingual school lest they get

God's Word along with the school. They were known to have killed each other in drunken brawls. As we worked through the different sins Paul mentions in Romans 3 — "swift to shed blood, mouth full of cursing and bitterness, none that does good" — I say to Casper Mountain, "This reminds me of the people of Sancachari." I proceed to tell him about our visit in that village and the people telling us they did not want God's Word.

Casper has never visited that place before, but he thinks about it for a while and says, "I think if I go there, they will listen to me as I tell them God's Word."

I don't say it, but I don't think they will. We eventually finish the translation of Romans and it is again time for my furlough. Sad to say, I don't even think about the people of Sancachari during that busy furlough.

When I return to the Amueshas and Casper Mountain and I are again translating Scripture, he casually begins to tell me about going to Sancachari. "I went to Sancachari, he begins, "I remembered you said that they did not want God's Word, so I did not call any meeting. I just lived with the head man and his household" (which usually includes married daughters, their husbands, and their children).

It is quite normal in Amuesha culture for a single man to live with a family. If he helps get the firewood for cooking and does his share of keeping the jungle cut back, he can stay and eat with the family. In the evenings after eating, the family talks together for a while before retiring.

Casper Mountain says, "In those evening times as I sat with the family, I would first start to hum one of our Christian tunes. After a while, some of the children would say, 'That's a pretty tune. Sing it again so we can learn it.' I would hum it several times so the children could learn it well before we went to sleep.

"The next evening, the children wanted to sing it again. 'Does this tune have any words?' they would ask. 'Yes, it has words.' I would sing the words for them. 'Jesus loves me; I know this because our Father's Word tells me so.' Then they would ask me to sing it several times so they could learn it well.

"The next evening, they would want to sing it again. So I would ask them, 'Do you know where these words come from?' 'No,' they replied. 'Where do they come from?' Then I would take out my Scripture book of God's Word and read to the children from John 3:16. 'Our Father God loved all the people of the world so much that he sent us his Son Jesus.' 'That's good,' the children answered. 'We want to learn that.' Then the parents would say, 'What was that? Read that again.' As I read it again, they said, 'That's good; we didn't know God loves us. We want to learn that, too.'

"The next evening, the children wanted to know if I knew more songs. Then I would teach them another song and read to them from God's Word, where the song came from. The parents and other older ones became interested and listened too. Slowly, starting with the songs they loved so much, I could teach them the way of salvation from God's Word, and they listened and said they wanted to believe.

"After they were all believing, I would move to another household and start all over again. It was several months before I finished with all the families and went back home. Then they would send for me to come back and teach them more."

I sit there dumbfounded taking in Casper Mountain's story. The people of Sancachari listened to God's Word and believed. I marvel at the wisdom and patience that Casper used in dealing with his own people in leading them to accept and believe God's Word. I think about how differently he approached the situation than an ordinary missionary would: call a meeting, ask for a show of hands, and hurry off. How beautiful it is to see Casper and other Amuesha believers using innovative methods to win over their own people. We need to let the Gospel work in the lives of the new Christians and through them within in their culture, recognizing that the same Holy Spirit who leads us is at work in them and leading them to the truth.[1] Thank you, Lord.

The time comes when the people of Sancachari call for Casper Mountain to baptize them, from the headman on down to the children. Out of great appreciation, the headman offers his daughter to Casper Mountain as a wife. "I watched to see if she minded her parents, which she did, so I knew that she would mind her husband also," Casper tells me later. Juana, too, becomes a believer. She and Casper Mountain enjoy reading the Scriptures together. She learns much from him.

Julio is now the second teacher in the school at Singing Water which allows him to live in his home area. I am greatly surprised when he comes one morning and informs me that his mother has died up on the mountain where they live. "She refused to take her medicine," he says. This is the little, old woman that Julio and his sister, Kosepa, have led to believe in Jesus. I can only thank God that she did believe.

Julio invites me to come sit with them in the evening and through the night. I take along some food that we can share with the others who will come to join Julio and Kosepa in their sorrow. I notice as I reach the house that I do not hear any wailing as Amueshas are accustomed to do.

After we have eaten the food, Julio stands up in the midst of the people, with his provisional copy of I Corinthians (that he had helped me translate) in his hand, and begins to speak, "You notice that I and my sister, Kosepa, are not wailing as we Amueshas usually do. You may think that it is because we do not love our mother. That is not the reason. We know that our mother believed in Jesus to save her. We know that she is now safe with Jesus. That's why we are not wailing. We know that her body will rise to life again when Jesus comes. That's what God's Word tells us here in I Corinthians 15."

Julio proceeds to read from verse 42, saying how our mortal bodies are destined to die but when we rise again we will never "die" again. How my heart rejoices with Julio as I remember translating these words with him and now see these very words are bringing him peace and joy. I remember how Julio and Kosepa were so concerned that their mother also believe in Jesus. Thank you, Lord.

I happen to be with the Amueshas when the first U.S. moon landing is made. I have heard on my little radio exactly when the touchdown will occur. I hurry upstairs, just under the thatched roof where I sleep and keep the radio, to be sure I hear the landing from beginning to end.

In the meantime, two of the older, Amuesha ladies come to visit. I call to them that I will be down soon. "I'm listening to something very important on my radio," I say. As I hear that dramatic ending of the "giant step" onto the moon, I turn off the radio and rush down with all my excitement to tell the Indian women about "the first person who has ever walked on the moon."

The two Amuesha women look at each other in surprise and remark casually, "Why 'our mother' has been on the moon for a long time." (The Amueshas call the moon 'our mother.')

I continue to work with Casper Mountain on translation. As we start the book of Luke, we run into another problem. In Chapter 1, verse 15, the text reads (speaking of John the Baptist), "and he shall be filled with the Holy Spirit." The Amueshas have never associated their word for "fill" with anything except pots and baskets. How can a person be "filled"? Even their word for a full stomach is not the word for "fill."

We talk together about what "filled with the Holy Spirit" means (obsessed with or possessed by). The thought comes to me of what the Amueshas say about the shaman. They say that he can "wear" the spirit of the tiger, that they can tell when he is wearing the tiger spirit because he then will act like a tiger. Their word for "wear" is the same word as to "wear or put on a garment." Can this possibly be the way to say "filled with God's Spirit"? As I cautiously question Casper about this, his face lights up immediately. "Yes, that is the way we would say it, he is 'wearing' God's Holy Spirit."[2] What a neat parallel — when we are "wearing God's Holy Spirit, we act good like God; when we are wearing the devil's spirit, we act like the devil."

As we continue with this last Gospel to be translated, I realize that in the first three Gospels we translated early on, there is room for improvement. Over the years, I have learned so much more about good storytelling in Amuesha. In fact, I have written a paper called "Prominence and Cohesion in Amuesha,"[3] dealing with the features of their language which make for more understandable storytelling.

Cultural differences continue to be a problem in translating the Amuesha New Testament. They must be reckoned with in each case and passages must be translated in such a way that the Amuesha people will understand the author's original meaning, right down to the last book. Revelation 3:20 is no exception. Amuesha people do not "knock" on doors. Often their houses have no doors, just a doorway. Their cultural equivalent is to "call" at the doorway of the house. Now, many Amueshas are hearing Jesus "calling" at their doorways and are inviting Him to come in!

After finishing the translation of the New Testament, Casper Mountain and I take another two years, to retranslate the first three Gospels, incorporating the aspects of narrative discourse learned later in the translation process. We put in long hours.

Knowing how I am pressed for time, Santiago's mother (one of the early believers among the women) tells me she would like to help by serving Casper Mountain his noon meal. What a sweet expression of Christian love and concern. After Casper leaves at four o'clock to go back up on his mountain and do his chores before dark, I start typing the revised text we've finished that day, often not ending before dark. I light candles on both sides of my typewriter and continue typing there in the church (a new, large church the believers have built). Then I rush over to get my supper, bathe, and get ready for the next day. Occasionally at night, I talk by radio with my distant cousin, Lucy, who is now in Lima, telling her of our progress. When I awaken the first thing in the morning, under my thatched roof, I sing "When morning guilds the skies my heart awakening cries, may Jesus Christ be praised." The end of the translation work is in sight!

When we get down to the last ten verses of the final draft of the New Testament, Casper Mountain tells me to let Lucy know we are finishing our last ten-verse countdown tomorrow, and on time. Praise the Lord! We know that Lucy will pass the word on to all our colleagues who are anxious to rejoice with us. Although we still have the big read-through for proofreading ahead of us, we will do that later at Yarina Center where we have better facilities for this long, careful job.

I ask Francisco (the "Tail End" orphan of the school) to help with the proofreading because I remember from many years before how sharp he was in school, even in the first grade. I determined way back then that in the future, Francisco should help in proofreading the final New Testament text. He is now a grown man with his own family, and a strong believer. He says he will be happy to help in checking the text. Casper Mountain and his family also agree to assist us.

Both families come to Yarina for the five-month period that we will dedicate to simply read through the manuscript to make sure all the words are spelled correctly with their various diacritic markings. Most of the books have already been printed in provisional form and are in use, except Hebrews and Revelation. At this point, all of the revisions have already been made.

Francisco, Casper, and I each plan to read through the whole New Testament, separately marking any of the mistakes we see. After we finish the first read-through, Francisco is certain he has seen and corrected all the mistakes. I, knowing how easy it is not to see a misspelled word or a letter missing its diacritic mark, suggest we each read it through at least three times. On the second read-through, when Francisco finds a word misspelled that he didn't see on the first round, he can't believe it, expert speller that he is. He, too, realizes that each one of us needs to read the text at least three times, for a total of nine read-throughs, which we proceed to do.

We continue reading day after day, and I notice that Francisco is keeping notes on the side. I look a little closer and see that he has a number of subjects under which he is tabulating verse references he considers to be good. When I admire what he is doing, he smiles and says, "I am going to have so many good things to share with all my people when I go back" — sermons in the making! Casper Mountain, too, is making his notes as he reads.

One day, as we are busy at work, we get a call from our director asking if he can bring in the Catholic cardinal, who happens to be visiting the Center. He would like to see a translation in process. He and his entourage are not all able to enter our small room. I show him all the checklists that we are following to make sure each part of the manuscript is well checked.

As I introduce my helpers, Francisco, who knows some Spanish, starts speaking with the cardinal, telling him how he learned to read in the Amuesha Bilingual School in his village. That's how he is able to help in translating God's Word into his language, he adds. Casper Mountain, in his limited Spanish, says, "I, too, even as an adult, learned to read in our Bilingual School. That's why I am able to help in the translation." Their compliments of our work make it seem as if I had prompted them to say these things, but I hadn't. As the cardinal concludes his visit and starts to leave, he takes my hand and says, "Let me congratulate you on doing a very noble work."

On the last day as we finish the five-month job of proofreading the Amuesha New Testament,[4] we each break into spontaneous prayer praising God. Francisco, just having read Revelation 5:9, ". . . you purchased men for God from every tribe and language and people and nation," prayed his thanks to God: "Thank you, our Father, that you wanted us Amuesha people to have your Word in our language." Thank you, Lord, for your great faithfulness!

"... great is your faithfulness."

> – the Prophet Jeremiah, (Lamentations 3:23 NIV)

"The Lord gave the Word; great was the company of those that published it."

> (Psalm 68:11 KJV)

"The entrance of thy Word giveth light ..."

> (Psalm 119:130 KJV)

# 49

# The Printing
# and Dedication
# of the New Testament

Can you believe it? They used the wrong glue!

On the night that we finish the final read-through of the New Testament, our Center Director calls a meeting for the whole group to gather and celebrate with our Amuesha team. Despite us being dog-tired, we rejoice with all our colleagues at Yarina who have had a part in producing the Amuesha New Testament. Beaming with happiness, Casper Mountain says, "Let's sing our song of praise to God, *'Ya'ye'choĉhtatoñña Yompor.'*"

The next day, I get a radio call from my friend, Bob, who is out in the Amarakaeri area distributing Scripture books among the people he works with. He has heard the radio news that the Amuesha translation is finished. He congratulates me and asks, "What are your plans now?"

"Well, I have to get the entire manuscript to Dallas where they will start the layout and typesetting for printing," I reply. "It's time for my furlough anyway, so I will be going home soon." I completely forget that it is time for Bob's furlough also, since we returned to Peru at the same time together.

In just a few days, I receive a letter from Bob — with a marriage proposal!

Since we have been very good friends for a long time, it is not altogether a shock. Instead, it's a great joy. My New Testament is now finished, and we can both work together as Bob finishes his translation. The only problem is, I have no way of telling him my answer!

With ten indigenous churches already functioning among the Amueshas, I feel I am not needed in Amueshaland any more. These are churches that the Amueshas themselves have established, where they are doing the preaching and teaching using their Amuesha Scriptures. In fact, I know that allowing them to continue on their own is the best thing to do. I should let the new churches develop within the Amueshas' own cultural setting. Once there is an understandable translation of the Scriptures, and believers who are able and willing to read and share God's Word with their people, there is no need for the missionary.[1]

Since there is no way for Bob to receive my answer to his proposal, he has to wait until he arrives back at Yarina. Once he knows that my answer is "yes," we make preparations to leave immediately for the U.S. as Bob is already planning his furlough. Looking over our schedule, we only have one week before we head home. With this tight schedule, we decide not to announce our engagement to our fellow workers at Yarina because such an announcement would surely bring all kinds of social kindnesses which we would appreciate but feel we don't have time for. Preceding our departure for the airport, we do, however, announce our engagement at a farewell meal with our closest friends.

News spreads fast at Yarina. Shortly after we arrive at the airport, our friends arrive, complete with rice to give us a loving send-off. Friends in Lima also get the happy news before we land there. They meet us at the gate and have signs up, and my room is adorned with flowers. House parents, Dick and Nadine Clark, prepare a banquet for the occasion. Jim Wroughton suggests that we sing a "fitting song": "Seek Ye First the Kingdom of God and His Righteousness and All These Things Shall Be Added Unto You."

Bob and I buy festive Quechua hats to wear home on the plane. The Gammons and others greet us in Miami and make sure our news is true. Bob's parents meet our plane in North Carolina to take us to their beautiful, new home in Tryon, North Carolina and help us get ready for the wedding.

In less than a week Bob and I are married there in a lovely Fall ceremony that takes place amidst the colorful leaves and matching chrysanthemums I have used to decorate the mantle over the fireplace in his parents' new home. Bob's old Navy buddy is happy to marry us and provide the music. Both of our sisters are on hand to make our family wedding complete. My nephew arrives just in time to "give me away." Following a delightful wedding dinner for all at the Pinecrest Inn, Bob and I are off on our honeymoon in the Smoky Mountains.

When we return back at Bob's parents' home, we find they have already left for their winter condominium in Florida, which leaves us the full use of their North Carolina house. Bob and I soon move on to Dallas to start processing the New Testament for printing. This turns out to be no small job because the whole manuscript has to be keyboarded again, which of course requires yet another round of proofreading. (Personal computers were not available in Peru at the time.) A special font has to be created to take care of the diacritical markings that some Amuesha letters require. The commercial typesetter that our group is using causes us extra problems. However, after final instructions for the printer to be sure to use glue that will resist the moisture of the jungle, we are again off to Peru for the dedication of the Amuesha New Testament.

Bob and I set up housekeeping in a new, large house we have purchased at Yarina Center. While waiting for the printed New Testaments to arrive, we start preparing for the dedication. We make a preparatory trip to Singing Water to make plans for holding the upcoming dedication there. Many people from the U.S. have told us that they want to attend. We are happy to have them come, but have no idea how we can get so many people transported out to this remote area. Since our planes cannot fly directly into the village, what can we do?

As we ponder these problems, I happen to be talking to Will Pritchard (fellow member who works at our center in Yarina). He suggests the possibility of using our Bluebird bus and he even volunteers to drive. Since there is now a road to the village, maybe the bus can get there. His wife, Marcia, volunteers to take charge of food and bedding for the group. Thank you, Lord. Even a generator for lights, and many more New Testaments can go on the bus.

Plans are proceeding well, and the New Testaments arrive in Peru. How could we ever know that our biggest problem yet is just about to knock us out. We can't believe it — the printer did not use the synthetic, moisture-resistant glue on the covers of the New Testaments as instructed! *What can we do so the books will be ready on time for the date already set for the dedication?*

Phyllis Woodard is an angel in disguise. She volunteers to take over the job of seeing that all the old glue gets scraped off the covers of thousands of New Testaments (Amuesha and four other languages) and is replaced with our own moisture-resistant glue. She also hires a crew of young people to do the job. It's a good thing for us that the date the Amueshas have chosen for the dedication will not come too soon for everything that needs to be done. *Thank you, Lord.*

We have loads of help in taking care of our many visitors at Yarina before we even leave for the dedication. Miss Shirley Wood, the librarian from Columbia Bible College (CBC) where I worked, and Miss McClarty, my Spanish teacher from CBC, stay with us. The newly reglued books are scarcely ready when they are loaded by pilot Doug Deming and John Bush on the plane for the first leg of their journey to Amueshaland. They will continue on by bus from San Ramon.

What a delight to finally arrive at Singing Water and see the large, palm frond arbor the people have made for this special occasion. Although the new, larger church was built some time ago, it surely cannot hold all the people who are coming from the upriver region.

Only one special person will not be here: my closest friend Kosepa, the one for whom I felt I was especially translating the New Testament. I am told she died some time ago. How I would have loved to put the New Testament in her own hand and seen the look in her eyes. But it will be here for her husband and children, and I'm sure she is rejoicing with us.

Marcia goes into action with her food and bedding business. The villagers inform us that we can use the second floor of the new church building (not yet walled in) to put down sleeping bags and mosquito nets for our twenty-five visitors from the U.S. It appears a little like a rescue mission with all the nets set up side by side, but everyone sleeps well there.

The Amueshas want our celebrations to go on for three days. Our fellows get the generator set up and the lights go on for the first time in Singing Water! Since we knew we would have electricity, we brought along a slide projector to finally show the Amueshas the pictures we have made over the years, pictures they have always wanted to see. This presentation becomes a little sideshow after the evening singing. Santiago and others of the young Christian leaders direct the singing sessions, even accompanying songs with guitars they have learned to play.

I get together right away with all the Christian leaders to see what they are planning for the dedication service. They have planned that each of the groups coming from the various villages have their own little program, headed up by their bilingual teacher in charge. They plan to read Scriptures and sing songs.

What a joy it is to see the children and older Amueshas reading from the very first copies of the Amuesha New Testament: "Heaven and earth will pass away, but my words will never pass away." (Matthew 24:35 NIV). "The grass withers and the flowers fall, but the word of the Lord stands forever." (I Peter 1:24-25 NIV).

Santiago directs the entire dedication program. Both Pedro and Valerio (teacher of the Amuesha Bible School) speak in appreciation for all the

Amuesha people. When the first complimentary copies of the New Testament are presented to those who have helped with the translation, I remember Kosepa, who helped check some of the Scriptures. But Kosepa is not here to receive her copy. How she would have delighted in it! Although her husband, Ambrocio, is here to represent her, I miss Kosepa terribly. As I present the New Testament to him he says, "I want God's Word. Kosepa and I had planned to teach God's Word together to our children, which I now plan to do."

Of course, the greatest joy is presenting the New Testament to Casper Mountain, who has really dedicated his life to the translation. Pedro and Julio receive their complimentary copies also. Pedro beams with joy in seeing his people receive God's Word in their language, fulfilling his greatest desire. Carlos represents his beloved teacher, Tomas, whose position he has vowed to fill, as he receives his copy. Would we ever think that Carlos' son, Asael, just a babe in arms now, will be working with his father, carrying on the work of the bilingual schools among the Amueshas as we ourselves leave Peru?

We have our U.S. visitors also help us present the complimentary copies of the Amuesha New Testament. After Miss McClarty hands a copy to one of the Amuesha, she tells us later, "It was the greatest joy I have ever had in my whole life." We had no idea that her earthly life was coming to an end in the very near future.

At the end of the program which lasts several hours, immediately the Amueshas adorned with their crowns, feathers, best tunics, drums, panpipes, and flutes start their native processional dances of praise and thanksgiving to the true "our Father." Just as Casper Mountain had said, "I used to do these dances to the sun that we thought was 'our Father'; now I want to do my dances to the one I know is the true 'our Father, God.'"[2]

As they finish their dance and stand in file to thank the true "our Father," I hear Santiago's mother, who is closest to me pray, "Thank you, our true Father, for giving us your Word in our language." How God must be rejoicing to hear His new Amuesha believers praising and thanking Him, the true God, in their own native ways!

It is now time for all the Amueshas to receive their own copies of "our Father's Word" *(Yompor Po'ñoñ)*. Since the Amuesha people put more value on a gift given by a loved one than on a bought article, we have decided not to charge a fee for the books. Instead, we tell the people that anyone may have a book who wants one, but books do take money to print. (The Bible League has paid for the printing.) Also, whoever has money and wants to pay for one or more books for those who have no money may do so. Any money given will be used to help another group receive God's Word. A "collection plate" has been fashioned from one of the emptied New Testament boxes. With a slit in the top of the box, it is placed near the books.

Following our instructions, pandemonium breaks loose as people rush to the table where the New Testaments are all stacked. Hands are giving, hands are receiving the "Wonderful Words of Life" in their own language. Some hands are putting money in the collection box, some are not. Casper Mountain shows me he is putting in five times the normal cost. "That's so that five children who cannot pay may have their copies also." At the end of the day, some two hundred copies of those books have gone into waiting hands. When

we count the funds we've received, it averages a little higher than the price per book we would have charged. Thank you, Lord.

On the final night of the three-day celebration, we once again are sleeping under our mosquito nets. From the loft of my little, old house, what a delight it is to hear Espiritu's voice nearby reading aloud from the new book of Revelation. Revelation and Hebrews are the only books the Amueshas have not already seen in provisional form.

After the Amuesha dedication, we head back to Lima to participate in yet another celebration. This time the special occasion is a five New Testaments dedication. Four other translation teams have finished with their New Testaments as well — in the Chayahuita, Cashibo, Bora, and Capanahua languages. Our Lima personnel take charge of this dedication. They invite Lima friends and officials to attend, including the head of the Peruvian Bible Society.

Francisco goes along with us to read, since they have requested a reader from each of the language groups be present to read the verse of Scripture (I John 4:7) in his own language. Fluently and beautifully Francisco reads this verse: *"Masheñneshacha 'ñaɱanočhaneshacha 'amueranna 'tpahuepa 'ch allohueney ɩ̃arro 'mar ñeñɩ̃pa' Yomporeshoɩ̃ huena."* "Dear friends, let us love one another for love comes from God." This is a favorite verse of Wycliffe founder, William Cameron Townsend. Who would ever think little orphan Poso'mer (the "Tail End" now a tall, young man called Francisco) would be reading God's Word in his own language for all these Lima officials? Thank you, Lord.

"The one who calls you is faithful and he will do it."
  – the Apostle Paul, (I Thessalonians 5:24 NIV)

". . . I have given them the words which thou gavest me . . ."
  – Jesus, (John 17:8 KJV)

"My word . . . will not return to me empty, but will accomplish what I desire."
  (Isaiah 55:11 NIV)

"Heaven and earth will pass away, but my words will never pass away."
  – Jesus, (Matthew 24:35 NIV)

(Thank you, Lord, for the great desire of the Amuesha people to have your Word in their language. May they use it to win many more of their people to you.)

# 50

# The Presentation of the Amuesha Grammar Book and the Dictionary

Do indigenous people want a grammar book of their language?

We spend most of our time now with Bob's language group, the Amarakaeri, while he finishes the translation of the New Testament in their language. These people live far to the south of Peru, near the Bolivian and Brazilian borders and a good distance away from the Amuesha nation. The languages of the two groups are very different.

Bob is nearing the completion of his translation but could use some help with the literacy work. I take this on as my job, along with continuing to work on a complete write-up of the Amuesha grammar book and the compilation of a dictionary in Amuesha. I am learning a little bit of the Amarakaeri language, but one can accomplish a lot in literacy without knowing much of the language.

It's fun working with these kids too. Just like the Amueshas, they want to learn to read in their own language. Easier than the Amuesha alphabet, in no time the young people are learning to read and write in Amarakaeri. And they are soon doing creative writing and composing little stories and legends. They begin reading some of the simplest Scripture stories that Bob has completed.

On a short trip back to the Amueshaland, I mention that I am writing a book of Amuesha grammar. Espiritu Bautista, one of the sharp Amuesha bilingual school graduates, takes great interest in this.

"When you finish that book, this is what we want you to do," Espiritu tells me in all earnestness. "Bring copies of it for each one of us. We want you to have a seminar and show all of us what the grammar of our language is." He is like many Amueshas who have been told their language has no grammar and that they should not be speaking it. People who talk this way about another language do not realize that every language has a concise system of grammar rules that operate, otherwise, there could be no communication between speakers. Espiritu not only wants to see that grammar book, but show it to the Spanish speaking critics.

I remember Espiritu's words as I work through the long grammar, describing all the intricate grammatical rules I find operating very precisely in this complex language. His words encourage me to keep working at it. I am sure that when the Amuesha people realize their language has grammatical structure just like any other language, they will have more pride and confidence in the use of it, despite what they have been told by the speakers of Spanish, the national language. This, in itself, will encourage the use of the Amuesha New Testament, which still touches their hearts more clearly and effectively, than does the New Testament in the Spanish language.

The dictionary compilation begun in our first days among the Amueshas continues simultaneously with the grammar book. As soon as the word classes are defined in the grammar, those same classes are used to identify each word in the dictionary. For example, nouns are identified as a category of words which may carry a certain list of affix morphemes, and verbs are a category of words which may carry another list of affix morphemes. All nouns have a common function in the sentence, all verbs another function. Thus, the Amuesha dictionary is very similar to the national language dictionary in its entry format.

All the bird, tree, and plant names also find their way into the Amuesha side of the diglot dictionary. Since there are hundreds of these names from all the Amazon rainforest species, rather than fill up the dictionary, I place them in a special appendix listing for those which have no special relationship to the culture and we have been unable to link with Spanish equivalents. The appendix also includes such cultural items as all the woven designs (along with drawings by Casper Mountain), names of the many panpipe and drum dances, names of legendary characters, and names of ancient clans. Simply, the Amueshas want to have a written record of their culture.

Francisco, the little "Tail End," who is now a six-footer and a devout Christian, is my chief consultant in identifying the meanings of all the words in the dictionary. He also learned some Spanish as a teenager, which helps with the entries on the Spanish side of the dictionary.

As Francisco and I are taking a little break from our dictionary work, at one point he starts telling me about their church at Singing Water as it functions now.

"There are six of us men who like and are willing to teach and preach in our church there, in addition to the head, indigenous pastor. As each one of us reads our Amuesha Scriptures, we keep in mind passages we would like to share with our people. We all meet together on Saturdays to pray for the following Sunday and to decide which of us will be the speaker for the next Sunday.

"One day, as I was going to the Saturday meeting, I was sure that after we prayed, they would all say I should be the next preacher. I had a very good passage of Scripture I felt God really wanted me to share with my people. But after we prayed that day, they all said one of the others should be the next preacher. I started to say, 'Stop, you've got it all wrong, I'm sure God wants me to be the preacher; I've got just the right message.'"

Francisco continues: "Just then I decided, 'Maybe I should just keep quiet.' Even so, I felt so bad, thinking they had made a mistake. But do you know what happened the next Sunday? When the chosen man got up to speak, he had the very same passage of Scripture that I was planning to use with the people, and he made practically the same comments on it that I would have!"

I sit there thinking about Francisco's story. I not only praise the Lord for the six volunteer preachers in the church, which is good news for me to hear since the distribution of the Amuesha New Testaments, but also for the great lesson He is teaching Francisco and me.

"Francisco, do you know that you are teaching me and my people something new from the Word? We don't always 'submit to one another' as willingly
as you did." Thank you, Lord, for teaching Francisco and me.

When the final pages of the two books — the Amuesha Grammar and the
Amuesha Dictionary[1] (a total of 971 pages) — are finished and printed, the
Amuesha teacher-trainees studying at Yarina Center are anxious to see and
study the completed products. They get so excited when it is confirmed that
their language really does have nouns, verbs, and other parts of speech like
any other language. Remaining enthusiastic even after we have been studying
the new Amuesha grammar book for several hours, the teacher-trainees are
surprised but greatly pleased to see how the grammatical rules operate. They
now realize what they have been told by national language speakers — that
their language has no grammar — is not true at all. Prestige for their mother
tongue has taken a quantum leap forward!

The teacher-trainees set the date for the presentation of the dictionary
and grammar books to the people. I have not forgotten about Espiritu's
request for a seminar on the grammar and we schedule it to begin the week
following the presentation. Teacher Carlos volunteers to host this event at
his village of Azules, which previously was the most remote of the Amuesha
areas.

Azules is not remote anymore. In the interim years, the marginal highway has been built east of the Andes Mountains and it passes right through
Azules. This means we can arrive by road rather than trekking for days as in
years past.

Carlos' son, Asael, a third-generation teacher-trainee, is now taking
the Teacher Training Course at Yarina Center. He plans to attend this
presentation but wants to get a preview of the Amuesha grammar contents
before that time. He asks that I review the new grammar book with him
and his buddy, another Amuesha teacher-trainee studying at Yarina. They
too are enthralled as they become aware of the grammatical structure of
their own language!

We load up our JAARS plane with the new grammar books and dictionaries
and take off for the presentation. We fly to the nearest airstrip and find a
vehicle that will travel up the new road to Azules. With all the books reloaded,

we head out in a pick-up truck. I can hardly believe we will now get to this remote area in just a few hours by road.

As the jungle trees whiz by and we near Azules, I start to see large, printed signs along the road. They read: "Primer Seminario" (the First Seminar). We pass so quickly I can't read the smaller type, but I wonder who could be having a seminar in this remote place. Crazy me. At the third sign, I realize that Carlos, efficient guy that he is, has had these neat signs printed and placed to announce the Amuesha Grammar Seminar. When we meet Carlos and I congratulate him on the good signs, he says, "I would have put them still farther out, but I ran out of time."

Carlos has been hard at work. The preparations he has made for this big event include appointed houses for the visitors, meal tickets, cooks for the four-day occasion, and seating arrangement for the seminar. We can certainly understand why Carlos ran out of time to place more signs. With all the things we have also brought — blackboard, books, theme sign, etc. — our jungle site is beginning to look like the location of a real seminar.

What fun it is to renew acquaintances with many the Amueshas from various areas. I have not seen them for a long time; children have grown up, and adults and teachers have grown older over the years.

After an early church service on Sunday morning, we gather again for the presentation of the grammar books and dictionaries. Carlos has the entire program planned, with various speakers, including former bilingual school student Agosto, who has been working in Lima with anthropologists. Agosto now has his own office and secretary, and has been involved with the construction project that created the new road. (Agosto, by the way, was the baby of the second wife who told me she had never heard of Jesus.)

I take my turn in speaking to the people, encouraging them to not abandon their Amuesha language. Carrying out the theme of our conference, I remind them that as they will be learning Spanish in the future, they should continue to speak Amuesha. " 'Two languages are better than one' is true, even as our theme says. Keep your identity as a people speaking a beautiful language, with a grammar more complex than Spanish or English. Teach it to your children." I feel that helping them to realize their identity as a people, with a fully adequate grammar and vocabulary in their language, is very important to their future existence as a people group.

The next day, as we begin the requested seminar, our students are ready with notebook and pen in hand. When I start to talk about nouns in the Amuesha language and how they can be identified, I notice a look of deep satisfaction come over the faces in my audience. Just to know they have nouns in their language, like other languages, is the most pleasing thing that they can hear. After all the ridicule they have endured about their Amuesha being inferior, to realize now that they have nouns, verbs, and other standard parts of speech in their language similar to Spanish and English, is a great encouragement.

As I continue, and show them how to identify nouns in Amuesha, the pens are moving quickly. The group is taking notes, just like any college-age students would. I look out to see who they are. Right in the front row is Santiago, who started in the bilingual school as a little six-year old. Now he is a mature adult and the organizer of the Amuesha Church Association. Through the years, he has been going out to all the Amuesha areas where the number of believers has been increasing, baptizing them as they request it, and helping them organize their churches. Right beside him is Andres, who, as a little six-year old in the school, always had sore ears. Today Andres is the leading Christian in the church. And there are others, each with their own story. I am suddenly overcome with emotion at God's great faithfulness to the Amuesha people. I regain my composure and carry on with the nouns as the pens scratch away. Thank you, Lord.

At the end of the first class of the seminar, on how to identify nouns in their language, I hand out printed copies of one of their best-known Amuesha legends. Their test is to identify and mark the nouns. Asael helps me check the papers. I can hardly believe it, Amueshas identifying nouns in their own language!

The house to which Bob and I are assigned is the same house to which Santiago and the present head of the Amuesha Church Association are assigned. During the evening, I hear the other two talking together in Amuesha about the plans they have for the "forty-five churches."

"Did you say forty-five churches now?" I ask.

"Yes, forty-five churches," they answer.

"Amuesha churches?" I question again, not believing what I am hearing. "Yes, forty-five Amuesha churches. Thank you, Lord!

Since the dedication of the Amuesha New Testament and my leaving the Amuesha group, God has multiplied believers in a real people movement. With God's Word in hand, in their own language, and in their hearts, it has resulted in a church planting movement. Thank you, Lord. Praise the Lord for what He has done through His Word in the mother tongue of the Amuesha people.

". . . I will build my church; and the gates of hell shall not prevail against it."

– Jesus, (Matthew 16:18 KJV)

End

# Epilogue 1

We hear that Casper Mountain has been taken to jail on charges of working cocaine — not only he alone, but his father-in-law and his son-in-law. We are sure that these charges are not true, but what can we do except visit him in prison and pray the truth will be known?

Casper Mountain makes the most of his prison time. Since he had previously led his father-in-law to know the Lord, he never had enough time to really disciple him in the Word, as he says. Now is the time! With his Amuesha New Testament, which he carried into the prison with him, he reads to him every day, teaching him more about the Lord. He also underscores verses that he especially likes, wanting to share them with his wife, Juana.

One day, Casper cannot find his New Testament that he always keeps in his *poshac* (man's handbag). It is nowhere to be found. The other prisoners are watching him with great delight. Finally, they let him know they have taken it, and he will have to pay to get it back. He scrapes up all the little money he has and offers it in exchange for his New Testament. Once it is returned, his studies continue.

His deriders become curious. They decide they would like to know what is written in that book he is reading to his father-in-law every day in Amuesha. So Casper starts to teach the prisoners also, as best he can in Spanish. No doubt his son-in-law helps him out since he is more bilingual than Casper. Songs, too, ring out through the prison as Casper Mountain continues his "prison ministries." He says he is happy to have this time to study the Word and really knows it well now. He even memorizes the contents of each book in the New Testament as I am later to find out. When I happen to mention a story from the New Testament, he remarks, "Yes, that's what it says in Acts Chapter 6!"

Finally, the charges against Casper Mountain are dropped as false, and he finishes his "prison ministries." For Casper, with his commitment to spread the Word, it was time well spent. Thank you, Lord.

# Epilogue 2

My husband Bob and I continue to be involved with Wycliffe Bible Translators. Bob works as a personnel administrator at JAARS, in Waxhaw, North Carolina. I maintain friendly contact with the Amuesha Christian teachers and leaders by e-mail, FAX, and telephone. Mary Ruth Wise, my former co-worker, also continues to work with Wycliffe, working as editor at the Summer Institute of Linguistics in Dallas, Texas.

The latest good news that I have had from the Amueshas is that Asael, one of the second generation of bilingual teachers who recently received his official Teacher's Certificate, has been named by the Ministry of Education to supervise all the Amuesha bilingual schools. He has also been selected to teach Amuesha candidates in an institute of higher learning as part of a program which the Peruvian government is now offering to all the indigenous peoples of the jungles. It is a dream of the founder of Wycliffe Bible Translators, William Cameron Townsend, come true!

I was happy to hear that recently all the 45 Amuesha church groups — from upriver and downriver — came together for a spiritual celebration.

I trust that my book, *Jungle Jewels & Jaguars,* an account of my experiences in living and working with the Amueshas, may be an inspiration to others. It is my hope that it will help to bring many young people to decide that they too should become involved in Bible translation for the 2,200 language groups of people in the world today who are still without any of God's Word in their language.

Thank you, Lord, for your great faithfulness!
Martha Duff Tripp

*Additional Notes:*

Although translation of God's Word has been the central focus of our involvement with the Amuesha people, other community projects have taken place from time to time.

Dick and Jackie Rutter headed up an agricultural development project in the Villa America area where the people are more acculturated. Gerhard Fast did initial survey work in Amuesha areas on behalf of helping the people to acquire land titles.

Richard (Dick) Smith of the Peace Corps followed through in conducting land surveys, measuring land lots with Ministry of Agriculture surveyors, and acquiring titles for all the villages. Dick also originated the Amuesha Cultural House where several graduates of the bilingual schools were employed and trained in writing and printing Amuesha cultural books.

Vaccination teams have been sent from our Yarina medical department and from Public Health of Peru to various areas among the Amueshas. Several Amueshas have trained at Yarina as health promoters for many of the remote areas.

Occupational Courses provided by the Ministry of Education at the Yarinacocha Center have trained Amueshas in agriculture, cattle and poultry, mechanics, carpentry, economics, sewing, and other life skills. The Cattle Project, under the direction of Herbert Fuqua, has provided good stock cattle to upgrade the initial cattle projects of the indigenous people in some areas.

The Teacher Training Course provided by the Ministry of Education in Peru, in cooperation with SIL members, has produced trained indigenous teachers for hundreds of bilingual schools throughout the jungle. The result is a high literacy rate.

# Endnotes

Since many principles of indigenous work in missions, expressed in the book *Perspectives on the World Christian Movement* edited by Ralph D. Winter and Steven C. Hawthorne, agree with the principles already used in the work with the indigenous Amuesha (Yanesha') people of Peru, South America, extensive referencing to this book is made, along with other notes. Students of the *Perspectives* courses, when reading *Jungle Jewels & Jaguars,* will realize the validity of such principles when used along with the translation of God's Word into other languages.

Note:   Page numbers listed here for articles in *Perspectives (Third edition)* may be different in a later edition of *Perspectives.*

Chapter 1

1. JAARS International is a non-profit organization (originally Jungle Aviation and Radio Services) providing construction, technology, and transportation services for Wycliffe Bible Translators, Inc. and Summer Institute of Linguistics International.

2. Wycliffe Bible Translators is an international organization of more than six thousand workers whose mission is to assist the church in making disciples of all nations through Bible translation.

3. *Perspectives on the World Christian Movement,* edited by Ralph D. Winter, founder, U.S. Center for World Missions, and Steven C. Hawthorne, Director of Curriculum Development, Institute of International Studies, 1999:

Grimes, Barbara F., "From Every Language," 559-561;

Ladd, George Eldon, *The Gospel of the Kingdom,* (Our responsibility: to complete the task), 75;

Stott, John R.W., "The Bible in World Evangelism," 21-26;

Stott, John R.W., "The Living God is a Missionary God," 3-9;

Townsend, William Cameron, "Tribes, Tongues and Translators," 309-310;

Winter, Ralph D., "Four Men, Three Eras, Two Transitions," 260-261;

Winter, Ralph D. and Fraser, David A., "World Mission Survey" (Tribes: an endangered species), 363-364.

Chapter 2

1.Yarinacocha (Palm Lake) Center is often shortened to Yarina or the Center.

2. *Perspectives on the World Christian Movement,* edited by Ralph D. Winter, founder, U.S. Center for World Missions, and Steven C. Hawthorne, Director of Curriculum Development, Institute of International Studies, 1999:

Hiebert, Paul G., "Cultural Differences and the Communication of the Gospel" (Culture shock), 373-383.

Chapter 3

1. *Perspectives on the World Christian Movement,* 1999:

Beaver, R. Pierce, "The History of Mission Strategy" (Evangelism, education and medicine), 249-250.

Chapter 4

1. *Perspectives on the World Christian Movement,* 1992, 1999:

Adeney, David H., "Lifestyle for Servants of Christ" (Identification), D-282-283;

Hiebert, Paul G., "Social Structure and Church Growth" (Identification), 425;

Larson, Donald N., "The Viable Missionary: Learner, Trader, Story Teller" (Learner), 440.

2. Warren, Rick, *The Purpose Driven Life,* (The surrendered life), 77-84; (Made for a mission), 281-286; *Perspectives on the World Christian Movement,* 1999:

Winter, Ralph D., "Join the World Christian Movement," 718-723.

Chapter 5

1. Fast, Peter W., "Amuesha (Arawak) Phonemes," *International Journal of American Linguistics,* Vol. 19, 1953, 191-194.

Chapter 6

1. *Perspectives on the World Christian Movement,* 1999:

Brewster, D. Thomas and Elizabeth S., "The Difference Bonding Makes" (Establishing a sense of belonging), 444-448.

Chapter 7

1. *Perspectives on the World Christian Movement,* 1999:

Kraft, Marguerite and Crossman, Meg, "Women in Mission," 269-273;

Larson, Donald N., "The Viable Missionary" (Learner), 440.

Chapter 8

1. *Perspectives on the World Christian Movement,* 1992, 1999:

McGavran, Donald A., *Understanding Church Growth,* "Today's Task, Opportunity and Imperative" (the need of literacy), D-5-6;

Pierson, Paul, "A History of Transformation" (Establishing education), 266-267.

2. *Perspectives on the World Christian Movement,* 1999:

Winter, Ralph D., "The New Macedonia: A Revolutionary New Era in Mission Begins" (Different kinds of evangelism), 341-342.

3. *Mission Frontiers,* April 2000, "The Ten Common Factors" (of church planting movements), 1. Worship in the heart language, 41.


Chapter 9

1. *Perspectives on the World Christian Movement,* 1999:

The Lausanne Committee for World Evangelization, "The Willowbank Report" (Moral standards and cultural practices), 504-506.


Chapter 10

1. *Perspectives on the World Christian Movement,* 1999:

Brewster, E. Thomas and Elizabeth S., "The Difference Bonding Makes," 444-448;

The Lausanne Committee for World Evangelization, "The Willowbank Report " (Wanted humble messengers of the Gospel), 491-494.


Chapter 11

1. *Perspectives on the World Christian Movement,* 1999:

Beaver, R. Pierce, "The History of Mission Strategy" (Evangelism, education and medicine), 249-250;

Pierson, Paul, "A History of Transformation" (Bringing medical care), 267.


Chapter 13

1. *Perspectives on the World Christian Movement,* 1999:

Townsend, William Cameron, "Tribes, Tongues and Translators" 'Witchcraft, killings, superstition, ignorance, fear and sickness are giving way before the Light of the Word, literacy, medicine . . .' (quote), 309-310.


Chapter 14

1. *Perspectives on the World Christian Movement,* 1999:

Hiebert, Paul G., "Cultural Differences and Communication of the Gospel," 373-383.


Chapter 15

1. Tournavista is the center formed by the R. G. LeTourneau Co. for constructing a road in the Peruvian Amazon Basin.

Chapter 17

1. *Perspectives on the World Christian Movement,* 1999:

The Lausanne Committee for World Evangelization, "The Willowbank Report" (Cultural sensitivity in communicating the Gospel), 490.

Chapter 18

1. The article came out later in *Town Journal* magazine, "Teaching Headhunters to Read," May 1956.

2. *Perspectives on the World Christian Movement,* 1999:

Hiebert, Paul, "Social Structure and Church Growth" (Identification), 425.

Chapter 20

1. For a complete translation of this Inca legend see Appendix.

2. *Perspectives on the World Christian Movement,* 1999:

The Lausanne Committee for World Evangelization, "The Willowbank Report" (Cultural sensitivity in communicating the Gospel), 490-492.

3. Instituto Francés de Estudios Andinos, *"Al Este de los Andes: Relaciones entre las Sociedades Amazónicas y Andinas entre los Siglos XV y XVII."*

Chapter 21

1. Duff (Tripp), Martha, "A Syntactical Analysis of an Amuesha (Arawak) Text," *International Journal of American Linguistics,* Vol. 23, 1957, 171-178.

2. Duff (Tripp), Martha, *Diccionario Yanesha' (Amuesha) — Castellano,* Serie Lingüística Peruana, No. 47 and *Gramática del Idioma Yanesha' (Amuesha),* Serie Lingüística Peruana, No. 43.

Chapter 24

1. *Perspectives on the World Christian Movement,* 1999:

The Lausanne Committee for World Evangelization, "The Willowbank Report" (Cultural sensitivity in communicating the Gospel), 490.

Chapter 25

1. Duff (Tripp), Martha, *Tabet — José,* (Historias de David y José del Antiguo Testamento), 1956.

2. *Perspectives on the World Christian Movement,* 1992, 1999:

Glasser, Arthur F., *Crucial Dimensions in World Evangelization,* "The Missionary Task: An Introduction" (Making disciples), A-122;

Piper, John, *Let the Nations Be Glad,* "Discipling All The Peoples," 113.

Chapter 26

1. For a translation of the complete story of *Tempo* see Appendix.

Steffen, Tom A., *Passing the Baton,* "Why Communicate the Gospel Through Stories?" (Back to the power of story), 404-407.

2. *Perspectives on the World Christian Movement,* 1992, 1999:

Dayton, Edward R. and Fraser, David A., "Mission and the Church" (The kingdom of God and mission), D-21-22;

Ladd, George Eldon, *The Gospel of the Kingdom,* (Our responsibility: to complete the task), 75;

The Lausanne Committee for World Evangelization, "The Willowbank Report" (The convert and his culture), 495-496.

3. *Perspectives on the World Christian Movement,* 1999:

The Lausanne Committee for World Evangelization, "The Willowbank Report" (Culture in the biblical revelation, Form and meaning), ('recurring symbols in Scripture'), 485-486.

4. For a translation of the complete story of *Tempo* see Appendix.

Steffen, Tom A., *Passing the Baton,* "Why Communicate the Gospel Through Stories?" (Back to the power of story), 404-407.


Chapter 28

1. Summer Institute of Linguistics (SIL) is Wycliffe's sister organization, involved in linguistics, Bible translation, literacy, and training around the world.


Chapter 29

1. Resolución Suprema 2420, June 23, 1945; Resolución Suprema 909, Nov. 28, 1952;

*Perspectives on the World Christian Movement,* 1999:

Pierson, Paul, "A History of Transformation" (Establishing education, Bringing medical care), 266-267.


Chapter 30

1. *Perspectives on the World Christian Movement,* 1999:

Smalley, William A., "Cultural Implications of an Indigenous Church" (The nature of an indigenous church), 475-478;

Winter, Ralph D., "The New Macedonia: A Revolutionary New Era in Mission Begins," 339-342.


Chapter 31

1. *Perspectives on the World Christian Movement,* 1999:

Beaver, R. Pierce, "The History of Mission Strategy," 245, 251;

McGavran, Donald A., *The Bridges of God,* 323-338;

Winter, Ralph D., "The New Macedonia: A Revolutionary New Era in Mission Begins," 339-353.

Chapter 32

1. *Perspectives on the World Christian Movement,* 1999:

The Lausanne Committee for World Evangelization, "The Willowbank Report" (Identification), 493-494;

Reyburn, William D., "Identification in the Missionary Task" (Symbolic value of food), 453-454.

2. *Perspectives on the World Christian Movement,* 1992, 1999:

Beaver, R. Pierce, "The History of Mission Strategy" (Since World War II), 251-252;

Kraft, Marguerite and Crossman, Meg, "Women in Missions," 272;

The Lausanne Committee for World Evangelization, "The Willowbank Report" (Renunciation; Identification), 493;

McGavran, Donald A., *The Bridges of God,* (People movements), 323-338;

Parshall, Phil, "God's Messenger" (Ministry), 459;

Richardson, Don, *Eternity in Their Hearts,* "The Hidden Message of 'Acts,'" (Churches for the Gentiles), A-116-117;

Tippett, Alan R., "The Evangelization of Animists," 628-629;

*Mission Frontiers* (WSCWM), April 2000:

"What is a Church Planting Movement?", 36;

"The Ten Common Factors" (of a church planting movement) 7. On-the-job training for church leadership, 9. Outsiders keep a low profile, 42.

Chapter 33

1. *Perspectives on the World Christian Movement,* 1999:

Kietzman, Dale W. and Smalley, William A., "The Missionary's Role in Culture Change," 482;

The Lausanne Committee for World Evangelization, "The Willowbank Report" (Cultural barriers to the communication of the Gospel), 489.

Chapter 34

1. The Bilingual School Program was established in Peru in 1952 by the Ministry of Education, with the cooperation of the Summer Institute of Linguistics, for training indigenous, young people to be teachers among their own language groups of people, starting the teaching in their own native language (Resolución Suprema 909, Nov. 28, 1952). These schools have been very successful in bringing the literacy rate to a high degree among indigenous people of the jungle areas. See *Who Brought the Word* by Wycliffe Bible Translators, Inc. in cooperation with the Summer Institute of Linguistics, 1963, 52-53, 80.

2. *Perspectives on the World Christian Movement,* 1999:

Grimes, Barbara F., "From Every Language" (Bible translation: How many languages to go?), 560-561.

Chapter 36

1. *Perspectives on the World Christian Movement,* 1999:

Beaver, R. Pierce, "The History of Mission Strategy" (Evangelism, education, and medicine), 249- 251;

The Lausanne Committee for World Evangelization, "The Willowbank Report," 8. Church and culture, 497-506;

*Mission Frontiers* (WSCWM), "The Ten Universal Elements" (of church planting movements), 4. Scriptural authority, 39.

Chapter 37

1. *Perspectives on the World Christian Movement,* 1999:

Piper, John, *Let the Nations be Glad!,* (The call of God), 54;

Robb, John D., "Strategic Prayer," (Reaching unreached peoples), 150.

Chapter 38

1. *Perspectives on the World Christian Movement,* 1999:

Bosch, David J., *Witness to the World,* 59-63;

Dearborn, Tim, *Beyond Duty,* 90-93;

Hawthorne, Steven D., "Mandate on the Mountain," 108-112;

Piper, John, *Let the Nations Be Glad,* "Discipling All The Peoples" ('nations' = people groups), 113-117.

Chapter 40

1. Duff (Tripp), Martha, "Amuesha (Arawak) Syntax 1: Simple Sentence Types," *Série Lingüistica Especial No. 1,* 1959, 172-237.

2. Also while on furlough, Martha Duff (Tripp) and Mary Ruth Wise were featured, along with other fellow Wycliffe linguist-translators, in a Reader's Digest article entitled "Two Thousand Tongues to Go," written by Clarence W. Hall (August, 1958). Later a full-length book, *Two Thousand Tongues to Go,* was written by Ethel E. Wallis and Mary A. Bennett, Harper and Brothers, New York. At the time, Martha Duff was contacted by Harper and Brothers about writing a book of her own experiences. She declined, feeling that she did not want to delay at that critical time in the work with the Amueshas. Also, Martha Duff was featured in a *Time* magazine article, "Alphabet for Amueshas" (January 1959);

*Perspectives on the World Christian Movement,* 1999:

Townsend, William Cameron, "Tongues, Tribes and Translators," 309-310.

3. *Perspectives on the World Christian Movement,* 1999:

Winter, Ralph D., "The New Macedonia: A Revolutionary New Era in Mission Begins" (Different kinds of evangelism), 341-342.

Chapter 41

1. *Perspectives on the World Christian Movement*, 1999:

The Lausanne Committee for World Evangelization, "The Willowbank Report" (The content and communication of the Gospel), 488-489.

2. *Perspectives on the World Christian Movement*, 1999:

Coleman, Robert E., *The Master Plan of Evangelism*, "The Master's Plan" (Men were his method), 101;

McGavran, Donald A., *The Bridges of God*, 323-338.

3. *Mission Frontiers*, April 2000, "The Ten Common Factors" (for church planting movements), Worship in the heart language, On-the-job training for church leadership, Leadership authority is decentralized, Outsiders (missionaries) keep a low profile, 41-42;

*Perspectives on the World Christian Movement*, 1999:

Hawthorne, Steven, "Acts of Obedience" (Cross-cultural communication), 125.

Chapter 42

1. *Perspectives on the World Christian Movement*, 1999:

McGavran, Donald A., *The Bridges of God*, 323-338;

Mott, John R., "The Responsibility of the Young People for the Evangelization of the World, 317-322;

Mulholland, Kenneth B., "A Church for All Peoples," 135-136.

Chapter 43

1. *Perspectives on the World Christian Movement*, 1999:

Hesselgrave, David J., *Communicating Christ Cross-Culturally*, "The Role of Culture in Communication" (The Bible culture context), 394-396;

Johnstone, Patrick, "Covering the Globe" (Scripture translation), 546-547;

The Lausanne Committee for World Evangelization, "The Willowbank Report" (Culture in the biblical revelation, Form and meaning), 485-487.

2. *Perspectives on the World Christian Movement*, 1999:

Winter, Ralph D., "The New Macedonia: A Revolutionary New Era in Mission Begins" (Different kinds of evangelism), 341;

Winter, Ralph D. and Koch, Bruce A., "Finishing the Task: The Unreached Peoples Challenge" (The essential missionary task), 516-518;

*Mission Frontiers*, April 2000, "The Ten Universal Elements" (of church planting movements), 4. Scriptural authority, 39.

Chapter 44

1. *Mission Frontiers*, April 2000, "The Ten Common Factors" (of church planting movements), Evangelism has communal implication, Rapid incorporation of the new converts into the life and ministry of the church, 41-42

2. *Perspectives on the World Christian Movement*, 1999:

Kraft, Charles H., "Three Encounters in Christian Witness," 408-413.

3. Ibid.

4. Ibid.

5. Ibid.

6. Ibid.

7. Ibid.

8. Ibid.

9. Warren, Rick, *The Purpose Driven Life*, "Formed for God's Family" (The importance of small group meetings of believers), 117-123.


Chapter 45

1. *Perspectives on the World Christian Movement*, 1992, 1999:

Hesselgrave, David J., *Communicating Christ Cross-Culturally*, "World View and Contextualization" (Adapting the message to world view), C-45-46;

Hesselgrave, David J., *Communicating Christ Cross-Culturally*, "The Role of Culture in Communication" (The respondent culture context), 395-396;

Kraft, Charles H., "Culture, Worldview, and Contextualization," 384-391;

Richardson, Don, "Redemptive Analogy," 397-403;

Smalley, William A., "Cultural Implications of an Indigenous Church" (Indigenous churches start apart from missions), 479.

2. *Perspectives on the World Christian Movement*, 1999:

Winter, Ralph D., "The New Macedonia: A Revolutionary New Era in Mission Begins" (Different kinds of evangelism), 339-342.

3. *Perspectives on the World Christian Movement*, 1999:

The Lausanne Committee for World Evangelization, "The Willowbank Report" (Individual and group conversions, 496-497;

McGavran, Donald A., *The Bridges of God*, (The group mind and group decisions), 325-326;

Tippett, Alan R., *Let The Earth Hear His Voice*, "The Evangelization of Animists," 628-631;

Winter, Ralph D., "The New Macedonia: A Revolutionary New Era in Mission Begins," 339-353.

4. *Mission Frontiers*, April 2000, "The Ten Universal Elements" (of church planting movements), 4. Scriptural authority, 39.

Chapter 46

1. Duff (Tripp), Martha, "El grabado en papel," *Peru Indígena*,Vol. X, No.24-25, 1963, 79-81; Wise, Mary Ruth, "Six Levels of Structure in Amuesha (Arawak) Verbs," *International Journal of American Linguistics*, Vol. 29, 1963, 132-152.

2. *Perspectives on the World Christian Movement*, 1992:

Glasser, Arthur F., *Crucial Dimensions in World Evangelization*, "The Missionary Task: An Introduction," A-121-123.


Chapter 47

1. *Perspectives on the World Christian Movement*, 1992, 1999:

Glasser, Arthur F., *Crucial Dimensions in World Evangelization*, "The Missionary Task" (Planting churches), A-122-124;

Hian, Chua Wee, *Let The Earth Hear His Voice*, "Evangelization of Whole Families" (Evangelizing families in other cultures), 614;

The Lausanne Committee for World Evangelization, "The Willowbank Report" (Understanding God's Word today), 487-488, (Church and culture), 497-503;

McGavran, Donald A.," A Church in Every People," 617-622;

Tippett, Alan R., *Let The Earth Hear His Voice*, "The Evangelization of Animists," 623-625;

Richardson, Don, *Eternity in Their Hearts*, "The Hidden Message of 'Acts'" (Churches for the Gentiles), A-116-117;

Schwartz, Glenn, "Dependency," (How to destroy local initiative), 592;

Snyder, Howard A., *Community of The King*, "The Church in God's Plan," 137-141;

*Mission Frontiers*, April 2000, "The Ten Common Factors" (of church planting methods), 41-42: 1. Worship in the heart language, 2. Evangelism has communal implications, 3. Rapid incorporation of new converts , 4. Passion and fearlessness, 7. On-the-job training for church leadership, 8. Leadership authority is decentralized, 9. Outsiders (missionaries) keep a low profile.

"Nine Obstacles to Church Planting Methods,": 1. Imposing extra-biblical requirements for being a church, 2. Loss of a valued cultural identity, 4. Non-reproducible church models, 5. Subsidies creating dependency, 6. Extra-biblical leadership requirements, 45-46.

2. Ibid.

3. Ibid.

4. *Perspectives on the World Christian Movement*, 1999:

Kraft, Charles H., "Three Encounters in Christian Witness" (power, truth and allegiance), 408-413;

Tippett, Alan R., "The Evangelization of Animists" (power encounters), 629, (indigenous from the beginning, fellowship-forming or church-planting), 629.

Chapter 48

1. *Perspectives on the World Christian Movement,* 1999:

Hian, Chua Wee, *Let The Earth Hear His Voice,* "Evangelization of Whole Families" (Evangelizing families in other cultures), 614-615;

Hiebert, Paul G., "Cultural Differences and the Communication of the Gospel," 379-380;

McGavran, Donald A., "A Church in Every People," 617-621;

Smalley, William A., "Cultural Implication of an Indigenous Church" (Indigenous churches start apart from missions), 479.

2. *Perspectives on the World Christian Movement,* 1999:

Hesselgrave, David J., *Communicating Christ Cross-Culturally,* "The Role of Culture in Communication," 395;

Hiebert, Paul G., "Cultural Differences and the Communication of the Gospel," 373-383;

The Lausanne Committee for World Evangelization, "The Willowbank Report" (Culture in the biblical revelation, Form and meaning, 'dynamic equivalence'), 485-486.

3. Duff (Tripp), Martha, *Yompor Po'ñoñ,* El Nuevo Testamento, La Liga Bíblica, 1978; "Prominencia y cohesión en la narración Amuesha," 1981.

4. *Perspectives on the World Christian Movement,* 1992:

Glasser, Arthur F., *Crucial Dimensions in World Evangelization,* "The Missionary Task: An Introduction" (Planting churches), A-121-124;

*Mission Frontiers,* April 2000, "The Ten Universal Elements" (of church planting movements), 4. Scriptural authority, 39.


Chapter 49

1. *Perspectives on the World Christian Movement,* 1999:

Parshall, Phil, "God's Messenger" (Ministry), 459; *Mission Frontiers,* April 2000, "Ten Practical Handles for Church Planting Movements" (Model, assist, watch and leave), 44.

2. *Perspectives on the World Christian Movement,* 1992, 1999:

Hiebert, Paul, "Culture and Cross-Cultural Differences" (Syncretism versus indigenization), C-21;

The Lausanne Committee for World Evangelization, "The Willowbank Report" (Moral standards and cultural practices), 504-505;

Smalley, William A., "Cultural Implications of an Indigenous Church," 475-477.


Chapter 50

1. Duff-Tripp, Martha, *Gramática del idioma yanesha' (amuesha),* Serie Linguüística Peruana No. 43, 1997;

Duff-Tripp, Martha, *Diccionario yanesha' (amuesha)*, Serie Linguüística Peruana No. 47, 1998.

# Appendix

Translation of the Inca Legend

Inca, this one, had taken god's daughter, our god. He was very angry. He was very angry. Inca beat our mother. He was jealous of our mother, Palla. Our mother, Palla, this one he took. He is going to beat her very much. They drink. They make merry. Then he follows her. Then he beats her. He beats her. She goes inside. He doesn't like it. He said, "I'm going to follow her." Chief Mopooll said, "He's not going to beat you. Don't you listen to him. Tomorrow morning I'm going to take you. I'm going to leave you at your mountain namesake. From there you will go to where your father is. He is very mad at you. Very much you cause the heads to be cut off of our dead ones." Thus he said to her.

Then all night they kept going on singing. Then they were talking. They made fun of him in song. They said, (song) "Inca, our mother, Inca our . . . he loves, our mother, Inca, our mother." Her husband said to her, "Alalala, you are making your harlots make fun of me in song." He was mad at her.

The next morning they left. They will go and be lost out of sight. They kept on going. Her children cried for her. Her children cried for her. He said, "Alalala, don't cry for your mother. She will come back tomorrow." Then they went five days. "Don't cry for her." Three days passed.

Suddenly, in the morning he remembered her. In the morning he remembered her. He said, "Alalala, now I will play the flute for you. Your mother will come." He played the flute in the morning. He didn't play his flute well. He cried. "Alalala, now your mother is lost again. We won't see her." Then he played the flute. This one went. He went to look for her. He opened all up the places where the non-Amuesha people were. His wife might be there. He didn't see her. He opened all up the places of the non-Amuesha and then left. He said to his children as he left, "You close it all up. I will go to look for your mother." He went. He went to look for his wife. He went to look for her. He went downriver. He didn't see her. He piled up water. He piled up this rock in the water. Then he climbed up high. The sour gnats arrived. He said, "Where are you going?" They said, "We are going to leave. We are going to go visiting upriver." "Alalala, where do you get drunk?" "Far over there we get drunk. We are licking our mother Palla's strainer for her." "Alalala, you show me where she finally is." They took him. They took him to where his wife was. Then he went and went. Inca was a very, very angry person. Then he went. He arrived at this lake. It was a large lake, very large. The lake stretched out far. Then he said there, "How will I ever cross?" Then the sour gnats left flying and arrived and stood over on the other side. He saw a spider. It was sticking there. He said to it, "You take me across, Alalala, you take me across." It said. It sang, (song) "I will carry you, Inca. Isn't it Cuzco over there? Inca is crying." Then it jumped him across. He arrived all the way near to the shore. He jumped off. He broke all the spider's little hands. It went then out of sight. Let it be lost out of sight.

Then he arrived there. He arrived there. What now? He went and went and went. He saw his wife. He arrived on the other side. She came then. His wife came. She said there, "Inca, you've come." "I have come, Alalala here where you finally are." "Here I am, Inca. Now you just be humble. Father in his house there is very powerful. You kneel there. From there father will forgive you for as many heads as you used to cause to be cut off of our dead ones. Thus you will pay there. But father is just a little mad at you. He will forgive you there. You ask for forgiveness. He will forgive you there. Don't by any means talk bad." Inca said, "Alalala, your father comes to an end just as I do." She said, "Don't talk so, Inca. Talk all the way good. When you come, in a little while he will forgive. Father is just a little mad, just a little. Then he will get over it." He (father-in-law) threw it out (the chief's seat). He comes now, he comes. He follows there. "Alalala, so you are saying, Alalala, your father is very powerful. Shouldn't he be just as I am?" "Don't, Inca, be talking so. You just pray right there to father."

Then he came up near. He (Inca) said to him (father-in-law) when he came. He (Inca) greeted him when he came. He (father-in-law) gave him when he came the chief's seat. "You will sit there." He threw it out for him.

He (Inca) jumped and jumped on it. Let it be all broken down. Shouldn't it be all broken? He bumped hard his buttocks on the chief's seat

Then his father-in-law got up. He talked a little loudly to him (Inca). "Now you come here. Here you will pay for the number of my dead ones whose blood you used to shed. Now here you will see it. You will grab all out as many times as you used to cut off heads. Now you come, Inca. They weren't your people whose heads you caused to be cut off. It wasn't from their own sins. Now here you will pay. You will not get up again. Even forever. Even from the past. You will not pay back. You will not get up again. Now I leave you here."

Inca said, "Alalala, I will pay all. Inca will get up again forever, Inca will get up again. Even forever."

"Inca will not get up again. You will be grabbing out on my earth. From there your roots will grab out as many times as you used to cause the heads to be cut off of people." Thus our god said to him.

Then he was stopped from talking. He went now. His roots went out in all directions. He rooted far out in all directions like trees do. Then he did not get up again. He punished him. Inca cried and cried. "Now how will I ever get up again. Already roots grow from our buttocks." Then truly, it was that way. They put on him a whirlwind, a strong wind. From there the tree will not grow again. He will not get up then. "Forever you will be grabbing on my earth as many times as you used to shed the blood of our dead ones. Day after day you used to hurt them. Her, too, my daughter you used to beat. You used to be jealous in various ways. Now here you will pay for it all. Even forever. You will not get up again." What now? I've finished. It's ended.

## Translation of the *Ĩempo* (branch minnow) story

A non-Amuesha person *(oc)* came to the stream and dipped me up in her bucket. She carried me back to her house. Then she said, "I dipped up a *ĩempo*." Then she took hold of me and threw me out on the ground. There I jumped and flipped.

Another *oc* saw me and came to me and picked me up. She loved me and put me in a glass of water. If she had not put me in water, I would have died. There I breathed again. My heart became good again.

When it was morning again I looked all around and moved again. A little more and I would have died. There I slept again.

The next day, they took me back to my house. When I saw my buddies again, I told them all that had happened: "An *oc* grabbed me. There was another *oc*, a lover, so that I didn't die. It was the lover that picked me up so that I didn't die. If she had not done that, we wouldn't be seeing each other again.

I looked all around at the *oc's* things. All kind of things they had — all kind of plates, spoons, pots. They had their cook-fire up high. It lighted all around. All kind of things they had.

I am happy again to arrive back at my house. I was sad when this happened. But they did bring me back.

Now, never again will I step into an *oc's* house. Before, I didn't know that they would grab me. Now I know. When I see an *oc* coming, I will swim far away."

# About the Author

Martha Duff Tripp, a member of Wycliffe Bible Translators, served 47 years in Peru, South America. After learning to speak the Amuesha language, she analyzed its grammar and reduced the language to written form. She then translated the New Testament and Old Testament portions. She also wrote a 283-page book on Amuesha grammar, a 688-page bilingual dictionary (Amuesha-Spanish), and many school textbooks and storybooks. Her linguistic technical articles have been published in the International Journal of Linguistics.

In cooperation with the Ministry of Education of Peru, Mrs. Tripp established bilingual schools, resulting in a high degree of literacy among the Amuesha people. Forty-five churches have been established by the people themselves using the translated Scriptures.

Mrs. Tripp is a graduate of Columbia Bible College (presently Columbia International University) and studied linguistics at the University of Oklahoma.

Through her incredible story, *Jungle Jewels & Jaguars*, the author wishes to encourage Christian young men and women to consider serving as Bible translators.